POLITICS OF HATE

Celebrating
30 Years of Publishing
in India

POLITICS OF HATE

Religious Majoritarianism in South Asia

Edited by

FARAHNAZ ISPAHANI

HarperCollins *Publishers* India

First published in India by HarperCollins *Publishers* 2023
4th Floor, Tower A, Building No. 10, DLF Cyber City,
DLF Phase II, Gurugram, Haryana – 122002
www.harpercollins.co.in

2 4 6 8 10 9 7 5 3 1

P-ISBN: 978-93-5629-355-7
E-ISBN: 978-93-5629-001-3

Typeset in 11.5/15.7 Adobe Garamond Pro
Manipal Technology Ltd, Manipal

Printed and bound at
Thomson Press (India) Ltd

MIX
Paper
FSC FSC® C010615

This book is produced from independently certified FSC® paper
to ensure responsible forest management.

To all those who have lost their lives fighting for the right to peacefully practise their faith and those battling religious persecution and majoritarianism across South Asia today

Contents

List of Abbreviations

ACMC	All Ceylon Muslim Congress:
ACTJ	All Ceylon Thawheed Jamaat
AIML	All India Muslim League
AIMPLB	All India Muslim Personal Law Board
AIMIM	All India Majlis-e-Ittehad-ul-Muslimeen
AL	Awami League
AQIS	al-Qaeda in the Indian Subcontinent
BBS	Bodu Bala Sena
BCS	Bangladesh Chattra Shibir
BGB	Border Guard Bangladesh
BHBCUC	Bangladesh Hindu Buddhist Christian Unity Council
BJP	Bharatiya Janata Party

BJS	Bharatiya Jana Sangh
BJeI	Bangladesh Jamaat-e-Islami
BNP	Bangladesh Nationalist Party
BSD	Bangladesher Samajtantrik Dal
CAA	Citizenship Amendment Act
CPC	Country of Particular Concern
CPB	Communist Party of Bangladesh
CSDS	Centre for the Study of Developing Societies
DSA	Digital Security Act
HI	Hefazat-e-Islam
ICT	International Crimes Tribunal
INC	Indian National Congress:
IPS	Indian Police Services
IRFA	International Religious Freedom Act
IS	Islamic State
ISIL	The Islamic State of Iraq and the Levant
JI	Jamat-e-Islami
JeI	Jamaat-e-Islami
JHU	Jathika Hela Urumaya
JMI	Jammiyathul Millathu Ibrahim
JSD	Jatiya Samajtantrik Dal
JUI	Jamiat-e-Ulama-e-Islam
JUH	Jamiat-e-Ulama-e-Hind
JUP	Jamiat-e-Ulama-e-Pakistan

LTTE	Liberation of Tamil Tigers Eelam
NAP	National Awami Party
NBSA	News Broadcasting Standards Authority
NGO	Non-Governmental Organization
NRC	National Registry of Citizens
NSP	National Socialist Party
NTJ	National Thawheed Jamaat
NWFP	North West Frontier Province
OIC	Organization of Islamic Cooperation
PBUH	Peace Be Upon Him
PDS	Public Distribution System
PML	Pakistan Muslim League
PPP	Pakistan Peoples Party
PPC	Pakistan Penal Code
RAB	Rapid Action Battalion
RPP	Rastriya Prajatantra Part
RSS	Rashtriya Swayamsevak Sangh
SLMC	Sri Lanka Muslim Congress
SLFP	Sri Lanka Freedom Party
SLTJ	Sri Lanka Thawheed Jamaat
TLP	Tehreek-e-Labbaik Pakistan
TTP	Tehrik-e-Taliban Pakistan
UN	United Nations
UNP	United National Party

UPSC	Union Public Services Commission
USAID	United States Agency for International Development
USCIRF	US Commission on International Religious Freedom
USIP	United States Institute of Peace
VHP	Vishwa Hindu Parishad
WHO	World Health Organization
WP	Workers Party

Introduction

THE LAST DECADE OR MORE has seen a rise in majoritarian communalism across large parts of the world. The situation is particularly grim in South Asia, home to almost 2 billion people, which includes followers of every major and minor religious belief in the world. The rise in religious extremism in this religiously diverse subcontinent is often a function of politics.

The partition of the subcontinent in 1947 along religious lines seems to have exacerbated the desire of majorities within the countries of the region to further consolidate their dominance. Pakistan, which was created on the basis of religion, has had several phases of suppression of the relatively small remaining religious minorities. India, a country founded on secular nationalism, has also demonstrated a slide towards religious nationalism over the last several years.

There is clearly a regional trend, and there is a need to examine it. This edited volume seeks to offer a distinct and original take on the issue of extremist religious hatred within the context of South Asia's politics. Pakistan and India can both be cited as the prime examples of this phenomenon, though instances of communal majoritarianism undermining the rights and protections of minorities are also increasing in Bangladesh and in Sri Lanka.

By 2050, India will have the world's largest Muslim population, in addition to its majority Hindu population, alongside Christians, Sikhs, Buddhists, Jains, Zoroastrians and Jews.[1] Over the last few years, there has been a reported increase in violence targeting India's Muslims. This rise in religious violence, often by vigilante groups that are sometimes condoned by the state, has raised questions about India's religio-ethnic stability—something that could not even have been imagined in the first five decades of India's independence.

In December 2019, the Indian Parliament passed the Citizenship Amendment Act (CAA), which granted an expedited process of acquiring citizenship to Buddhists, Jains, Christians, Hindus and Sikhs from neighbouring countries—Afghanistan, Pakistan and Bangladesh—but not to Muslims. This was seen as a signal that the Indian government saw Muslims differently from how it saw other communities.

A few months later, in February 2020, at the same time as then US President Donald Trump was in Delhi, the capital city witnessed one of the worst anti-Muslim riots in decades. Reports by human rights watchdogs like Amnesty International and Human Rights Watch, Muslim academics, human rights activists, former police officers and journalists all alleged anti-Muslim bias in the investigation of the riots by New Delhi police.[2]

In September 2020, Amnesty International was forced to shut down its India office. The human rights watchdog 'accused the government of pursuing a "witch-hunt" against human rights organisations.'[3] India is the only democracy where Amnesty has been forced to shut offices.

Over the last few years, there has been a rise in religiously motivated attacks against non-Hindu communities in India, especially Muslims and Christians. During COVID-19, there has been a rise in attacks targeting and blaming Muslims for what was called, in the media, 'corona jihad'.[4] The local and central governments and the media blamed the spread of COVID-19 on a March 2020 conference held by the Islamic Tablighi Jamaat organization. Even though courts across India dismissed these charges, the damage had already been done.[5]

In July 2021, jailed tribal rights activist Father Stan Swamy died in a prison in Mumbai, at the age of eighty-four. A Jesuit priest, who suffered from Parkinson's disease, was arrested in October 2020 after being accused of terrorism along with sixteen other activists, academics and lawyers. Mary Lawlor, UN Special Rapporteur on Human Rights Defenders, had referred to this detention as 'inexcusable'.[6]

Pakistan, founded as the homeland for British India's Muslims, has over time become a country where all minorities—both Muslim and non-Muslim—have faced persecution and harassment. Where there were once 17 per cent non-Muslim minorities in areas constituting Pakistan at the start of 1947, today, minorities comprise only 3 per cent of Pakistan's population. Pakistan was ethnically cleansed of its Hindu and Sikh populations at the time of Partition and discriminatory policies and persecution have led to many Christians and Ahmadis emigrating from the country.

Pakistan has the strongest blasphemy laws in the world and is the only country whose constitution has sought to define who is—and is not—a Muslim. In early August 2021, an eight-year-old Hindu boy was accused of blasphemy and is being held in protective police custody in Pakistani Punjab, becoming the youngest person ever to be charged with blasphemy in the country.[7] When the boy was released on bail, a Muslim mob attacked the local Hindu temple, damaging statues and burning down the temple's main door.[8]

In May 2021, a Muslim mob attacked a Christian village in Pakistani Punjab after a quarrel between young Christians who cleaned the entrance to their church and a Muslim gentleman who passed by.[9] This is not the first time Christians have been attacked or their places of worship attacked in Pakistan.

Ahmadis have long been persecuted in Pakistan, and the Constitution of Pakistan does not even recognize them as Muslims. However, over the last few years, there has been a rise in attacks against Ahmadis.[10] According to human rights activists, this spike can be traced to the rise of the Tehreek-e-Labbaik Pakistan (TLP), formerly Tehreek-e-Labbaik Ya Rasool Allah (TLYRA), an Islamist militant outfit that rose to popularity on the issue of blasphemy.

Most Islamist groups argue that Pakistan's status as an Islamic republic justifies defending the sensibilities of the Muslim majority at the expense of the minorities. At different times in Pakistan's short history, various Islamist scholars have articulated the need for different treatment of Muslims and non-Muslims in the light of Islamic law. The country's hostility towards India has also resulted in nurturing, through textbooks and the media, an anti-Hindu sentiment.

Bangladesh differs from Pakistan in that it was founded as a secular Muslim country. But it has, over the years, become a battleground for Islamist groups who would like to lead the country down the path of an Islamic state. In March 2020, hundreds of supporters of Hefazat-e-Islam, a radical Islamist group in Bangladesh, attacked houses belonging to Hindus in the country's north-eastern Sylhet division. These protests spread to the capital city, Dhaka, with thousands of Islamist activists marching in the streets.[11]

Sri Lanka's ethnic conflict, originally pitting the majority Sinhalese against the minority Tamils, has also taken on a religious dimension. Buddhist Sinhalese have started targeting Sri Lanka's Muslims, some of whom have attacked Christians. In April 2019, suicide bombers attacked churches and hotels across Sri Lanka on Easter Sunday, killing more than 290 people.[12] Attacks against Sri Lankan Muslims have increased since the Easter attacks. Many Muslim-owned businesses face informal boycotts and anti-Muslim riots broke out in two provinces one month after the Easter attacks.[13]

There have also been efforts to deny Muslims the right to be buried in accordance with their religion. In February 2021, the Sri Lankan government first announced that it would only allow cremation for those dying from COVID-19. After doctors' groups, the World Health Organization (WHO), the United Nations (UN) and local human rights activists protested, the government backed off and allowed burial for Muslims and Christians.[14]

One month later, in March 2021, Sarath Weerasekara, Sri Lanka's minister of public security, announced that the government planned to ban the burqa, and would close more than 1,000 Islamic schools across the country. The minister was quoted as saying that 'the burqa was a sign of religious extremism and had a direct impact on national security'.[15] After protests from human rights organizations, the government rescinded this policy, which nevertheless reflected the growing anti-Muslim sentiment in Sri Lanka.

The Universal Declaration of Human Rights grants to everyone the right to believe and practise their religion, as well as the right to change those beliefs. But over the last decade, governments across South Asia have taken legal measures to prohibit religious conversions from the dominant religious group. These anti-conversion laws are a violation of the individual's right to choose their religious faith.

The motivation behind these laws, though not officially stated as such, is to protect the dominant religious tradition from a perceived threat from minority religious groups.

The methods of preventing conversion vary. In India, several state legislatures have adopted laws limiting conversions away from Hinduism. In Pakistan, national blasphemy laws are used to criminalize attempts by non-Muslims to convert Muslims. Moreover, governments in India, Pakistan and Nepal are tightening their control over non-governmental organizations (NGOs), especially foreign missionary groups.

The rise of majoritarianism, and the desire for religiously 'purer' communities, is also manifested in the heightened sensitivities among majority populations over interfaith marriages or marriages predicated on the conversion of one spouse.

In Pakistan, poor Hindu and Christian girls, sometimes underage, are converted through forced marriages but since the conversion is in the direction of the majority, the legal system tends to ignore the element of coercion. In India, even interfaith marriages resulting from romantic relationships between adults are described as 'love jihad'. Despite the persistence of these allegations, credible data has not been presented to demonstrate the extent and nature of these allegedly coerced conversions. In fact, the National Investigation Agency in India in October 2018 closed an investigation of alleged love jihad and found that accusations of a Muslim plot to convert Hindu women were unfounded.

Overview

This edited volume includes chapters that cover the rise and the spread of religious extremism in each country, how each country's state apparatus has viewed this rise, and the various legislations implemented within each country (the anti-conversion laws, anti-blasphemy laws, laws targeting foreign and local NGOs).

In 'Religious Majoritarianism in a Diverse Region', Husain Haqqani explains how, since their emergence as modern nation states, all countries in South Asia have witnessed a rise in religious majoritarianism and moved towards religious national identity. This has happened despite the region's history reflecting long phases of inclusivity and pluralism, with only short spurts of communal conflict. Haqqani explains the phenomenon as a function of 'otherization' for political mobilization. Generating hate against 'the other' is an easy way to garner votes and keep attention away from issues of inequitable distribution of economic and political power.

In 'Muslimophobia in India: Reasons and Remedy', A. Faizur Rahman traces the rise of Muslimophobia within Indian society and politics, the rise of Hindutva politics, and the fears of many that Nehruvian secular India appears to be moving towards a Hindu rashtra (state). Rahman traces how, viewed over time, it appears that the long-cherished idea of India as a benign, inclusive state appears to be collapsing and giving way to a less pluralistic, less inclusive and less tolerant country where patriotism has often become indistinguishable from chauvinism, and democracy metamorphoses into one-man rule.

In 'Hindu Majoritarianism and Unmaking the Idea of India', Niranjan Sahoo traces the last seven decades of modern India's rise as a secular pluralist country despite being an overwhelmingly Hindu majority country. Sahoo traces the rise of the Hindu nationalist Bharatiya Janata Party (BJP) and the resurgence of its sister organizations, like the Rashtriya Swayamsevak Sangh (RSS). Sahoo argues that the brand of majoritarian pro-Hindutva politics that the ruling dispensation has pushed over the last few years comes at the cost of key constitutional principles and India's pluralist history.

In 'The Indian Media's Role in Fuelling Communal Violence: Media Divides and Hates for Profit', Maya Mirchandani examines the role of the Indian media in furthering social divides primarily based on identity and normalizing hate speech. The key group that the media, both mainstream and social, has focused on are religious minorities, especially Muslims. Over the last few years, communal rhetoric has become mainstreamed within the Indian political and media space, with use of terms like 'love jihad' and 'corona jihad', among others.

In her chapter, Mirchandani unpacks how the media can foment division and incite hatred. The chapter examines the interaction between traditional mainstream media and social media and the role the latter has played in amplifying voices of hate.

In 'Islamophobia and Sinhalese Buddhist Nationalism in Sri Lanka', Neil DeVotta undertakes an in-depth analysis of the interaction between an assertive Sinhalese Buddhist nationalism and the rise of Islamophobia in the island nation of Sri Lanka. DeVotta points out that over the last few decades, growth in Wahabi–Salafi teachings have resulted in Sri Lanka's Muslims becoming more conservative and insular and separate from their Sri Lankan and South Asian heritage.

DeVotta states that there is a rise in a Sinhalese Buddhist majoritarian identity that believes that 'minorities who do not recognize their subordinate place' need to be 'put in their place', if need be, by force.

In 'Fear, Radicalism and Violence: Sri Lanka's Cyclical Crisis,' Gehan Gunatilleke examines the 'cyclical' relationship between majoritarian Sinhalese nationalism and Islamist radicalism. The chapter hypothesizes that the communal crisis in the island nation has socio-political roots. Gunatilleke's chapter lays out these socio-political factors, examines their ties to Buddhist majoritarian identity and anti-Muslim violence, and then offers thoughts on how this violent cycle could be broken.

In 'Christians in Pakistan: Retrospect and Prospect', former bishop, Michael Nazir Ali, traces the history of the spread of Christianity to South Asia, including to Pakistan. Ali argues that contrary to the views expressed by many in the subcontinent, some Indian Christians assert that Christiniaty came to the Indian subcontinent in the early centuries of the Christian era. Ali also lays out policy recommendations for the government of Pakistan to ensure freedom of expression, belief and worship instead of a theocratic state where only one kind of narrative is allowed to prevail.

In 'Genesis of the Shia Predicament in Pakistan', Mohammad Taqi traces how the predicament faced by Shias in Pakistan led to the evolution of a Shia religio-cultural identity that competed with Sunni and Sufi coreligionist. Taqi shows how the Shia communal identity was well-defined and distinct from other Muslim sects, and yet syncretic with them as well as with the majority Hindu population. Taqi's chapter provides an in-depth historical overview of the evolution of this Shia identity in the medieval era, in colonial times and then after the creation of Pakistan.

In 'Constitutional Issues and the Treatment of Pakistan's Religious Minorities', I have attempted an in-depth examination of how Pakistan has failed to fulfil its obligations towards its minorities under the Universal Declaration of Human Rights. The trend of religious immoderation can be traced to the earliest days of Pakistan's emergence as an independent state and continues till today. Pakistan's constitution declares it an Islamic republic. The interpretation of what an Islamic republic means has varied at different times during the seventy years that Pakistan has existed as an independent state.

In 'Understanding the Radicalization of the Bangladeshi Society and Politics', Ali Riaz examines the root causes of radicalization within Bangladeshi society and politics. He presents a multilayered argument tracing the phenomenon to 'highly contentious rivalry among two political parties', rising authoritarianism, a 'constructed binary on national identity' and the emergence of two 'contesting social movements' in 2013. Riaz uses all these factors to trace the radicalization process in Bangladesh.

In 'Religious Intolerance in Bangladesh', C. Christine Fair and Parina Patel undertake an examination of the rise of sectarian and communal intolerance in Bangladesh using a data set derived from a 2017 nationally representative survey of Bangladeshi society. Fair and Patel's analysis shows support for Sharia law among the respondents, high levels of religious intolerance against non-Muslim minorities and sectarian intolerance against Muslim sects.

Read collectively, these essays highlight the trends of religious intolerance and the dominance of majoritarianism across South Asia. It is the hope of the volume's editor and contributors that studying the trend of expanding political support among the majority by targeting minorities would help advance a discourse of greater tolerance both within society and political leaderships of these countries.

Farahnaz Ispahani

1

Religious Majoritarianism in a Diverse Region

HUSAIN HAQQANI

THE SOUTH ASIAN SUBCONTINENT IS home to almost 2 billion people, or a quarter of the world's population. The region's history reflects long phases of inclusivity and pluralism, with only short spurts of communal conflict. Since emerging as modern nation states, all South Asian countries have witnessed a rise in religious majoritarianism and have moved towards religious national identity.

Majoritarianism is defined as 'the idea that pre-existing ethnic, racial or religious majorities have a natural right to dominate a certain political entity'.[1] In India, it means the Hindus; in Bangladesh and Pakistan, it means Muslims; and in Sri Lanka, it means the Buddhists. But in each of these countries, various religious minorities have coexisted alongside the majority for years. The majoritarian trend undermines that coexistence.

In each case where a majority asserts an inherent right to dominate, its narrative portrays the minority as a threat either to its beliefs or its way of life. In some cases, the minority is labelled as being tied to a country's real or perceived enemies. Majoritarianism is often sustained by conspiracy theories and fear. It usually takes only one populist movement to set the majority against minorities. Majoritarianism plays on otherization of the minority, but, if history is any guide, seldom enhances stability or peace in a society.

After several decades of asserting its secular credentials, the world's largest democracy and the most populous South Asian country, India, has witnessed a rise in Hindu majoritarianism and attacks against religious minorities, especially Muslims and Christians. India's religious make-up, as per the 2011 census, was 79.8 per cent Hindu, 14.23 per cent Muslim, 2.3 per cent Christian, 1.7 per cent Sikh and less than 1 per cent Buddhist, Jain and others.[2]

In December 2019, the Indian Parliament passed the controversial CAA. The act amends India's decades-old citizenship law, which currently prohibits illegal migrants from becoming Indian citizens. The new bill makes an exception for these communities—members of six religious minority communities: Hindu, Sikh, Buddhist, Jain, Parsi and Christian—in the process of obtaining citizenship, if they can prove that they are from Pakistan, Afghanistan or Bangladesh. Primarily, it seeks to keep out Muslims, the only religion explicitly omitted in the bill, as a virtual statement of a new policy.

In February 2020, the capital city Delhi witnessed large-scale anti-Muslim riots. These followed a series of other occurrences in the preceding years that targeted India's minorities: attacks on Muslims based on allegations of cow slaughter, attempts to convert Muslims and Christians to Hinduism (*ghar wapsi*) on the grounds that these communities had grown as a result of wrongful conversions over the centuries, and blaming Muslims for spreading COVID-19 ('corona jihad'). Even though the courts have ruled against allegations of 'love jihad' or 'corona jihad' and attempts to misuse the law against cow slaughter, the damage to communal harmony has already been done.[3]

Just as India's secular foundations are being shaken, South Asia's second most populous country, Pakistan, has continued its slide into an even less tolerant quasi-Islamist state. Muslims comprise 96.47 per cent of Pakistan's population. Hindus are around 2 per cent, Christians number 1.27 per cent, and Ahmadi Muslims less than 1 per cent. But their overwhelming numbers are not enough for some Muslims, who still see a danger to Islam and Muslims that must be fought by oppressing the minorities.

Non-Muslim minorities in Pakistan have claimed that the latest census figures have undercounted their numbers. The 2017 census, released in May 2021, shows a rise in the percentage of Muslims and a decline in the percentages of minorities.[4]

Pakistan has one of the world's strictest blasphemy laws, which continues to target the country's beleaguered minorities, including Ahmadis. In 2020, around 200 people were accused of blasphemy, compared to eighty-two people in 2019. The accused are primarily Shia and Ahmadi Muslims, along with some Christians and Hindus.[5]

In July 2020, the government of Imran Khan first allowed the construction of a temple in Islamabad and then backtracked after protests from religious clerics and parties. In 2020, the government of Pakistani Punjab passed measures against Ahmadis and many government officials openly engaged in anti-Ahmadi rhetoric.[6]

In August 2021, the absurdity of Pakistan's blasphemy laws was on full display when an eight-year-old Hindu boy was accused of blasphemy after he urinated in the library of an Islamic school (madrasa). After he was released on bail, the local temple in his village was vandalized by a Muslim mob. A community must be unusually insecure to feel that its faith is threatened by an eight-year-old urinating in the library of a religious school.[7]

The frenzy of Pakistani mobs against small religious minorities is assisted by a political structure and government that defines nationalism through religion. As a US Department of State report on international religious freedom explained, 'Perpetrators of societal violence and abuses against religious minorities [in Pakistan] often faced no legal consequences due to a lack of follow-through by law enforcement, bribes offered by the accused, and pressure on victims to drop cases.'[8]

One would have thought that after breaking away from Pakistan in 1971, Bangladesh would maintain its founders' secular and religiously tolerant outlook with some passion. But its economic and political success notwithstanding, Bangladesh has not been able to keep at bay the religious passions tormenting its neighbours. Over 90 per cent of Bangladesh's population is Muslim, while Hindus are 8 per cent. Buddhists and Christians remain at under 1 per cent.

Several incidents over the last few years show the rise in extremism within Bangladeshi society. In July, a Sufi Muslim was attacked and killed outside a Sufi shrine in Gazipur, and the same month, local residents exhumed the body of an Ahmadi Muslim infant from the cemetery claiming her family members were 'infidels'.[9] In October 2020, a mob of several hundred beat a Muslim to death outside a mosque in Rangpur on the grounds that he had desecrated the Quran.[10]

Attacks against Hindus have been reported in Sylhet and the capital city Dhaka, with homes being set afire and temples attacked.[11] According to the Bangladesh Hindu Buddhist Christian Unity Council (BHBCUC), there was a rise in communal violence against minorities during the COVID-19 pandemic.[12]

Being the larger countries in the region, India, Pakistan, and Bangladesh have larger problems. But the relatively smaller states are also not free of religious friction and the desire of majorities to assert even greater dominance than their numbers already confer.

The Nepali constitution prohibits religious conversion, proselytizing and 'harming the religious sentiment' of any caste, ethnic community or class. The largest religious group is Hindus at 81.3 per cent of the population, followed by Buddhists at 10 per cent, Muslims at 4 per cent and Christians at around 1 per cent. Here, the rise of the Hindu nationalist Rastriya Prajatantra Party (RPP), which seeks to re-establish the country as a Hindu state, has led to a rise in attacks on Muslims and Christians in recent years.

Nepal treats Hinduism and Buddhism as local religions and treats Muslims and Christians differently. For example, some Christian pastors were arrested in 2020 for violating COVID-19 lockdown regulations and for seeking to convert Hindus to Christianity, even though Hindu priests and Buddhist monks were not targeted for similar violations.[13]

The only officially recognized religious organizations that are allowed to own property or operate legally are Buddhist monasteries. Other religious groups, including Muslims and Christians, need to register as non-profit organizations.[14]

Similarly, Sri Lanka's constitution accords 'foremost place' to Buddhism while it recognizes Islam, Hinduism and Christianity as religions practiced by Sri Lankans. Seventy per cent of Sri Lankans are Buddhists, with Hindus at 12.6 per cent of the population, Muslims around 10 per cent, and Christians at around 8 per cent. Human rights organizations have long complained that the Sri Lankan state has engaged in systematic discrimination against religious minorities and that the discrimination is getting sharper with time.

According to the US Department of State report on international religious freedom, 'Reports stated that local government officials and police responded minimally or not at all to numerous incidents of religiously motivated discrimination and violence against minorities. Religious minorities reported government officials and police often sided with Buddhists and did not prevent harassment of religious minorities and their places of worship.'[15] According to Human Rights Watch, in April and May 2020, social media was used to call for a boycott of Muslim-owned businesses.[16]

India

At independence in 1947, the modern Indian state defined Indian nationalism in secular, pluralist and territorial terms. In *The Idea of India*, Sunil Khilnani argues that modern India was shaped by a 'wager' of India's educated urban elite on modern ideas and modern agencies.

'It was a wager on an idea: the idea of India,' Khilnani notes, adding that India's 'nationalist elite itself had no single, clear definition of this idea'. According to him:[17]

> one of the remarkable facts about the nationalist movement that brought India to independence was its capacity to entertain diverse, often contending visions of India ...Indian nationalism before independence was plural even at the top, a dhoti with endless folds...It contains people from markedly different backgrounds yet whose trajectories were often parallel.

Indian secularism as crafted by the Indian national movement and defined in the Indian Constitution was different from American and French Jacobin secularism. Indian secularism meant the state would treat all religions as equal and provide constitutional provisions to ensure there was no discrimination based on religion. Further, it would ensure that the various religious minorities (and even ethnic and linguistic minorities) felt they had equal say, there would be constitutional provisions that allowed minorities to establish educational, cultural and religious organizations, and the state would support this endeavour.

According to Kanchan Chandra, 'It was this secular idea that created India in 1947, not as the Hindu mirror of a Muslim Pakistan, but as the pluralist opposite of majoritarian nationalism. Now, things have changed. With the BJP's rise to become India's governing party, the idea of India is being redefined to mean a Hindu polity. Through acts of violence as well as words and laws, India is debating not whether the country's political system should recognize Hindu identity, but the precise way in which it should be recognized.'[18]

The rise of Hindu majoritarianism is not new. For decades there has been a section of the populace in India which saw Hindu society and Hinduism as under attack, both from what they perceived as centuries of foreign rule (Muslim rule) and from Christian missionaries during the colonial era. The growth of the Arya Samaj (Society of Nobles) in the nineteenth century and its use of *shuddhi* (purification or baptism) and *sangathan* (organization) to force reconversion (ghar wapasi) of Muslims and Christians back to Hinduism was representative of this perspective.

There is remarkable consistency in Hindu conservative thought over the decades: even today, reconversion (ghar wapsi) of non-Hindus back to Hinduism, protection and reconversion of mosques back to temples (Ayodhya's Babri Masjid–Ram Janmabhoomi controversy), and cow protection remain the dominant issues for rallying the Hindu community.

The colonial era and the Indian national struggle gave rise to the question 'who is a Hindu?' This led to the notion that civilizational India's purity has been tarnished by millennia of alien influence and created the demand for rebuilding India as a uniform nation, with one culture, one language and one religion.

In his 1925 tract, 'Hindutva: Who Is a Hindu?', Vinayak Damodar Savarkar attempted to lay out a vision for the 'land of the Hindus'. According to Savarkar, 'A Hindu means a person who regards this land of Bharatvarsha, from the Indus to the Seas, as his fatherland as well as his holy land that is the cradleland of his religion.'[19]

Hence, it was not enough to be born in India or live in India for centuries, rather you needed to treat India as your holy land. This definition excluded Muslims and Christians from their Hindu neighbours, since their religions originated in the Middle East and not in the Indian subcontinent. Savarkar argued, 'although the root meaning of Hindu and Hindi may mean only an Indian, yet it would be straining the usage of words too much if we call a Mohammedan a Hindu because of his being a resident of India.'[20]

The same year Savarkar published his pamphlet and Maharashtra doctor Keshav Baliram Hedgewar founded the Rashtriya Swayamsevak Sangh (RSS—National Volunteer Corps) as a Hindu nationalist ideological organization. Hedgewar and his organization were deeply influenced by the writings of Savarkar.

The RSS also found ideological symbiosis with the All India Hindu Mahasabha (All India Hindu Grand assembly), a political organization formed in 1907—one year after the Muslim League's creation—to pursue a Hindu rashtra (homeland for Hindus). But the conservative current of Hindu thought was not strong enough at the time to forestall the momentum of the unified struggle for India's independence from British rule.

In his book *We or Our Nationhood Defined*, Madhavrao Sadashivrao Golwalkar, the second *sarsanghchalak* of the RSS, wrote, 'Hindusthan is the land of the Hindus and is the terra firma for the Hindu nation alone to flourish upon.'[21] Blaming foreign invaders for destroying Hindu India, Golwalkar spoke of the need for 'national regeneration'. Unlike the Nehruvian idea of India, Golwalkar rejected the concept of 'territorial nationalism' and championed the idea that 'our "Nation" means, and independently of the question of majority always must mean, the Hindu Nation and nothing else'.[22]

The anti-Muslim rhetoric was extremely strident in Golwalkar's thought; he wrote, 'Ever since that evil day, when Moslems first landed in Hindusthan, right up to the present moment, the Hindu Nation has been gallantly fighting on to shake off the despoilers. The Race Spirit has been awakening.'[23] Periodically, alarm bells have been raised about the prospect of Hindus in India being turned into a minority, through higher Muslim birth rates or conversion, including conversion based on marriage.

That such a view is still prevalent is obvious from a recent speech given on 21 July 2021 by the current sarsanghchalak of the RSS, Mohan Bhagwat, who defended amendments to the citizenship act on the grounds that 'Since 1930 there have been planned attempts to increase the Muslim population in India, so that the community becomes a dominant force, and the nation slowly turns into Pakistan. This happened in Punjab, Sindh, Assam, and Bengal. The plan somewhat worked as the Partition happened. But not entirely since Assam got saved because it did not go to Pakistan, even though part of Bengal and Punjab got divided.'[24]

Modern India built a progressive political and economic system but found it difficult to transform society. The element of Indian society that embraces a conservative attitude towards identity and community has stood firm and gained ground at the expense of the liberal component.

These organizations sought to create a 'Hindu political consciousness'—indeed, a Hindu public sphere for causes that were close to their hearts, like banning cow slaughter, Hindi as the national language (with the rejection of Urdu and a pushback against

English), protests against the Hindu code bill, and rejection of the secular Indian Constitution. Over the years, the pull of conservative Indian religious identity proved resistant to top-down attempts to modernize Indian culture.

These beliefs coalesced into the views presented by the BJP as it arose in the 1980s. As Angana Chatterji points out, the rise of a notion of 'the moral force of a majority' helped the emergence of Hindutva politics: 'The success of the BJP has been based on its capacity to instigate anti-minority violence and then reap the electoral benefits of the emotional wave of aggression and fear that communal riots tend to generate.'[25]

Kanchan Chandra, a political scientist, lays out the argument of Hindu majoritarianism as being that 'India should adopt laws that privilege its Hindu majority, while giving non-Hindus diminished legal status'. Chandra notes that if 'majoritarianism were to prevail, India's non-Hindu minorities would become second-class citizens. Many Hindus might become second-class citizens, as well. To see this, consider the BJP's position that the Indian state should ban the slaughter of cows because the cow is sacred to Hindus.'

According to Chandra, the idea of a ban on cow slaughter 'has assumed a new urgency following a recent spate of lynchings of those, often Muslims, accused of killing cows. Some senior BJP leaders have openly backed the killings. But as with most beliefs associated with Hinduism, some Hindus hold cows sacred, and others don't. There are many perfectly traditional beef-eating Hindus, especially in southern and northeastern India. It should be no surprise that many of those lynched for cow slaughter have been Hindus … A ban on cow slaughter would discriminate against these Hindus and non-Hindus alike.'[26]

Tragically, such arguments touch on issues that were first debated in India's Constituent Assembly between 1946 and 1949, when some legislators tried to tie Indian citizenship to religion. During these debates, India's first prime minister, Jawaharlal Nehru; then Deputy Prime Minister and Home Minister Sardar Vallabhbhai Patel; and the draftsman of the Constitution, Dr B.R. Ambedkar, argued vehemently against the use of religion in defining citizenship. Nehru stated, 'You cannot have rules for Hindus, for Muslims or for Christians only.'[27] Patel championed citizenship based on *jus soli,* 'whereby citizenship is acquired by birth within the territory of the state, regardless of parental citizenship', not *jus sanguinis*, 'whereby a person, wherever born, is a citizen of the state if, at the time of his birth, his parent is one'.

While early attempts to tie Indian citizenship to the Hindu religion did not succeed, these ideas never lost currency. Over the last few years, India's secular pluralist credentials have taken a hit with a rise in Hindu majoritarianism and attacks on religious minorities, primarily Muslims. Ten of India's twenty-eight states have laws that restrict religious conversions, and there are numerous incidents of young Muslim men and their families being attacked on the grounds that the men committed 'love jihad', i.e., a Muslim man married a Hindu woman with an eye on the possibility that their children might grow up partially Muslim.[28]

The CAA has drawn criticism because it specifically excludes Muslims from the categories of people who can be given citizenship. The implication is that Muslims are not 'culturally Indian', and thus have no claim to Indian citizenship and cannot place obligations upon the Indian state. In Assam, the National Registry of Citizens (NRC) has been used to document migrants from Bangladesh, which is seen as targeting Muslim Bengalis. These measures reflect new and serious attempts by the current Indian government to create a more exclusive, non-Muslim definition of what it means to be an Indian.

Pakistan

The fear of erosion or submersion in a Hindu majority and a perceived threat to the Islamic way of life was the rallying cry that led to the idea of Pakistan. Pakistan's state ideology is defined through Islam, which now manifests itself in sectarian strife and unending fundamentalist demands. Ethnic cleansing in the territory now constituting Pakistan during the violence that accompanied Partition transformed Pakistan into an even more overwhelmingly Muslim country in demographic terms than originally envisaged.

The nexus between Islam and Pakistan's national identity has created an environment that portrays men of faith as defenders of Pakistan's ideology. Fundamentalists have taken advantage of this nexus, describing their harsh views and violent actions as acting aggressively to 'protect the faith' that defines the Pakistani state and nation. It is difficult for the Pakistani government to act against groups that wrap themselves in Pakistan's flag and claim to be fulfilling Pakistan's raison d'etre.

Pakistan's founders had simultaneously offered two visions of Pakistani nationalism in the process of garnering support for a new nation and state. The first of these is described by historian Faisal Devji as 'Muslim Zion': a land where the Muslim minority dispersed across a vast subcontinent could escape the majority's persecution, which they, rightly or wrongly, feared.[29] The other imagining of Pakistan has been described by another historian, Venkat Dhulipala, as 'New Medina': 'the harbinger of Islam's renewal and rise in the twentieth century, the new leader and protector of the global community of Muslims, and a worthy successor to the defunct Turkish Caliphate'.[30]

Depending on the audience, Pakistan's founder, Muhammad Ali Jinnah, and his lieutenants used the two visions alternately in their speeches and interviews in the run-up to Partition. After Independence, Jinnah attempted to set Pakistan's direction away from a theocracy. He told Pakistan's Constituent Assembly that he envisaged a Pakistan where, over time, 'these angularities of the majority and minority communities, the Hindu community and the Muslim community', would vanish.

Jinnah expressed the hope that ideally, 'In course of time, Hindus would cease to be Hindus, and Muslims would cease to be Muslims, not in the religious sense, because that is the personal faith of each individual, but in the political sense as citizens of the State.'[31]

That speech of Jinnah is often cited as representing a secular vision of Pakistan.

'You are free,' he said, 'you are free to go to your temples, you are free to go to your mosques or to any other place of worship in this State of Pakistan. You may belong to any religion or caste or creed—that has nothing to do with the business of the State.'[32] But one speech was not enough to clarify the deliberate ambiguity that had characterized the campaign for Pakistan's creation in the preceding seven years. A few months after stating that religion has nothing to do with the business of state, Jinnah went on to describe Pakistan as 'this mighty land' that had 'been brought under a rule which is Islamic'.[33]

The secular Muslim nationalist path was never taken and was abandoned in stages after Jinnah's death. When Pakistan's first prime minister, Liaquat Ali Khan, presented the 'Objectives Resolution' in the country's Constituent assembly in March 1949, it became the first formal step towards transforming Pakistan into an Islamic ideological state. The resolution outlined the main principles of a future Pakistani constitution, which it defined as democracy, freedom, equality and social justice 'as enunciated by Islam'. This opened the door for many controversies about what Islam required of a state.

The Objectives Resolution settled Pakistan's status as an Islamic ideological state. But creating an ideological state based on Islam that was compatible with modern times was not easy. Islam means different things to different people, which is why there are several Muslim sects and denominations. To sidestep problems that might emerge from letting clerics, or even the will of the people, define the contours of an Islamic state, permanent institutions of state (the military and the civil bureaucracy) took control of the process of building the new nation.

Pakistan ended up becoming a highly centralized state. The secular elite, beginning with Liaquat, assumed that they would continue to lead the country while rallying the people on the basis of Islamic ideology. For them, theologians and Islamist activists could be allies but they were not to be empowered to the point where they would start writing laws or running government departments. But the westernized elite's attempt at paying lip service to Islam received serious pushback from Islamists, who sought a greater share in power.

Through much of Pakistan's history, secular competitors for power have enrolled the help of clerics and religious agitators to put rivals on the defensive. Politicians and even civil servants and generals have plotted against each other by orchestrating criticism of rivals as 'un-Islamic'. Entire sects and communities have been tarnished in the advancement of political goals.

A major manifestation of the pitfalls of religion-based politics came in January 1953, when clerics of various Muslim denominations demanded that the Ahmadi sect be declared non-Muslim for legal purposes. Widespread riots soon followed, resulting in dozens of deaths and considerable loss to property. Reflecting what has been a consistent pattern in Pakistan's history, the religious demand also had a worldly purpose. Punjabi politicians had instigated the clerics in the hope of dislodging the government of the Bengali prime minister, Khawaja Nazimuddin, who had assumed office after Liaquat's assassination two years earlier.[34]

Pakistan's secular leadership succeeded in pushing back a religious demand and the army enforced order, putting the Islamists and their rioting followers in their place. Still, the events of that year highlighted three interlinked problems that have dogged Pakistan's internal politics since Independence: part of the state apparatus used religion and religious groups for a political purpose; the extent of the religious groups' influence and the sentiment unleashed by them could not be fully controlled; and the military stepped in to deal with the symptoms of the chaos generated by religious–political agitation, without making any effort to deal with its causes.

At the time, the government set up a Commission of Inquiry, headed by the chief justice of the Lahore High Court, Muhammad Munir (who went on to become Chief Justice of Pakistan), to look into the causes of the anti-Ahmadi disturbances. The most important statement of the commission, however, related to the differences among the clerics, which would divide Pakistanis more strongly than religion could unite them. 'The ulema were divided in their opinions when they were asked to cite some precedent of an Islamic State in Muslim history,' Justice Munir reported, pointing out that 'no two learned divines are agreed' even on the fundamental definition of who is a Muslim.

Since then, Pakistan has witnessed several rounds of religion-based violence. Pakistan's minorities have often paid the price as the country has Islamized further over the years. Curricula and textbooks have been standardized, presenting a version of history that ties Pakistan's emergence to Islam's arrival in the subcontinent instead of it being the outcome of a dispute over the constitution of postcolonial India. Young Pakistanis are taught to see the history of Islam not as the history of a religion or a civilization, but as a prelude to the creation of the Pakistani state.

In 1974, the Pakistani Constitution was amended to declare Ahmadis as non-Muslims. Islamist demands against the Ahmadis were no different this time around from those made almost two decades earlier. But in 1953, Prime Minister Nazimuddin had been willing to call in the army to stop the rioters and Justice Munir had written his report pointing out the problem with the state accepting demands to define which sect was or was not Islamic. This time around, Prime Minister Zulfikar Ali Bhutto failed to follow in Nazimuddin's footsteps and there was no one of Munir's stature to remind the government that it should not allow clerics to dictate legislation.

General Zia-ul-Haq's military dictatorship (1977–1988) marked the pinnacle of Pakistan's embrace of Islam as the national ideology. Examples of Zia's Islamization include the blasphemy laws, the creation of Shariat courts with powers to challenge and strike down laws that were deemed un-Islamic, the ordinances forbidding Ahmadis from engaging in any practice that might make them seem Muslims, and the introduction of *zakat* and *ushr* religious taxes. Zia also ordered heads of government departments to organize prayers for their staff every day,[35] creating an excuse for government officials to take time off from work, ostensibly for prayer.

'The ideology of Pakistan is Islam and only Islam,' Zia once thundered, declaring secularism to be a threat to the country. 'There should be no misunderstanding on this score. We should in all sincerity accept Islam as Pakistan's basic ideology,' he said, adding that if that was not done, Pakistan would 'be exposed to secular ideologies'.[36]

Although Zia was killed in a plane crash in 1988, Pakistan has not recovered from his Islamization. Several Pakistani leaders have publicly acknowledged the need for rolling back Islamic militancy and rationalizing Islamic laws such as those relating to blasphemy. But no one has been able to systematically reopen the debate on how Pakistan might make policy decisions based on economic and social necessities rather than on the basis of religious affectation.

There has been a rise in attacks against Shias, in addition to Ahmadis and non-Muslim religious minorities. In 2017, a row over proposed changes to the election law, which would have eased some of the barriers on Ahmadis participating in elections, led to street protests by the Khatm-e-Nubuwwat and Tehreek-e-Labbaik and ended in the government backtracking on its decision.[37]

In the summer of 2020, Pakistan witnessed anti-Shia campaigns on social media that demanded that Shia Muslims be declared heretics. The Punjab Assembly passed the Tahaffuz-e-Bunyad-e-Islam (protection of foundation of Islam) Bill, which supported only the Sunni interpretation of Islam. In September 2020, over 30,000 people joined a protest organized by extremist Sunni Muslim groups in Karachi for over two days and demanded that Shia Muslims be called 'unbelievers' and 'blasphemers'.[38]

Islamic ideology not only sets Pakistan apart from India, notwithstanding many commonalities of history, culture, and social mores. This ideology or Nazariya e Pakistan (Ideology of Pakistan) has also been used by the Pakistani state to resist policy pressures from major international powers. In some ways, it is a weapon amid weakness, even if it is a gun held to one's own head. Constant indignation at real or perceived indignities against Islam are a useful device for Pakistan's politicians and Islamists. It distracts from substantive economic and social issues. Often, religious rage is generated through falsehoods and rumours, which are systematically deployed as vehicles of policy.

The periodic outbreaks of protest over insults to Prophet Muhammad and to Islam are hardly spontaneous. In each case, the protesters do not react to something they see or become aware of in the ordinary course of life. Most of the objects of complaint—a remark made in private, a book published in the West or a movie that has not been released in Pakistan—are not widely available and yet, the public is whipped into a fury. The Islamists first introduce the objectionable material to their audience and then instigate outrage by characterizing it as part of a supposed worldwide conspiracy to denigrate Islam.

The emergence of social media and the swiftness of international communications have made it easier to choreograph global campaigns, and in Muslim-majority countries, Islamists tend to be among those who are most effectively organized to take advantage of technology for political ends. But Pakistan has been a particular centre of campaigns to 'protect Islam' and the 'Prophet's honour', each starting with frenzy and fizzling out without attaining its stated objective.

In the process of moulding a nation on the basis of Islam, Pakistan has ended up earning for itself the reputation for being home to the world's angriest Muslims. That anger results in periodic attacks on hapless minorities, constant legislation to further Islamize a country that has a 97 per cent Muslim population, and a majority that is still not satisfied with its dominance of the country.

Sri Lanka

The roots of Sinhalese-Buddhist majoritarianism and of the fear of the ethnic—Tamil—and religious—Muslim and Christian—

minorities are in the siege mentality of the Sinhala majority and the fear that these minorities are powerful elsewhere in the world and will use that leverage to impose decisions on the Sinhala Buddhists.

The Sinhalese comprise 75 per cent of Sri Lanka's population and the majority of them are Buddhists. Tamils comprise around 11 per cent of the population and are Hindus, Muslims and Christians. The Tamils in Sri Lanka comprise both, those who have been living on the island for centuries and those who were brought by the British during the colonial era. The colonial era, during which the Tamil minority benefitted from British largesse, left a bitter legacy for Sinhala-Tamil relations.

The Tamil question in Sri Lanka has long had an impact on Sri Lankan nationalism. Among the Sinhalese, there is a deep sense of insecurity, a fear of being absorbed by Hindu India and the belief that even those Tamils who have lived in Sri Lanka for centuries are 'Indian' or 'Indian agents'. The Sri Lankan Buddhist majority has long suffered from a minority complex.[39]

Like in India and Pakistan, Sinhala Buddhist nationalism's ideological origins lie in the Buddhist revival of the late nineteenth century, which began as a reaction to British colonial rule and the perceived attacks on Buddhism under a Christian imperial power.

According to Anagarika Dharmapala, a Sri Lankan Buddhist revivalist in the nineteenth century, 'There exists no race on this earth today that has a more glorious, triumphant record of victory than the Sinhalese. Sons of Aryan ancestors, they built their first city and called it Anuradhapura, after the prince Anuradha and the constellation Anura. Fifty-four years before the Battle of Marathon, the Sinhalese had conquered Ceylon; nine years after the conquest of the Kingdom of Candahar by Alexander the Great; and one hundred and eleven years before the destruction of the Carthegian Power; and forty-three years before the consolidation of the Roman Empire, the Religion (sic) of the Buddha was established.'[40]

Many Sinhala political leaders have used Dharmapala's arguments that Sinhalese Buddhists were the 'true owners' of Sri Lanka's historical civilization, which had been destroyed by 'barbaric vandals': Tamils, Muslims and then Europeans. Further, any appeals for tolerance and interethnic or interfaith harmony, according to this argument, are simply a ploy by Sri Lankan elites—who were at one time dominated by Tamils—to suppress Sinhalese Buddhists.

Such views came to the forefront of Sri Lankan domestic politics in the 1950s when the Sri Lanka Freedom Party (SLFP), led by Solomon West Ridgeway Dias Bandaranaike, won the elections. In an interview Bandaranaike gave to BBC News, he asserted that since 70 per cent of Sri Lanka was Sinhala, their language had to be Sinhalese. Tamil was no longer recognized as a state language. Bandaranaike's government was a nationalist one that gave Buddhism, the majority religion, a prominent place in the affairs of state.

The next two decades witnessed anti-Tamil riots and the rise of an insurgency which resulted in the creation of groups like the Liberation of Tamil Tigers Eelam (LTTE), a terrorist group, which fought for a separate Tamil state. As a Buddhist monk stated in an interview in the late 1990s, 'Get this straight and quote me. Sri Lanka is a Buddhist Sinhala country. Let no one make a mistake. Seventy per cent of the country consists of Buddhists and Sinhala people. Also make this clear that Sri Lanka is the only Buddhist Sinhala country in the world. If we don't live here, are the LTTE (Liberation Tigers of Tamil Eelam) and some of the Tamil parties asking us to jump into the sea? I got angry with Mr Premadasa because he chose to call Sri Lanka a multi-national and multi-religious state. No. It is a Buddhist Sinhala state.'[41]

Decades of civil war later, in 2009, the LTTE and its remnants were eliminated by Sri Lankan troops. What happened over these decades, however, was the rise of separate political parties that represent the Sinhala Buddhists and the Tamils.

According to a prominent politician from a Sinhala national political party, the Jathika Hela Urumaya (JHU), 'We know there are English in England, French in France, Thai in Thailand, and Japanese in Japan. They are the people who created the civilization in those countries. This doesn't mean there aren't minorities in those countries. Likewise, Sri Lanka is the country of the Sinhalese and Sinhalese civilization was born in Sri Lanka.'[42]

That these views are still prevalent is obvious from a statement given by Galagoda Aththe Gnanasara, the general secretary of the Bodu Bala Sena, in 2019 after the election of President Gotabaya Rajapaksa. 'We built an ideology that the country needs a Sinhala leader who does not bend down in front of minorities,' he declared, adding, 'Now that ideology has won. Halal, burqa, Islamic banks, Kathi courts, Shariah universities, those all destroyed social integrity that we do have. Gotabaya can establish one rule, one nation, one country.'[43]

There has also been a rise in Sinhala extremist groups like the Bodu Bala Sena (Buddhist power force, BBS), Sinhala Ravaya (Sinhala roar), and Ravana Balaya, which have been accused of attacks against non-Buddhist minorities, especially Tamils. The BBS was founded in 2012 with the goal of 'protecting Sri Lankan Buddhism from all kinds of external influence and to uphold the Buddhist way of life'.

According to the leader of the BBS, 'Sri Lanka is a predominantly Buddhist country. We want all other communities to respect Buddhist culture ... If a Muslim is attacked there are many countries to defend them, but no one is there to defend Buddhism except the people of Sri Lanka.'[44]

International criticism of Sri Lanka's policies against its Tamil minorities simply elicits the response that these minorities—Tamil or Muslim or Christian—are simply using their international connections to criticize Sri Lanka. 'If something happens to the Muslims and Tamils all the embassies will raise their voices. But if something happens to the Sinhalese, no one is there to protect (us).'[45]

Conclusion

It appears that a wave of majoritarianism is currently sweeping South Asia. In almost every country of the region, the majority's overwhelming numerical superiority is deemed insufficient and political leaders, as well as some intellectuals, have created a sense of insecurity that results in the majority fearing the minority. The minority is the 'other' against which the majority can be mobilized. Any number of arguments can be, and are, invoked to explain why the majority's dominance is necessary and why what seem like extreme measures are simply steps taken to protect the majority's beliefs, rights or sentiments.

In India, resentment against minorities has been bred for having the same faith as past conquerors (Muslim sultans, Christian British colonialists). In Pakistan, the country's national ideology and its aspiration to be the leader of a global Islamic revival have become the source of hostility towards people of other faiths. Stern blasphemy laws and mob violence are said to protect the Muslim majority's sentiments in Pakistan, without regard for the life and property of non-Muslims or even of the 'wrong kind of Muslim'. And in Sri Lanka, a narrative has been built that unless they victimize the minorities, the Sinhalese Buddhist majority runs the risk of being itself victimized.

At the moment, there appears to be relatively little support among the advocates of majoritarianism for the views expressed by Indian Supreme Court Judge D.Y. Chandrachud, who said,

> Majoritarian tendencies, whenever and however they arise, must be questioned against the background of our constitutive promise. Any semblance of authoritarianism, clampdown on civil liberties, sexism, casteism, otherization on account of religion or region upset a sacred promise that was made to our ancestors who accepted India as their constitutional Republic.[46]

2

Muslimophobia in India

Reasons and Remedy

A. FAIZUR RAHMAN

THE 'RIGHTWARD SHIFT' IN INDIAN politics that catapulted the BJP, led by Narendra Modi, to power in May 2014 has been a cause of concern for many. Some fear that Prime Minister Modi, through his successful promotion of Hindutva ideology, is poised to remake India into a Russian-style 'managed democracy'—one retaining all the trappings of democracy while operating as a de facto autocracy.[1]

Others are worried that the long-cherished idea of India as a benign, inclusive state is collapsing and giving way to a less pluralistic, less inclusive and less tolerant country where patriotism becomes indistinguishable from chauvinism, and democracy metamorphoses into one-man rule.[2]

Amplifying this sense of disquietude, the US Commission on International Religious Freedom (USCIRF), in its 2020 Annual Report released on 28 April 2020,[3] exhorted the American government to designate India as a Country of Particular Concern (CPC) 'for engaging in and tolerating systematic, ongoing, and egregious religious freedom violations, as defined by the International Religious Freedom Act (IRFA)'.[4]

One of the main reasons cited for this drastic recommendation was Uttar Pradesh Chief Minister Yogi Adityanath's alleged pledge to exact 'revenge' on anti-CAA protestors and his statement that they should be fed 'bullets not biryani'. The report also claimed that throughout 2019, 'government action—including the CAA, continued enforcement of cow slaughter and anti-conversion laws, and the November Supreme Court ruling on the Babri Masjid site—created a culture of impunity for nationwide campaigns of harassment and violence against religious minorities'.[5]

But the most serious imputation was the finding that mob lynching of persons suspected of cow slaughter or of consuming beef continued, that it occurred mostly in BJP-ruled states and that the lynch mobs 'often took on overtly Hindu nationalist tones'.[6] As evidence, the report cited the June 2019 mob attack in Jharkhand on Tabrez Ansari, a Muslim, who was forced to chant the Hindu slogan 'Jai Shri Ram' (Hail Lord Ram) before being beaten to death.[7]

Earlier, a survey had made the shocking revelation that every third Indian policeperson thinks it is natural 'to a large extent' or 'somewhat' for a mob to punish culprits when there is a case of cow slaughter.[8]

The Indian government was quick to reject the USCIRF report, calling it 'biased and tendentious'.[9] However, a news analysis published in *The Hindu* quoted Nirupama Menon Rao, former Indian ambassador to the US, as stating that the report could not be ignored outright because 'there is a reputational issue involved, for India, as the world's largest democracy that draws strength from the protection of diversity'.[10] Similar views were echoed by a constitutional law scholar who argued that while the government was right at the diplomatic level to reject the report, the criticism ought to be seen as an opportunity to reflect on the state of freedom of religion in India.[11] Meanwhile, in its 2021 Annual Report, the USCIRF again asked the US government to designate India as a CPC and 'condemn ongoing religious freedom violations and support religious organizations and human rights groups being targeted for their advocacy of religious freedom'.[12]

It cannot be denied that in the recent past, Muslims in India have been demonized, abused, suspected and some even lynched with impunity in the name of religion.[13] Such acts of intimidation and mindless violence rose sharply after it came to light that several participants in the Tablighi Jamaat's Delhi conference, held in March 2020, had tested positive for COVID-19.[14]

Local newspapers carried horrifying accounts of how Muslims were mercilessly assaulted on suspicion of intentionally spreading the coronavirus.[15] The brutalities included people putting up posters banning the entry of Muslims into towns and villages and the circulation of anti-Muslim videos.[16] One of the most brazen expressions of hate was encapsulated in a video which showed the principal of a medical college allegedly calling the Tablighis 'terrorists' who deserved to be 'locked up in dungeons' rather than treated in hospitals.[17] Among the international publications that reported these crimes prominently were *The Guardian*,[18] *The New York Times*,[19] *The Washington Post*[20] and *Time*.[21] The Organization of Islamic Cooperation (OIC) also voiced its 'deep concern' on the growing Islamophobia in India and urged the Indian government to take steps to protect Muslim minorities, who were being negatively profiled and facing discrimination and violence amid the COVID-19 crisis.[22]

The courts, on their part, highlighted how the psychological impact of this enervating onslaught could go beyond traumatizing its direct victims and have a demoralizing effect on all Muslims in India. Quashing a case filed against Tablighi Jamaat members under the Disaster Management Act of 2005 and Epidemic Diseases Act of 1897, the Aurangabad bench of the Bombay High Court (through Justice T.V. Nalawade) noted that:

> It can be said that due to the present action taken, fear was created in the minds of those Muslims. This action indirectly gave warning to Indian Muslims that action in any form and for any thing can be taken against Muslims. It was indicated that even for keeping contact with Muslims of other countries, action will be taken against them. Thus, there is smell of malice to the action taken against these foreigners and Muslim for their alleged activities. The circumstances like malice is important consideration when relief is claimed of quashing of F.I.R. and the case itself.[23]

Earlier, in the Tehseen Poonawalla v Union of India & Others case [(2018) 9 SCC 501], a three-Judge bench of Justices Dipak Misra, A.M. Khanwilkar, and D.Y. Chandrachud had recognized the psychological impact of persecutory bullying. While asking the Parliament 'to create a separate offence for [mob] lynching and provide adequate punishment for the same' the bench asked state governments to prepare 'a lynching/mob violence victim compensation scheme in the light of the provisions of Section 357A of CrPC' giving due regard to the nature of not just bodily injury, but 'psychological injury and loss of earnings including loss of opportunities of employment and education and expenses incurred on account of legal and medical expenses.'[24]

The Supreme Court was also forced was forced to restrain television channel Sudarshan News from broadcasting a programme which had promised to expose the 'UPSC jihad conspiracy'[25] to infiltrate the Indian bureaucracy. Suresh Chavhanke, the editor of the channel, had also allegedly claimed that India was meant to be a Hindu rashtra right from Independence.[26] A three-judge bench of the apex court did not mince words when it said that the purpose of the programme was 'to vilify the Muslim community' and to bring it 'into public hatred and disrepute'.[27]

In this context, a report released in March 2022 by the Akhil Bharatiya Pratinidhi Sabha (ABPS)—the highest decision-making body of the RSS—stated: 'There appears to be elaborate plans by a particular community to enter the government machinery. Behind all this, it seems that a deep conspiracy with a long-term goal is working. On the strength of numbers, preparations are being made to adopt any route to get their points convinced.' One wonders which particular Indian community the ABPS was warning about.[28]

It would appear, however, that even hard-hitting judicial pronouncements did not have the desired impact. Three states—Uttar Pradesh, Himachal Pradesh and Madhya Pradesh—in the name of preventing religious conversion for the sake of marriage, passed tough anti-conversion laws to address the myth of 'love-jihad', an unsubstantiated Muslim complot to convert Hindu women to Islam after luring them into marriage.[29] A former judge of the Supreme Court of India dubbed these laws as ill-conceived and unconstitutional for vilifying interfaith marriages and placing unreasonable obstacles on consenting adults in exercising their personal choice of a partner.[30]

Another independent commentator described this suspicious attitude as an attempt to misrepresent the Quranic concept of 'jihad' by inventing hyphenated terms such as love jihad, corona jihad and

UPSC jihad to project Muslims as some kind of conspirators actively scheming against India's Hindu majority.[31]

An interesting finding of a major (June 2021) Pew Research Center survey of religion across India is that 80 per cent of Indian Muslims believe it is very important to stop Muslim women from marrying outside their religion, and 76 per cent say it is very important to stop Muslim men from doing so.[32] This would not have been the case if the community was indeed conspiring, as alleged, to increase its numbers through interfaith marriage. As for religious conversion, the survey found that it has 'a minimal impact on the size of religious groups', and that Hindus gain as many people as they lose through 'religious switching'.

These findings, however, had little impact on Islamophobes. In December 2021, calls for the massacre of Indian Muslims were made from a Dharam Sansad (religious parliament) held in the north Indian city of Haridwar. Annapurna Maa, a saffron-clad 'religious' lady, said that she would 'pick up arms to protect Sanatan Dharma if any demon tries to become a threat to Hindutva'. She warned that the situation in India is alarming, and therefore 'I am willing to sacrifice myself to ensure a Muslim prime minister does not take over in 2029. We need to increase our population over them. If needed, we can kill them. We will be considered winners even if 20 lakh [two million] of their population is killed.'[33]

From an anthropological point of view, one wonders what enculturation process could explain the revulsion that these men and women feel for Indian Muslims. For, no ancient or modern exponent of the great Indian system of life—Sanatana Dharma—had ever philosophized about a world where hate rules in place of love.

Swami Vivekananda, the celebrated apostle of Vedanta, explained in 1898 that 'without the help of practical Islam, the theories of Vedantism, however fine and wonderful they may be, are entirely valueless to the vast mass of mankind'. He proposed harmonizing the Vedas, the Bible and the Quran to teach humanity that 'religions are but the varied expressions of the religion, which is Oneness, so that each may choose that path that suits him best'.[34]

Muslimophobia

But how and why did things deteriorate so quickly for Muslims? On the face of it, the suddenness of these disturbing developments may appear inexplicable. But Islamophobia in India has a long history.

Muslim presence in the subcontinent dates back to around 630 CE, when Islamized Arab merchants started arriving in the coastal regions of Konkan, Gujarat and Malabar in continuation of the trade links they had had with India from pre-Islamic times. The cordiality of this business relationship was such that it resulted in not just the spread of Islamic culture in India but also in the conversion of Indians to Islam. It flourished for a long time, unaffected even by the forays of invaders such as Mahmud of Ghazni (971–1030), Muhammad Ghori (1149–1206) and Muhammad bin Qasim, the Arab general of the sixth Umayyad Caliph Abd al-Malik ibn Marwan (674–715), who captured Sindh and Multan from Raja Dahir around 711 CE.

However, the procession of Muslim conquerors that followed Muhammad bin Qasim seriously damaged Indo-Muslim propinquity, and by the turn of the twentieth century, a deep mistrust had developed between Muslims and Hindus. The Muslims came to be seen as outsiders who had come to conquer and convert the original inhabitants of the subcontinent to Islam.

For instance, in the late 1800s, Dayananda Saraswati's Arya Samaj tried, as Nehru put it, 'to become a defender of everything Hindu, against what it considered as the encroachments of other faiths'. Nehru had no doubt that the Arya Samaj was a reaction to the influence of Islam and Christianity, especially the former.[35] Indeed, the emergence of the Tablighi Jamaat in the mid-1920s was partly in response to the reconversion (shuddhi) movement of the Arya Samaj.[36]

The Arya Samaj's systematic attack on Islam intensified Hindu–Muslim antagonism and resulted in fifteen major riots between 1883 and 1891 over 'kine slaughter' (cow slaughter).[37] The animosity lingered on, with the effect that in the run-up to the Partition, pan-Islamic politics surrounding the Khilafat Movement were imputed to the entire community and it was charged with harbouring extra-territorial loyalties.

Gandhi did his best to remedy the situation but failed. In a well-attended unity conference in 1925, when he lamented about how the Ali brothers—once his staunch allies in the Non-cooperation–Khilafat movement—had been unfairly accused of wanting to invite the Afghans to raid India, Arya Samaj leader Lajpat Rai's response was that Muslim protestations about their love for India and their 'readiness to resist foreign invasions' were so hemmed in by 'ifs' and 'buts' that they left an 'atmosphere of distrust in many Hindu minds'. This prompted Jinnah to bitterly complain against this 'illogical and unwarranted feeling of Lalaji' and announce that he was 'perfectly willing and ready' to do anything to alleviate it.[38]

Nonetheless, in April 1925, Rai resigned from the Congress and became the president of the Hindu Mahasabha, months after conceding that anti-Muslim sentiments were the raison d'être of this movement, which imagined India as a Hindu rashtra.[39] Rai's Hindu tilt and his ideological antipathy to the Congress were not new. As early as 1901, he had warned the Congress against attempting 'a chimerical and premature union of the various religious nationalities' in India, and accused it of sacrificing Hindu interests for the 'false ideal' of national unity.[40]

It is not surprising, therefore, that long before Jinnah could imagine Pakistan, it was Rai who, in 1905, spoke of 'a clear partition of India into a Muslim India and a non-Muslim India.'[41] The 'non-Muslim India' could only have been a euphemism for a Hindu rashtra to be constituted on the principles of Hindutva.

Hindutva

Hindutva owes its popularity to Vinayak Damodar Savarkar (1883–1966), the Hindu Mahasabha leader who had made it the pivotal theme of his 1923 essay 'Essentials of Hindutva' (retitled 'Hindutva: Who Is a Hindu?' in 1928). The idea itself, however, had been introduced in Bengal during the 1890s by Chandranath Basu (1844–1910) in his Bengali essay 'Hindutva—an Authentic History of the Hindus', which extolled the superiority of Hinduism over other religions.[42]

Around the same time, another Bengali writer, Bankim Chandra Chatterjee (1838–1894), invoked Hindutva to arouse the Hindus. His provocative 1882 novel *Anandamath* fictionalized Hindu nationalistic sentiments in Bengal by narrating how 'everyone was angry with the Muslims for the anarchy and lawlessness of their reign', and how Hindus were keen to establish a sense of Hindutva because 'Hindu rule of life had disappeared' (*hindudharmer bilope anek hindui hindutva sthapaner janya agrahacitta chila*).[43] Interestingly, even the concept of Bharat Mata and the Hindus-are-in-danger notion appear to have had their origins in nineteenth-century Bengal.[44]

However, it is Savarkar's interpretation that forms the basis of Hindutva today. It ideologically links Hindutva with the term

Hindu, which Savarkar defined as one who (1) regards the entire subcontinent as his fatherland (pitrubhu), (2) is descended of Hindu parents and (3) and considers this land holy (*punyabhu*).[45] These three conditions signify a common nation (rashtra), a common race (jati) and a common civilization (*sanskriti*), respectively. And together they form the foundation on which Hindutva rests.[46]

This understanding has a lot in common with the theory of Aryanism which postulates that the Hindu race, because of its pre-eminence in every department of human activity, is the greatest nation that has flourished yet on this earth.[47] And the religion of this nation, unlike 'other religions', is not a confession of weakness or an admission of human helplessness that relies on an external power for salvation. It is an embodiment of the dignity and independence of the 'supreme manhood' of its adherents.[48]

Their land (India) too is masculine (pitrubhu). In Aryan terms, it is called Aryavarta (the abode of the Aryas) and encompasses the Gangetic plains of north India, Rajasthan and Punjab, where the Aryas settled after defeating various local savage people. They are believed to be the descendants of the nomadic pastoralist people mentioned in the Rig Veda who came to India around 2,000 BCE.[49] However, for a section of the Hindu right today, the Aryas were not outsiders. The 'eternal and unhistorical' nature of their religion makes them the autochthonous inhabitants of Aryavarta.[50]

The emergence of India after Independence as a secular, democratic republic under Nehru saw the advocates of Hindu nationalism go into a state of political quiescence, especially after the assassination of Mahatma Gandhi in January 1948, which led to the ban on the RSS, a prominent Hindutva organization, on suspicion of being involved in the killing. This dormancy lasted beyond the assassination of Indira Gandhi, who had also banned the RSS during the infamous Emergency (1975–77).

But Hindutva could not be suppressed for long. It was back on form in the 1980s when the Vishwa Hindu Parishad (VHP), another Hindu nationalist organization, started a movement for the construction of a Ram temple in Ayodhya at the very spot where the sixteenth century Babri Masjid stood, claiming it to be the place where Lord Ram was born. The VHP's campaign came soon after the formal launch of the BJP in April 1980, which lost no time in announcing its support for the movement, perhaps as an act of political expediency. One of the BJP's prominent leaders, Lal Krishna Advani, embarked on a provocative pro-temple *rath yatra* (chariot journey) in 1990 to Ayodhya from Somnath in Gujarat. Since then, Hindutva has dominated the national discourse.

On 6 December 1992, the Babri Masjid was demolished by a huge mob, sparking riots across the country.[51] Although commitments were made to restore the status quo ante of the disputed site and rebuild the mosque at the same place, they were never honoured.[52] Meanwhile, thanks to Hindutva, the BJP widened its political footprint and found itself in the seat of power with a landslide victory in May 2014.

After assuming office, the party did try to arrange an out-of-court settlement of the mosque–temple imbroglio, but in vain.[53] Finally, in November 2019, within months of the BJP winning a second term, the Supreme Court of India decided the case in favour of the temple being built there. This was followed by the acquittal of all the thirty-two accused in the Babri Masjid demolition case, including L.K. Advani.[54]

Although this brought closure to the longest Hindu–Muslim dispute in the history of India, legal scholars criticized both judgments.[55] RSS chief Mohan Bhagwat was, however, certain that

'Hindutva is the essence of this (Hindu) Rashtra's 'swa' (selfhood). We are plainly acknowledging the selfhood of the country as Hindu.'[56] Soon, huge rallies were launched to collect funds for the construction of the new Ram temple in Ayodhya.

In one such VHP rally organized in Delhi in January 2021, provocative slogans were raised invoking Hindu *talwarein* (swords) and *trishul* (tridents) as a warning to those who presumed Hindus to be weak, but not just that—*kar sevaks* (volunteers) from the locality who were in Ayodhya during the demolition of the Babri Masjid were honoured.[57]

Reasons for Muslimophobia

A deeper analysis of the Hindu right's historical Muslimophobia would reveal that the main reason for it was not Islam but a sense of political insecurity born out of exaggerated fears of a Muslim demographic threat. These anxieties came to the fore in 1905 when Bengali Hindus vehemently opposed the partition of Bengal into the provinces of 'Bengal' in the west and 'Eastern Bengal and Assam' in the east. They apprehended that it would reduce them to a minority in the western province and launched such intense protests that the British were forced to revoke the decision in 1911.

In Punjab, too, it was feared that the Punjab Land Acquisition Act of 1900 would force Hindus—'sons of the soil and its most ancient inhabitants'—out of agriculture and into other competitive professions, because of which they were in danger of becoming a minority not just in Punjab, but in all of India.[58] The bogey of Muslim political domination was raised again when the Indian Councils Act of 1909 introduced separate electorates for them. While the cry of 'Hindus in danger' was raised by certain Punjabi Hindus led by Lajpat Rai, Lal Chand and Munshi Ram, others sought to convince the Hindus of the importance of *shuddhi* and *sangathan*. That apart, petitions for cow protection were circulated, and steps were taken to form separate associations for the Hindu and Muslim press.[59]

What is astonishing is that even a great liberal-minded jurist like B.R. Ambedkar suspected the loyalty of Muslims. His fear was that with the Indian army being predominantly Muslim in its composition, and with most of these Muslims being drawn from Punjab and the North West Frontier Province (NWFP), in the event of a foreign invasion from the north-west by a Muslim neighbour like Afghanistan, Muslims might join the invader rather than defend India, and would almost certainly disobey orders if India were to ever decide to invade Afghanistan.[60]

Ambedkar, therefore, wanted Hindus to welcome Pakistan's separation from India so as to have a 'safe army'. He also rhetorically asked them whether it was better to have the Muslims 'without and against or if they should be within and against'. The best option, therefore, was to concede the territory of Pakistan, for that was 'the only way of getting rid of the Muslim preponderance in the Indian Army'.[61]

Ambedkar had another important reason for conceding Jinnah's demand for a separate Muslim state. He felt that without Pakistan, the 'communal problem' would involve 65 million Muslims, while after its creation, it would involve only 20 million Muslims in India. This would greatly reduce the proportion of Muslim to Hindu seats in central and provincial legislatures in India, which would fall even further once weightage was cancelled. It would also 'free the Hindus from the turbulence of Muslims as predominant partners'.[62]

In fact, long before Hindutva parties accused the post-Partition Congress of Muslim appeasement, Ambedkar had warned the party, saying that its policy of appeasement and concession would only exacerbate Muslim aggressiveness, for they would interpret it as a sign of Hindu defeatism. The Hindus might thus find themselves in the same fearful situation that the Allies found themselves in as a result of their appeasement policy towards Hitler.[63]

Notwithstanding Ambedkar's shocking views, one would have expected the Hindu right's unfounded worries of Muslim ascendancy to end or subside after India's independence. But they continued to be highlighted periodically. In September 2004, the VHP working president of north Gujarat region, Chinubhai Patel, expressing alarm at the 36 per cent rise in the decadal growth of Muslims reported in the 2001 census, said that the community was 'conspiring to convert "Hindu rajya" into Muslim country' and urged the Hindus to get united and organized in 'defeating' the 'purpose' of the Muslims.[64]

VHP leader Ashok Singhal brought up the issue again in February 2014 by warning Hindus that their population was fast declining and if it continued at that pace, they would become a minority in India. He wanted Hindus to have five children so as not to let Muslims and Christians outnumber them through conversion or marriage with Hindu girls.[65] More recently, BJP leader Surendra Singh said that Hindutva will become endangered in the next fifty years unless population control laws are enacted in the country.[66]

On 15 August 2019, in his Independence Day speech, Prime Minister Modi also flagged the issue of population explosion and said that having a small family was a form of patriotism.[67] His comments came a month after BJP Member of Parliament Rakesh Sinha introduced the Population Regulation Bill 2019 in the Rajya Sabha, the upper house of the Indian Parliament.

The bill inter alia states that whoever, in contravention of the small family norm, produces more than two children will receive reduced benefits under the Public Distribution System (PDS), will be eligible for loans from financial institutions but at higher than the existing interest rates, and will receive lower interest rates on saving instruments. Besides, such a citizen shall be disqualified from being chosen as a member of either the house of Parliament or of the state legislature or of any body of local self-government, i.e. panchayat or municipalities. Three years later, in April 2022, Sinha withdrew his bill when the federal Union Health Minister, Mansukh Mandaviya, said that 'population control should happen by creating awareness among people and it should not happen by force and being made compulsory'.[68]

Significantly, just a few days before this bill was introduced, hundreds of people gathered in Delhi along with some BJP leaders, including Union Minister Giriraj Singh, to demand a Population Control Law to 'tackle the problem of declining Hindu population and to stop the rise of non-Hindu population'.[69] It is astonishing that, Hindu leaders who speak in support of population control laws in India frame the discussion provocatively in terms of Muslims conspiring to numerically overwhelm the Hindus or to aggravate poverty. For instance, the chief minister of Assam, Himanta Biswa Sarma, urged Muslims in his state to adopt 'decent family planning' norms to bring down poverty and control social problems.[70] On 5 October 2022, speaking at a programme in Nagpur on the occasion of Vijayadashmi, the RSS chief, Mohan Bhagwat, warned that 'population control and religion-based population balance is an important subject that can no longer be ignored', because 'population imbalances lead to changes in geographical boundaries. Alongside the differences in birth rate, conversions by force, lure or greed and infiltration are also big reasons.'[71] Once again, the RSS chief did not clarify what he meant by 'religion-based population balance' and which religion or religions he was referring to.

Given this reality, medical anthropologist Nayantara Sheoran Appleton was forced to go on record stating that the idea of a 'population explosion' lends credence to the country's already surging anti-Muslim sentiment which, she pointed out, is based on false concerns that the population growth of Muslims in India is quickly outpacing that of Hindus.[72]

Similar concerns were expressed by another disinterested non-Muslim commentator, Gurdeep Singh Sappal, against the CAA, passed in December 2019. He wrote that under this law, the majority of Hindus and other non-Muslims would have nothing to complain about when their citizenship was confirmed, but Muslim citizens who failed the citizenship test could go to detention centres or perhaps live as disenfranchised and disempowered people.[73]

Muslim Response

There can be no doubt that the stridency of the accusatory onslaught has rattled the Muslim community to such an extent that it has not been able to mount a concerted intellectual response to overcome the climate of suspicion and distrust that prevails against it. Muslim religious organizations such as the All India Muslim Personal Law Board (AIMPLB) don't look beyond religion, and therefore, have shown little interest in engaging Hindutva ideologues in a meaningful dialogue. Their public pronouncements have mostly been limited to the shariah-in-danger kind of theologically emotive issues such as triple talaq and the law that was enacted in July 2019 to criminalize this practice after the Supreme Court invalidated it in August 2017.[74]

The Muslim intelligentsia, on the other hand, came up with two kinds of responses. One was a dispassionate and balanced countering of the arguments in support of triple talaq and citizenship laws, and a severe condemnation of the physical violence against Muslims. The authors of these responses were Muslim reformers, legal experts, journalists and independent researchers who wanted to educate Muslims about their constitutional rights and the legal options available to them, while attempting to wean them away from such un-Islamic concepts as extremism, misogyny and religious supremacism.

The second kind of response came mostly from Muslim bureaucrats who tried to lay the blame on the Muslims themselves. Although some of them did grudgingly acknowledge that the community has cause to complain, they also accused 'ordinary Muslims' of having adopted an obsessive persecution complex, and derided them for making victimhood their 'favorite dope' to get over the melancholic depression caused by the historical disasters they endured.

Such priggish self-flagellation from within the community consisted of ramblings about the huge population of Muslims, their caste system, their aversion to reform, the preponderance of mosques, madrasas and maulvis in post-Independence India, and the Islamist concepts of Dar-ul-Harb and Dar-ul-Islam. The idea was to somehow establish a nexus between these overdramatized facts and the non-existent 'victim mentality' of Muslims.

A disturbing aspect that characterizes some of these sanctimonious commentators is their reticence about the hate crimes perpetrated against the Muslims, which do not find a mention in their one-sided narrative. This cold-hearted silence on Islamophobia raises questions about their intellectual honesty and exposes the artificiality of their bombastic moralizing which, in any case, is of no use to the beleaguered community.

In a way, the arrogant preconceptions of the Muslim religious and bureaucratic elite about Indian Muslims validate Jean-Pierre Faye's much-criticized horseshoe theory which, in the context of political science, asserts that in certain situations, the far left and the far right bend like a horseshoe and come within touching distance of each other to present an eerie resemblance. Obviously, the far right and the far left ideologies have little in common, but what Faye meant was that there are times when the combined effect of these schools of extremist thought could have deleterious consequences for the cause they seek to espouse.

In the same way, the negative impact of the combined armchair philosophizing of Muslim religious leaders and bureaucrats, and their failure to provide a way out of the sustained demonization of Muslims, has pushed the community into the arms of Muslim political parties.

The biggest beneficiary of this shift has been Asaduddin Owaisi's All India Majlis-e-Ittehad-ul-Muslimeen (AIMIM), which made major gains even outside its home state, Telangana, by winning five important seats in the November 2020 Bihar assembly elections. All seats came from the Muslim-dominated Seemanchal region. In the 2015 assembly elections, the party had not won any seats in Bihar.[75] Spurred by this transformative success, AIMIM now plans to contest the upcoming assembly elections in West Bengal[76] and in Tamil Nadu.[77] Even provocative televangelist Zakir Naik tried to fish in troubled waters by asking Muslims to form their own political party and migrate to the non-BJP state Kerala to escape persecution.[78]

Researcher Asim Ali of the Delhi-based Centre for Policy Research attributes the new Muslim upsurge to their political disempowerment caused by their plummeting representation in the civil services, the police, the army and legislative bodies. For instance, in 1980, Muslim members of Parliament were at 9 per cent. Today, this figure is down to 5 per cent. Even India's most populous state, Uttar Pradesh, has just twenty-five Muslim members in a 404-member legislative assembly, the lowest in twenty-five years.[79]

However, political pundits have expressed their alarm at the sudden rise of a 'Muslim party'. Yogendra Yadav, a psephologist-turned-politician, believes that the rise of 'Muslim exclusive politics' at the national stage could end up becoming a catalyst for Hindu majoritarian politics as it would further polarize the electorate and hinder efforts to bridge the Hindu–Muslim divide.[80] Similar concerns were echoed by social activist Kancha Ilaiah Shepherd, who wrote that Owaisi's rise as a visibly Muslim leader is as much BJP's need as the AIMIM's and may lead to national disorientation and gradual disaster.[81]

But Yadav did recognize Muslim perturbations when he empathized with their fear of being reduced to second-class citizens in their own country, with much worse to come. This, he said, is bound to help politicians like Asaduddin Owaisi expand their base. Yadav, for some reason, missed flagging the other two contributing factors discussed above—the inadequacy of Muslim academic response and the balefulness of Muslim bureaucratic slurs.

If the Hindu right's distrust of Muslims in India is summarized from the foregoing arguments, it can be reduced to two broad, interlinked perceptions: one, the belief that Hindus are the original inhabitants of India and others are outsiders, and two, the worry that Muslims may numerically swamp the 'original dwellers' if their population growth is not regulated. A subtle reference to the doctrine of Hindu autochthony and Muslim alienness can be seen in a recent statement attributed to RSS chief Mohan Bhagwat, wherein he said that Muslims in India were the happiest people in the world because 'the Hindus are tolerant and believe in inclusiveness'.[82]

Bhagwat was also quoted as stating, 'Hindustan was divided at that time so that Muslims could live in Pakistan. According to the situation at that time, Hindus should have had a sway in Bharat, but our Constitution never said that either you go to Pakistan or you would have to be subservient to Hindus here.'[83] He went on to claim that India was the only country in the world where a foreign religion that ruled over its people still exists.[84]

The fact is that India was neither ruled by any 'foreign religion' nor was it divided to send all Muslims to Pakistan. Besides, one wonders why the happiness of Muslims should be dependent on Hindu tolerance, to say nothing about the fact that in the eighth World Happiness Report of 2020, India is ranked 144 out of 153 countries.[85]

The Way Forward

India's historical greatness lies in the fact that despite its religious and cultural heterogeneity, it has always been a secular polity. Efforts to homogenize the diverse ethnicities, religions, castes, theistic schools of thought and atheistic philosophies under the 'Hindu' identity have invariably failed because of their sheer richness, variety and spread across the length and breadth of the country. This means that it is almost impossible to formulate and enforce a parochially uniform concept of nationalism that is acceptable to all Indians, especially the Hindus, whose traditions are more diverse than those of the other communities.

Historian Rajmohan Gandhi perhaps had this reality in mind when he wrote, 'Counting Dalits and Adivasis in the Hindu fold, Hindu radicals reserve their public ire for Muslims. "Hindu consolidation" against Muslims is the political equivalent in India for the American call, open or subtle, for white supremacy.' He went on to say that if 'enough is enough' will not escape the lips of political leaders, 'everyday Hindus must utter the words, in their homes to kith and kin, outside their homes to fellow citizens'.[86]

The good news is, Hindus seem to be saying those words already. A survey of 24,236 voters conducted in 2019 by the Centre for the Study of Developing Societies (CSDS) across 211 parliamentary constituencies in twenty-six states revealed that nearly 75 per cent of Hindus (who use social media) were for an India that belonged to all religions.[87] This was confirmed by the aforementioned Pew Research Survey, which found that 85 per cent of Hindus feel that respecting all religions was very important to being truly Indian, and 80 per cent of them say that it is a very important part of their religious identity.[88]

Muslim secular and religious leadership must take heart from this fact and seek to increase the percentage of Hindus who believe in inclusive nationalism. This may be done by promoting Hindu–Muslim harmony through massive information campaigns to counter the deluge of disinformation in at least the following five areas.

1. Demographic threat: There must be a sustained nationwide effort to inform the Hindu masses that Muslims do not pose a demographic threat to them. The Hindus must know that in 1941, the Muslim population of India was 92 million (about 24 per cent of the total population),[89] but Partition brought this figure down to 35 million (9.8 per cent) in 1951. Although it reached 172 million (14.2 per cent) in 2011, the growth rate of the Muslim population has been steadily declining since 1991, when it was 32.87 per cent. It fell to 29.52 per cent in 2001 and 24.6 per cent in 2011.[90]

According to the Sachar Committee Report, India's population growth will eventually cease and possibly decline for all communities as the process of demographic transition progresses. By the end of the twenty-first century, India's Muslim population will stabilize at 320–340 million (in a total of 1.7 to 1.8 billion), about 18–19 per cent of the total population.[91] In other words, at 19 per cent of a stabilized total population, the question of Muslims overtaking the Hindu population does not arise.

These findings were more or less confirmed by a recent study published in *The Lancet* which suggested that by 2048, India's population will peak at about 1.61 billion and decline to 1.093 billion by 2100. And if India is able to meet UN Sustainable Development Goals for education and contraceptives, the population would peak earlier and decline to 929 million by 2100.[92]

The political import of these scientific projections is momentous. It explodes the myth that Muslims in India are plotting a 'demographic-jihad' to capture power. Hence any legislative attempt to regulate population based on unfounded fears would be as counterproductive as China's failed population policy, which not just affected the sex ratio, but reduced the productive workforce and resulted in an ageing society.[93] The Communist state is now considering 'more inclusive population policies' to boost the birth rate.[94] But they are not expected to be able to improve the situation. There is a lesson to be learnt from this.[95] Indeed, Roshan Kishore of *Hindustan Times* warns that if the Indian government were to formulate any policies which exclude families with more than two children, 83 per cent of the affected families would be Hindus. Not only is such a policy regressive, the article said, it will hurt the 'have-nots' more than the 'haves', and 'will also fail to achieve its communal design as more Hindus will suffer than Muslims'.[96]

2. Muslim religious rule: Similar misinformation prevails regarding Muslim rule in India, which often portrays Muslims as products of Islamic intrusions into India. Renowned historian Richard M. Eaton writes that modern textbooks routinely characterize the advent of Persianized Turks in India as a 'Muslim conquest', and the entire period from the thirteenth to the eighteenth centuries as India's

'Muslim Era'. 'That is to say, the agent of conquest is not a people as defined by their ethnic heritage or place of origin, but rather, a religion, the Islamic religion,' he laments.

In comparison, even though the sixteenth century Spaniards justified their conquest of Mexico in religious terms, modern texts never speak of a 'Christian conquest' of America, nor is the post-1492 period ever called America's 'Christian Era'. It is always the 'Spanish conquest' of Central and South America and 'European settlement' in North America.

Eaton blames medieval Indo-Persian chroniclers for promoting the notion of an 'Islamic conquest' of India and identifying Islam with the fortunes of their royal patrons. However, Sanskrit sources claim that from the eighth to the fourteenth centuries, Rajput, Brahman and other contemporary Indian elites referred to the invaders not by their religion but by their linguistic identity—typically as Turks or Turuska. These findings, says Eaton, permit dramatically new ways of conceptualizing the character of cultural encounters at the dawn of the appearance of Muslims in north India.[97]

3. Conversion: The belief that Muslims ruled India as Islamists, and not as covetous conquerors who happened to be Muslims, spawned several theories about the spread of Islam in the subcontinent. Some of the suppositions were (a) Muslim rulers used 'the sword' to convert Hindus, (b) Indian Muslims are the descendants of immigrants and invaders who settled in India, (c) Indians converted to Islam to avoid taxes or to seek the patronage of the ruling class, and (d) Hindus from the so-called lower castes, impressed by the egalitarian teachings of Islam, converted en masse to socially liberate themselves from the tyranny of the 'high-caste' Hindus.

While historians differ on the 'immigration', the 'patronage' and the 'social liberation' theories, they reject the sword theory.

According to Eaton, if Islamization had ever been the result of military or political force, regions exposed most intensively to Muslim rule would, in modern times, contain the greatest number of Muslims. Yet, the opposite is the case. Areas where the most dramatic Islamization occurred, such as eastern Bengal or western Punjab, lay on the fringes of Muslim political power, where the means of coercion were weakest.[98]

Citing the 'decentered perspective' of recent scholarship, Eaton explains that South Asians actively engaged with and creatively incorporated Islamic traditions into their lives and cultures, thereby making them their own. This led to the harmonization of the universal truth claims of Islamic traditions with the particularities of South Asian cultures. Put differently, there is no single explanation for the appearance of sizeable Muslim communities across South Asia. Their social and ethnic diversity emerged under very different historical circumstances.[99]

4. The Aryan theory: As has already been pointed out, most right-wingers in India believe that the 'noble' Arya were the original inhabitants of India and the Hindus descended from them. However, new studies have disproved this dogma, which seeks to alienate and otherize certain Indian communities.

Researcher Tony Joseph, first in his pioneering 2018 study *Early Indians: The Story of Our Ancestors and Where We Came From*[100] and then in an article, showed[101] that the Arya were central Asian Steppe pastoralists who arrived in India roughly between 2,000 BCE and 1,500 BCE, and brought Indo-European languages to the subcontinent. In other words, Indians are a multi-source civilization drawing their cultural impulses, traditions and practices from a variety of heredities and migration histories.[102]

In an interesting passage, Joseph describes,

> how the Indian 'pizza' got made, with the base or the foundation being laid about 65,000 years ago, when the Out of Africa migrants reached India. The sauce began to be made when the Zagrosian herders reached Balochistan after 7000 BCE, mixed with the First Indians, and then together went on to build the Harappan Civilization. When the civilization fell apart, the sauce spread all over the subcontinent. Then came the 'Aryans' after 2000 BCE, and cheese was sprinkled all over the pizza, but a lot more in the north than in the south. Around the same time arrived the major toppings which we see today in different regions in different amounts—the Austroasiatic and Tibeto-Burman-language speakers. And then, much later, of course, came the Greeks, the Jews, the Huns, the Sakas, the Parsis, the Syrians, the Mughals, the Portuguese, the British, the Siddis—all of whom have left small marks all over the Indian pizza.[103]

In short, says Joseph, almost all population groups of India carry 50–65 per cent of their ancestry from the First Indians (Out-of-Africa migrants), no matter where in the caste hierarchy they stand, what language they speak, which region they inhabit or what religion they belong to.[104]

5. Terrorism: This is another issue which has been used to target Muslims in India despite the community having rejected the worldview of terror outfits such as the al-Qaeda and ISIS. In its October 2017 report, The Soufan Center, 'a non-partisan strategy center dedicated to increasing awareness of global security issues in the United States and around the world', listed seventy-five Indians as 'foreign fighters' who had gone to join violent extremist groups in Syria and Iraq.

The report quoted Turkish authorities as documenting a total of 53,781 individuals from 146 countries whose state of residence feared they might attempt to join the fight in Syria and Iraq. This figure was as of mid-June 2017.[105] Although joining a terror outfit is a highly criminal and condemnable act, the number of Muslims from India (seventy-five out of 53,781) who volunteered to fight for such groups was insignificant. In terms of the number of the Muslims in India, this figure—seventy-five out of an estimated 200 million—is even more minuscule, and shows that the community as a whole has shunned violent extremism, thereby justifying the faith Prime Minister Narendra Modi has in its peaceability and loyalty to the country.

In September 2014, soon after assuming office, in an interview to CNN's Fareed Zakaria, the Prime Minister said:

> My understanding is that they (terror outfits such as al-Qaeda) are doing injustice towards Muslims of our country. If anyone thinks Indian Muslims will dance to their tune, they are delusional. Indian Muslims will live for India. They will die for India. They will not want anything bad for India.

This was in response to Zakaria's question on whether he was worried about an al-Qaeda video announcing the attempt to create a base in India.[106] Three years later, Home Minister Rajnath Singh echoed the Prime Minister's confidence when he said, 'I can say with full responsibility that despite such a large population (of Muslims in India), the ISIS has not been able to set foot.'[107]

A factual confirmation of India's top leadership's faith in the Muslim community was provided yet again by The Soufan Center. Its January 2019 report revealed how Indian Muslims had managed to ignore the lure of jihadi narratives, despite being precariously close to the geographical hub of al-Qaeda. The report also contains al-Qaeda leader Asim Umar's lament about the lack of jihadi spirit in Indian Muslims in a video message released in June 2013. Umar had provocatively asked them, 'Why is there no storm in your ocean?' only to be humiliatingly cold-shouldered.[108]

Rethinking Muslim Theology

The categorical rejection of terrorism by the entire Indian Muslim community in the face of taunting incitements is testimony to the fact that they don't believe in violence and have never harboured extra-territorial loyalties. It was this nationalistic fidelity that was also the reason for their rejection of the idea of Pakistan in the 1940s and their decision to choose a democratic state over a theocratic one. Yet, if Muslims continue to be suspected even decades after India's independence, there must also be reasons other than strategic Islamophobia. And these reasons are rooted in their theological acts of omission and commission. Historically, it was not just the Hindus who saw Muslim rule in India as 'Islamic rule'. Muslims themselves promoted this myth.

When the Mughal empire started tottering after Aurangzeb, it was thought that apart from the problems created by the Marathas, the 'grave breakdown of public morality' among the Muslims and the 'deep crisis in character' that they suffered from was the cause. Shah Waliullah (d. 1762), the renowned Hanafi theologian and Naqshbandi Sufi from Delhi, believed that the best way of remedying this situation was to revive Muslim rule in India. To this end, he combined his reformism with military action to prevent the Marathas and the Jats from completely decimating the floundering Mughals, and invited the Afghan ruler Ahmad Shah Abdali to invade India to liberate it from the Marathas.[109]

Abdali acceded to Waliullah's request, perhaps also encouraged by similar messages from several Muslim states and nobles. This ultimately led to the historical Third Battle of Panipat in 1761 in which the Marathas suffered a humiliating defeat. Shah Waliullah had expected Abdali to build the Muslim empire anew but Abdali had his own compulsions. According to historian I.H. Qureshi, it was the withdrawal of Abdali after the Battle of Panipat that unwittingly paved the way for the establishment of the British rule in India through the East India Company because neither the emaciated Mughals nor the defeated Marathas were in any position to resist.[110]

Waliullah's son Shah Abdul Aziz (d. 1823) tried to carry his father's revivalist movement further. He issued a controversial fatwa which declared that India was no longer Daar al-Islam (abode of Islam) as the British rule had rendered it Daar-ul-Harb (abode of war). A legal implication of the ruling was that it was the duty of every Muslim to restore the region (India) to its former status of Dar-ul-Islam.[111]

In various periods of Mughal history, writes scholar Ahmet Kuru, there were always conservative ulema who insisted on the emperors' 'duty' to convert the Hindu 'infidels' to Islam, but the rulers, including even Aurangzeb, did not pursue such a policy.[112] In fact, the emperor was so unimpressed with the madrasa-style classical education he himself had received from the ulema that he accused them of wasting the precious hours of his youth 'in the dry, unprofitable, and never-ending task of learning words (the Arabic language).'[113]

These facts clearly show that when it comes to Islam, the ulema are more loyal than the king. They took on even the mighty Akbar when he tried to promote a syncretic creed called Tawheed-e-Ilahi (a.k.a. Deen-e-Ilahi). In the forefront of this revolt were two well-known Sufis, Shaikh Abdul Haqq Muhaddis of Delhi and Shaikh

Ahmad of Sarhind, who had always wanted to raise orthodoxy 'to a place of partnership in the Empire'.[114]

Thus, it was not the Muslim rulers but the ulema who had conceived of India as an Islamic territory, a fact that has riled the Hindus ever since and led to gross mistrust between the two communities. If this suspicion persists today, it is because a section of Muslim clerics and televangelists in India continue to publicly display their supremacist arrogance.

For instance, advisories such as *ghair Muslimon ko unke tehwar par wish karna haraam hai* (wishing non-Muslims on their festivals is prohibited) are routinely issued during festivals such as Diwali and Christmas.[115] The trend was started by Zakir Naik, who doesn't lose an opportunity to callously mock Hindu deities and urge his followers to tell their non-Muslim friends how wrong their religion is, and why their gods are not really divine.[116] The Darul-Uloom Deoband too has issued a fatwa stating, 'Wishing merry Christmas to Christians on 25 December is not right. Likewise, congratulating people of other religions on their festivals is not correct.'[117]

Zakir Naik shocked many recently when he exposed his ill-informed belief in the concept of salvific exclusivity by asserting that even 'good non-Muslims like Ravish Kumar' (a prominent TV journalist in India) will not enter paradise because they commit the 'major sin' of *shirk* (belief in gods other than Allah). Only conversion to Islam can rescue them from hell, he said.[118] Naik is also on record stating that Muslim countries should not permit non-Muslim places of worship because Islam is the only true religion on earth.[119]

In July 2020, in the context of the construction of a Hindu temple in Pakistan, he reiterated this 'fatwa', saying that non-Muslims in a Muslim state do not have the right to construct their places of worship even with their own funds, and went on to castigate Muslim countries which allow temples or churches on their soil.[120]

However, in the context of the Hagia Sophia, Naik hypocritically declared that it is permissible for Muslims to convert a non-Muslim place of worship into a mosque after conquering their land.[121]

Such horrifyingly eccentric statements go against the Quran, which mentions with respect non-Muslim holy places such as *sawaami'u* (monasteries), *biya'un* (churches) and *salawaatun* (synagogues), and states that the name of God is invoked in them in abundant measure (*yuzkaru feeha usmullahi kaseera*).[122] Even anti-Quranic pronouncements could have been ignored had they been the isolated babble of attention-seeking grandstanders. But the bigoted preachers who issue them command a huge base of blind rooters and if the Muslim community fails to question and stop these fanatics, it would be unwittingly contributing to Islamophobia. If the truth be told, Muslims have failed to publicly challenge and reject televangelists such as Naik. On the contrary, they appear to be under their influence.

This is evident from the conspicuous absence of condemnation from Muslims in India when Hindus, Christians, Ahmadis, Shia or other minority communities and their places of worship in Muslim countries (especially Pakistan) come under attack. But they are quick to highlight (and rightly so) the sufferings of the Rohingya in Myanmar and the Uyghurs in China.

Similar hesitation prevails when it comes to condemning draconian laws in Muslim countries such as those pertaining to blasphemy in Pakistan, whose blatant misuse has resulted in the murder of both Muslims and non-Muslims.[123] This reluctance is also the cause of a terrifying pan-Islamic solidarity when it comes to justifying wrongful acts of Muslim majoritarianism. The AIMPLB's tweet that tacitly supported Turkey's conversion of the Hagia Sophia into a mosque can be cited as a classic example of this theological arrogance. It read:

> #BabriMasjid was and will always be a Masjid. #HagiaSophia is a great example for us. Usurpation of the land by an unjust, oppressive, shameful and majority appeasing judgment can't change its status. No need to be heartbroken. Situations don't last forever. #ItsPolitics.[124]

Although the tweet was removed and reformulated after severe criticism, the insinuation in it was clear: that the day is not far when Muslims would convert the temple to be built in Ayodhya into a mosque. The tweet was also an allusion to Muslims ruling India again because implementing the warning it contained is not possible in the absence of political power. It would be the height of naiveté to presume that the implication of such an ominous suggestion was lost on the people of India.

The shocking ideas contained in the deleted AIMPLB tweet are rooted in a fabricated statement attributed to Prophet Muhammad on the so-called *ghazwa al-Hind* (war against India), in the context of which he is supposed to have said that two notable groups of Muslims will be saved from hell—the group that invades and conquers India (*taghzu al Hind*), and the group that will stand with Prophet Jesus.[125]

Little do the extremists who exploit this narration realize that the Prophet could not have made such a statement because of his categorical declarations in the Quran that he was not a clairvoyant (*laa a'lamul ghaib*)[126] to predict the future, which God alone knows (*innamal ghaibu lillaah*),[127] and that he does not know what will be done with him or others (*maa adri maa yuf'alu bi wa laa bikum*).[128] But ghazwa al-Hind continues to be invoked by the Hindu right[129] to question the loyalty of Muslims, and thus, along with the aforementioned reasons, it forms the basis of Hindu-Muslim mistrust.

Among the many ways of eliminating this lack of confidence in Muslims is for the Indian ulema to emphatically declare the concept of ghazwa al-Hind to be un-Islamic. They must also collectively clarify that India is not Daar ul-Harb (abode of war), the word kafir has no pejorative overtones and that it does not refer to non-Muslims.[130] Apostasy and blasphemy must be removed from the list of capital crimes under Islamic law.

The idea of *dawah* (invitation to Islam) as a tool of Islamic supremacism must also be given up, for Prophetic Islam is not a churchy or propitiative religion, but a system of life that defines a 'Muslim' as one who seeks to achieve human progress through peaceful means. Hence, the Quran does not expect its readers to 'convert to Islam' or 'have faith' in its message, but 'be convinced' of the truth after examining it deeply. Even God is not to be blindly 'believed in' but recognized based on scientific evidence and logical substantiation.[131] This approach, which intends to wean Muslims away from doctrinaire arrogance, also shuts the door on any display of theological supremacism by them. Put simply, the Muslim clerical obsession with making the whole world 'Islamic' has no Quranic basis.

Another Muslim belief that is closely related to the conversion-fixated dawah is the power-hungry dream of a global caliphate. Barring the glorious thirty-year Caliphate of Prophetic Companions Abu Bakr, Umar, Usman and Ali (known as Khilafat-e-Raashida or the Rightly Guided Caliphate), no Muslim political rule measured up to the standards laid down by the Quran and the Prophet. In fact, there never existed a global caliphate in the history of Islam. Even the Golden Age of Islam (800–1,258 CE) does not offer a prototype of the ideal caliphate. During this period, three opposing caliphates competed with each other for the loyalty of Muslims: the Baghdad-based Abbasid Empire, the Cordoba-based Umayyad rule, and the Fatimid Shia caliphate headquartered in Cairo. Therefore, it is time Muslims are freed from the caliphate delusion, and the sooner the better.

In short, what is needed in India today is a radical rethink of Muslim theology. Renowned Indonesian scholar of Islam and the general secretary of the Nahdatul Ulama Supreme Council, Yahya Cholil Staquf, calls it the 'recontextualization' of the teachings of Islam. It involves drawing on the peaceful aspects of Islam to encourage respect for religious pluralism and the fundamental dignity of every human being. Citing the example of Catholics and Protestants who 'routinely killed each other' a few centuries ago but now coexist peacefully, Staquf says that the same type of change can occur within Islam in one or two generations provided it is developed and promulgated by those with religious and political authority in the Muslim world.[132]

As this is not possible in India with the outdated madrasa curriculum in existence, the 'religious authority' here, especially the Darul Uloom Deoband, must seriously consider revamping it completely to harmonize the pluralistic teachings of Islam with modernity. This entails a shift in focus from *taqlid* (zealous imitation) to *ijtihad* (a process by which Islamic principles are deduced from the original sources).

In doing so, Deoband will be opening up Islam to modern interpretations within, of course, the framework of its original sources. In the long run, it would inculcate a sense of tolerance among Muslims for different points of view and equip them to respond positively to the requirements of a multicultural society like India.

Even Saudi Arabia has realized the importance of modernizing and moderating the religious curriculum and started removing anti-Semitic and misogynistic content from school textbooks. Textbook editions introduced in 2019 no longer contain Quranic misinterpretations that say men are in charge of women and that rebellious wives may be struck by their husbands.[133]

This is an excellent example for Indian madrasas to follow. If they dither, then the Muslim laity must organize itself and challenge the hegemony of the ulema over the interpretation of Islam. For this, the community will have to become theologically informed, develop a secularized consciousness, and be bold enough to raise questions. Failing to do this would mean letting the ulema keep the Muslim masses forever engaged in emotive and haram–halal issues.

But if Muslims manage to assert their independence and succeed in pressuring the self-appointed custodians of Islam in India into modernizing their thought, it could herald the beginning of a transformative relationship with Hindus in which confrontation will give way to cooperation. With the fear of a shariah-obsessed Muslim community gone, ordinary Hindus would begin to realize that a fantasized confrontation between Islam and Hinduism, which they have been made to believe in, is not purely a Hindu-Muslim problem but concerns the entire nation, and could seriously affect its development if allowed to continue. It is well-known that poverty and backwardness are mainly the result of violent internal conflict. Pakistan is a classic example of this malady.

As the foregoing arguments have shown, Hindu-Muslim mistrust in India today is based on imaginary fears. Both communities are not responsible for what their respective ancestors did. But they would be if they buy into the politically motivated propaganda that seeks to keep them divided. If the larger goal is to make India an epitome of peace, stability and progress, the communities have no option but to work together.

Sant Eknath (1533–1599) in his *bharud*[134] titled *Hindu-Turk Samvad*, drives home this point through an imaginary Hindu-Muslim argument. His drama-poem (as translated by historian Eleanor Zelliot) begins with the lines:

> The goal is one; the ways of worship are different
> Listen to the dialogue between these two
> The Turk calls the Hindu 'kafir'!
> The Hindu answers, 'I will be polluted—get away'
> A quarrel broke out between the two;
> A great controversy begins …

After a lengthy polemical confabulation, the disputants end up saluting and embracing each other with great respect. Eknath's final lines capture this moment beautifully.

> You and I quarreled
> To open up the knowledge of the high truth,
> In order to enlighten the very ignorant.
> In place of karma—awakening!
>
> 'In place of words we have established the word's meaning'
> The highest truth pierced them both
> Enlightenment was the purpose of this quarrel.
> Both have been satisfied
>
> The argument was about oneness.
> The argument became agreement.
> Eka Janardan[135] says, 'Self-knowledge
> And great bliss came to both'.[136]

If a Hindu–Muslim argument can become agreement in the sixteenth century at the height of Muslim power in India, there is no reason why the two communities cannot live together in concord within the borders of the world's largest secular democracy, especially in the age of information technology, where it is not difficult to identify the 'fakeness' of animosity-provoking propaganda and disinformation.

3

Hindu Majoritarianism and Unmaking the Idea of India

NIRANJAN SAHOO

Introduction

WITH ONE-SIXTH OF HUMANITY, INDIA, as the world's largest democracy, is known for its mind-boggling diversity and pluralism. Despite being an overwhelmingly Hindu majority state, the country, largely owing to its founding fathers' vision, had maintained secularism and plurality in the decades since its independence from British rule in 1947. While India is no stranger to a mix of religion and politics, its Constitution had kept religion separate from politics by making it a secular republic.

However, in recent decades, particularly with the spectacular rise of the Hindu nationalist BJP and the resurgence of its sister organizations under the RSS, India's secular credentials are under great stress. Under the leadership of Prime Minister Narendra Modi, the BJP has not only won two back-to-back national elections with sweeping majorities, it has been able to strengthen its national footprint, capturing power in most states, thereby dominating politics, policymaking spaces and nearly every other aspect of the young republic.

The problem, however, is that the brand of majoritarian politics and pro-Hindutva politics that the ruling dispensation and its affiliates are unabashedly pushing and promoting come at the cost of the country's secularism and of the key constitutional principles such as the protection of minority rights. Over the last seven years, the country has witnessed growing instances of attacks on minorities, their religious practices, food habits, their systematic exclusion from democratic spaces and key decision-making bodies and an overall atmosphere of fear and anxiety.

The recent incidents of abrogating Article 370, which provided special status to India's only Muslim-majority state of Jammu and Kashmir, of the passing of the discriminatory CAA and a host of other coercive measures have alarmed the supporters of a secular and plural India. The chapter aims to analyse the trajectory of religious nationalism from the pre-colonial era to the present day, the key drivers facilitating the phenomenal rise of the Hindu right and the major implications on India's secular tradition, diversity and inter-religious relations.

The Colonial Origin of Hindu Majoritarianism

India's slide into majoritarianism is not a post-2014 development, although this process was hastened thereafter. India had embarked on this path even before the country got independence in 1947. The division between secular and Hindu nationalist visions of Indian identity has its roots in the colonial period. The two clashing visions of the 'idea of India' that emerged then continue to collide to this day.[1]

One strand of thought viewed India as a secular and pluralist nation, while the other camp defined India as a Hindu rashtra. During British colonial rule in the late nineteenth century, this binary became an increasingly prominent issue in the writings of Gopal Krishna Gokhale (1866–1915), the moderate face of the Indian National Congress (INC), and Bal Gangadhar Tilak (1856–1920), the champion of the Hindu right.[2] Whereas Gokhale pitched for Indian nationhood based on territoriality, Tilak defined it based on the culture and religion of India's Hindu majority.[3]

This contestation intensified as Gandhi began leading the struggle for Indian independence. At a time when Gandhi was trying to transform the INC into a mass organization to resist British rule, Hindu nationalism had begun to offer a political alternative that challenged Gandhi's commitment to non-violence and his conception of Indian nationhood.

Contrary to the perspective of Gokhale and other Congress leaders, Gandhi, a devout Hindu himself, viewed the Indian nation as a harmonious collection of religious communities that deserved to be treated as equals. He promoted a syncretic and spiritual brand of the Hindu religion.[4] The other notable Congress Party leader, Jawaharlal Nehru, who would serve as India's first prime minister (1947–64), criticized Hindu nationalism as a 'communal' ideology that resembled those of Muslim and Sikh separatists.[5]

In opposition to Gandhi and Nehru's vision, Hindu nationalists in the 1920s argued that Hindu culture defined Indian identity and that minorities needed to assimilate by showing allegiance to the symbols of this majority culture. Many Hindu nationalists coalesced behind the Akhil Bharatiya Hindu Mahasabha (All-India Hindu Grand Assembly), a conservative, Hindu nationalist party founded in

1915. V.D. Savarkar, who was leading the then Hindu Mahasabha, coined the term Hindutva (Hindu nationalism) to challenge Gandhi-Nehru's territorial and secular concept of Indian nationhood.[6]

In his book *Hindutva: Who Is a Hindu?* published in 1923, Savarkar argued for the idea of the Hindu rashtra. Like many European nationalisms that are based on religious identity, Savarkar defined the concept of Hindutva in terms of three essential elements: a common nation, a common race and a common culture or civilization.[7]

In 1925, the Hindu political activist K.B. Hedgewar turned Savarkar's idea of Hindutva into a mass movement when he founded the RSS, a paramilitary volunteer organization dedicated to promoting Hindu nationalism. The main goal of founding the RSS was a more centralized and assertive promotion of the Hindu rashtra.[8]

The RSS soon emerged as the fountainhead of the promotion of a Hindu rashtra. The RSS was able to mobilize critical support for its idea of the Hindu rashtra from sister organizations commonly known as the Sangh Parivar, or 'family of organizations'.[9] Thus, whereas Gandhi and Nehru's idea of India was secular and plural, the Savarkarite idea of India can be characterized as ethnonationalist in the way it elevates the concept of Hinduness.

Post-Independence Trajectory

Although the bloody Partition of India and Pakistan in 1947 heightened sectarian tensions, until the late 1970s, the hegemony of the Congress Party kept Hindu nationalism from occupying centre stage in national politics. The deft political leadership of Nehru further tempered polarization.

Polarization between the two conflicting visions of India increased dramatically when Pakistan was created as a Muslim state. Tensions only rose further when Nathuram Godse, a former pracharak (volunteer) of the RSS, assassinated Gandhi in 1948 over the issue of the latter's alleged 'sympathy' for the Muslim-majority Pakistan.[10]

The interim government under Nehru immediately banned the RSS and its affiliated organizations and took stringent measures to check their activities. The ban was lifted shortly afterwards, in 1949. It had proved futile as the RSS and its affiliates could pursue their mission and activities. Moreover, nation-building and other compulsions pushed the new government to be more open to the ideas of the RSS and other Hindu nationalist organizations.[11]

At the same time, the Hindu right movement moderated its extremist methods and took conscious steps to pursue its agenda culturally and politically as well. In 1951, its key leader, S.P. Mukherjee, left his post as president of the Hindu Mahasabha and formed a new political party, the Bharatiya Jana Sangh (BJS), to compete in India's first general elections, slated for 1952.

The BJS and the RSS accused the Nehru government of favouring religious minorities and strongly objected to the government's proposed Hindu Code bills, which sought to codify Hindu personal laws[12] (relating to issues such as marriage and inheritance) and bring them under the purview of the judiciary, while exempting Muslims from similar reforms.

The BJS and the RSS were also at the forefront of agitation against codes that allowed Muslims to have separate personal laws and to slaughter cows, a practice firmly opposed by the majority of Hindus and many others in India.

After years of Congress rule, however, the authoritarian and polarizing manoeuvres of Prime Minister Indira Gandhi (1966–77, 1980–84) provided the BJS and other opposition parties with a crucial opening. Indira Gandhi, the daughter of Jawaharlal Nehru, was an extremely divisive figure, and her tenure was marked by extreme centralization of power, intolerance of the Opposition and the press, and finally, the imposition of a state of Emergency between 1975 and 1977.[13]

The Emergency—which led to the arrests of hundreds of Opposition leaders and included various other draconian measures—galvanized the entire political opposition, including the Hindu nationalist BJS, to unite and form the Janata coalition, which defeated Indira Gandhi in the 1977 general elections.

Although the Janata coalition government collapsed soon afterwards in 1979 due to internal squabbles, it hugely benefitted the BJS and brought many of its leaders to national prominence. Yet, given the secular and socialist composition of the Janata coalition government, which contained many former members of the Congress Party, the Hindu right failed to advance its ideological project during this period.

A rising BJP and Hindu nationalism (1980–2004)

The divisions over Indian national identity became increasingly sharper with the formation of the BJP, a Hindu nationalist party, in 1980. After repeated failures to unseat the hegemonic Congress Party, Hindu nationalists from the BJS and the Janata coalition (with which the BJS had merged in 1977) formed a new political party in 1980.

Under the leadership of two leaders, Atal Bihari Vajpayee and L.K. Advani, the BJP began taking on the Congress with the help of the Sangh Parivar. In the mid-1980s, Advani pandered to Hindu sentiments and sought to mobilize the majority community on the basis of religious identity in the Hindi heartland, while Vajpayee employed a moderate approach to expand the new party's footprint beyond the so-called 'Hindi belt', a linguistic region in north-central India where the Hindi language is widely spoken.

The RSS and Sangh Parivar provoked communal tension by launching the Ram Janmabhoomi movement, which aimed to build a temple to the Hindu deity Ram on the site of the controversial Babri Masjid, a mosque in the city of Ayodhya. Through this movement, the RSS entered into a tacit understanding with its sister organization, the VHP, to relaunch an ethno-religious project that would revive the idea of a Hindu rashtra.

The two organizations started the Ram Janmabhoomi movement to reclaim for Hindus the land upon which the Babri Masjid was built, which some Hindus believe to be the birthplace of Lord Ram. In the sixteenth century, the army of Jalaluddin Muhammad Akbar, the Mughal emperor who conquered a large part of northern India, including the city of Ayodhya, is alleged to have demolished a Hindu temple there and built the Babri Masjid.

Given its incendiary history, this religious site remained a major source of conflict between Muslims and Hindus and was the cause of numerous riots.[14] With the tacit support of the BJP, in 1989, the RSS and the VHP launched a massive national campaign demanding the restoration of the original Hindu temple. This mobilization greatly contributed to the BJP's success in the 1989 general elections, in which the right-wing party won as many as eighty-five seats and in some ways, deprived the Congress of a legislative majority.

However, it needs to be noted that the Congress Party has been criticized by many for often following contradictory policies under Nehru's successors, policies which critics say contributed significantly to the success of the Hindu right and its tactics of religious polarization. Prime Minister Indira Gandhi openly stoked the anxieties of India's Hindu majority in election campaigns in the

1980s. More importantly, her son, Prime Minister Rajiv Gandhi, also employed similar tactics to woo the majority community. Yet, in 1985, the Congress Party faced a backlash over its reaction to the Indian Supreme Court's decision in the Shah Bano case, as its critics claimed that the party was allowing Muslims to live under a very different civil code.[15]

Rajiv Gandhi tried to win over Hindu hardliners who were very upset with his government by opening the gate of a Hindu temple in Ayodhya in 1988. Rajiv Gandhi's actions, which appeared to show his political weakness in pandering to the Hindu right, emboldened leaders like the Sangh Parivar to further politicize the mobilization against the Babri Masjid in Ayodhya.[16]

BJP leader Advani made the most of the political opportunity by launching a famous 10,000 km Rath Yatra to mobilize support for the construction of a temple to Lord Ram on the disputed site. Tensions ultimately culminated in the destruction of the Babri Masjid by kar sevaks on 6 December 1992, leading to a series of violent communal riots (with 1,200 reported deaths) between Hindus and Muslims across the country.

While the Babri episode isolated the BJP and made it a pariah party for some time, by the late 1990s, the party carefully shifted its strategy to capture political power. Realizing that it could not win power on its own and that it needed to form alliances with other regional parties, it toned down its inflammatory Hindu nationalist rhetoric.[17]

The Vajpayee-Advani duo's deft strategy of moderating Hindutva and mixing it with promises of economic development allowed the party to gain support from fifteen coalition partners in 1998 and run the first successful non-Congress coalition to complete a full five-year term between 1999 and 2004.[18] The BJP's dependence on its coalition partners meant that the party was forced to set aside contentious proposals such as building a Hindu temple at Ayodhya and adopting a Uniform Civil Code (which would end the practice of having different civil codes for different religious communities).

The rise of hardline 'hindutva' and rise of majoritarianism (2014–Present)

With a Congress-led government in power between 2004 and 2014, the BJP's majoritarian push was briefly halted. Despite propelling high economic growth, a series of scams and scandals and most importantly, the party's cynical use of identity politics against the purported threat of right-wing violence, created critical openings for the Hindu right in the decisive 2014 elections.[19]

The BJP's unprecedented electoral victory in 2014, where it secured a majority of seats in the lower house on its own, breaking a three-decade trend in coalition politics,[20] suddenly gave a new lease of life to Hindutva and its majoritarianism agenda, which were always in the party manifesto and slogans.

It may be noted that during its rule between 1998 and 2004, lacking a full majority, the BJP had toned down its Hindu nationalist rhetoric. Due to coalition compulsions, Prime Minister Vajpayee had made relatively subtle moves to advance the BJP and Sangh Parivar's ideological agenda. However, after the 2014 electoral landslide, the BJP, under Narendra Modi, emerged as an unapologetic advocate of Hindutva and the majority community's primacy in social, political and economic life.

In power, the BJP began rewriting Indian history to emphasize the country's Hindu heritage and its glorious past, aggressively promoted Sanskrit and packed important historical and cultural institutions with party ideologues or supporters.

The real game changer was the spectacular rise of Narendra Modi, who skilfully combined promises of economic development with Hindu nationalist appeals. A three-time chief minister in the state of Gujarat, Modi was known as an able administrator, a strong leader and a pro-growth politician who single-handedly turned Gujarat into one of India's top investment destinations.

Modi's pro-development record gave the BJP formidable electoral appeal, and the rising 'aspirations of the new Indian masses' contributed significantly to the party's landslide victory in 2014.[21] Yet, the single biggest factor explaining the BJP's phenomenal performance was sharp religious polarization in the Hindi heartland states.[22]

Modi was a deeply polarizing figure for his strong stance on Hindutva and his alleged role in the 2002 Gujarat riots.[23] Critical to the BJP's phenomenal rise was Modi's image as an unapologetic Hindu nationalist—his followers fondly address him as Hindu Hriday Samrat, or 'ruler of Hindu hearts'. Not only has Modi reversed the gradual slide of the Hindu right from its back-to-back electoral defeats in 2004 and 2009, but the BJP under him witnessed unprecedented electoral success across many regions of the country.[24]

In the 2019 general elections, the Hindu right under Modi won another spectacular mandate, much bigger than that in 2014. This was largely achieved by campaigning on the Hindu nationalism and national security planks. Prime Minister Modi campaigned in a Presidential style making the elections a sort of referendum on his leadership, chose to deploy every means to polarize the election processes for electoral gains.

The high point of the ruling party's polarizing tactics was the nomination of Pragya Singh Thakur,[25] a controversial *sadhvi* or saffron-clad preacher and a terror accused in multiple cases, including the Malegaon serial blasts in 2008, as a candidate for a parliamentary seat. Further, the 2019 general elections saw an extreme level of polarization and majoritarian consolidation based on Hindu nationalism, heavily benefitting the right-wing party.

In short, within a span of six years, the BJP under Modi has become the central pole of Indian politics, with a hegemonic presence in every aspect of the republic, particularly the religious and cultural spheres.

Implications of Hindu Majoritarianism

The implications of Hindu nationalism and the growing ascendancy of majoritarianism are very much visible in terms of altering the nature of Indian politics and society. The rise of divisive political rhetoric and the increasing deployment of polarization tactics by the Hindu right have brought about sharp changes in the national conversation. However, the most worrisome outcome is the growing trend of religious violence and the gradual marginalization of minority groups.

The growing culture of intolerance and the rising number of attacks of secular traditions by right-wing idealogues and their foot soldiers are threatening the very idea of a plural and secular India.

Breaking of the social and cultural fabric

The most damaging outcome of the rise of Hindu nationalism and the consequent majoritarianism is the breaking of the social fabric. Through daily abuse, stigmatization and demonization, sometimes taken to the extreme of violence and intimidation, minorities have been sent into a severe state of insecurity.

Majoritarian violence orchestrated by vigilante Hindu mobs with impunity is creating deep anxiety and insecurity among minorities and groups that are opposed to the Hindu right's ideology. The biggest casualty of such majoritarianism is that it is eating away the social capital, which is vital to maintaining a cohesive social fabric in an extremely diverse and large country.

What is more worrisome is India witnessing a rising tide of violence perpetrated by vigilante groups behaving as a sort of 'moral police'. In several instances, vigilante groups are allowed (by state silence) to determine what people should think, write, eat, drink and wear. Writers, scientists and intellectuals are being attacked and routinely derided with abusive language for expressing even the slightest difference in perspective.

The scale and degrees of intolerance witnessed in India today are alarming. Majoritarian mobs have attacked minorities, human rights advocates and activists with impunity. For instance, as the data portal IndiaSpend indicated, as many as 97 per cent of cow-related violence reported between 2010 and 2017 has occurred since the BJP government assumed power in May 2014. In 2017 alone, as many as eleven Muslims were killed in incidents of cow vigilantism across the country, the highest toll on record in recent years.[26] Those who oppose this are often taunted with slogans like 'go back to Pakistan'.[27]

However, intolerance is not restricted to divisions over the status of cows. Even personal life and personal liberty are under attack. This is most vividly seen in the case of a spate of legislations passed by BJP-ruled states to regulate interfaith marriages after raising the bogey of love jihad.[28] Love jihad is used to discourage interfaith relationships and marriages by claiming that Muslim men are deliberately wooing Hindu women in order to force them to convert to Islam upon marriage.

Rewriting history and cultural appropriation

For a long time, the Hindu right nurtured deep grievances against the Congress and other secular parties for denying them their rightful place and recognition. Jawaharlal Nehru, Indira Gandhi and other Congress leaders blocked the Sangh Parivar's Hindutva project, and the Congress filled key cultural and educational institutions with people sympathetic to its ideology.

After their massive electoral success in 2014, Modi and other Sangh Parivar leaders have not only derided secularism (which they call 'pseudo-secularism'), the right-wing government has also moved aggressively to give recognition to its icons, RSS and BJS figures such as Deen Dayal Upadhyaya and Shyama Prasad Mukherjee, and fill institutions with people who support and advance its ideology.

Beyond this, there are systematic efforts being made to rewrite history to reflect the Hindu majoritarian worldview. This is because the RSS sees cultural hegemony as more enduring than political power. While the rewriting of history project faced strong resistance from coalition partners during Vajpayee's tenure, between 1999 and 2004, there have been no such troubles in Modi's tenure. In most BJP-ruled states, school and higher education curricula are being changed to reflect the Hindu right's sentiments and worldviews.[29] In short, the government is openly and aggressively pursuing its cultural and political agenda by filling up key cultural and educational institutions with its own ideologues and sympathizers.

Increasing irrelevance of Muslims in electoral process

The most serious outcome of Hindu nationalism is the rapid shrinking of minority rights and their political representation. Since the 2014 general elections, Muslim representation in the Lok Sabha (lower house) of India's Parliament and in several state assemblies has fallen drastically.[30]

To expand, although Muslims represent more than 14 per cent of India's population (as per the 2011 census), in 2018, they held only

4 per cent of the seats in the Lok Sabha, the lowest since 1957.[31] In the 2019 general elections, the number of MPs from the community improved marginally. There are only twenty-seven Muslim MPs in the current Lok Sabha, none of them from the ruling party.[32] The BJP fielded just six Muslim candidates in various states, and none won the elections.[33]

Further, Muslims also have negligible representation in the ruling BJP: of the party's 1,418 state assembly members, only four are Muslim. Even more troubling is that during the 2014 general elections, the BJP chose not to field a single Muslim candidate in Uttar Pradesh, a state where Muslims constitute more than 20 per cent of the population. As a consequence, the largest minority community's representation in the state assembly fell from 17.1 per cent to 5.9 per cent. There is only one Muslim minister in the entire Uttar Pradesh cabinet—which is headed by a Hindu monk, Yogi Adityanath of the BJP.[34]

Constitutional routes to majoritarian state

After it won by another electoral landslide in May 2019, the BJP unveiled the real face of its majoritarianism by introducing a series of major constitutional changes to alter the secular nature and character of the republic. The first major legislative move, soon after it won the mandate, was the passage of the Triple Talaq Bill (The Muslim Women [Protection of Rights on Marriage Bill]) in July. The Bill, which criminalized instant divorce by Muslim men, had been one of the core aims of the BJP and its sister organizations, or the Sangh Parivar, for many decades.[35]

However, the most decisive step towards a majoritarian state was taken in August, when the Hindu right government, fresh from its massive electoral success, decided to repeal Article 370 of the Constitution, which had granted the only Muslim majority state, Jammu and Kashmir, semi-autonomy and certain specific constitutional guarantees.[36]

This had been a long-standing demand of the BJP and the Sangh Parivar and the move received overwhelming approval from the foot soldiers of Hindutva.[37] Not only was the state dismantled into three Union Territories, the key leaders of the state were put under detention for over a year.

In the same month (August 2019), the BJP-led central government implemented the NRC in Assam, which required all the residents of the state to furnish physical proof of citizenship. Many analysts suspect the NRC was deployed as a tool to deny citizenship to Muslim migrants from Bangladesh and render them stateless.[38]

However, the much bigger constitutional changes towards the majoritarian project came in December 2019, when the central government passed the CAA, which allowed fast-tracking of citizenship to all Hindus, Buddhists, Sikhs, Parsis, Jains and Christians facing religious persecution in neighbouring countries. Analysts claimed that by dividing these immigrants or refugees into Muslims and non-Muslims, the new law openly discriminates against citizens based on their religion.[39] Thus, the CAA and NRC combo has the potential to turn India into a majoritarian state.

Bringing Hindutva to the centre stage

The BJP's aggressive use of the Hindu majoritarian card and selective use of cultural and religious symbols to profit from identity politics has only given rise to competitive Hindutva politics. Given that the Congress Party is identified as a secular party, one would have expected it to vociferously oppose the BJP's polarization tactics.

However, the Congress and several regional parties are found aping and matching the right-wing party's Hindutva tactics. In order to counter the BJP's allegations of Congress being a pro-minority party, Rahul Gandhi, the senior leader of the Congress, has been making frequent visits to major Hindu temples, including an arduous pilgrimage in 2018 to Kailash Mansarovar in the Himalayas, to add to the party's Hindu credentials.[40]

In another example of this turn towards 'soft Hindutva', Arvind Kejriwal, the chief minister of Delhi and a bitter critic of Modi and the Sangh Parivar, did a complete U-turn during the assembly elections in 2020. While addressing an election rally, he took the opportunity to shore up the image of his 'Hindu-ness' by reciting the Hanuman Chalisa (hymn to Lord Hanuman) and announced a slew of freebies for his Hindu constituency.[41]

Many Opposition-ruled states have been following or even trying to outdo what the BJP and the Sangh Parivar are doing to showcase their majoritarian credentials. In short, a race to the bottom on identity politics is under way, which only aids the BJP's majoritarian Hindutva project.[42]

Conclusion

The majoritarian worldview of the Hindu right, which appeared to be remote and unlikely less than a decade ago, looks like it is shaping reality today. The politics of religious polarization, successfully deployed by the BJP and its affiliates, is keeping India in a permanent state of tension and conflict.

India's civic sphere resembles a war zone in which opposing groups, particularly religious minorities, are seen as enemies. Such a divide is taking a heavy toll on the fragile social relations in the country, which had weathered riots, ethnic skirmishes and inter-religious conflicts in previous decades. Even at the height of the polarization resulting from the Ram Janmabhoomi movement, which caused many deaths and rioting, the divide was never as deep as it is now.

While India's strong culture of regionalism, interfaith dialogue and plural and tolerant Hindu faith may offer some resistance to majoritarianism, these may not endure in the longer run. This is because the Hindu nationalist government, and a slew of the institutional and legislative changes that it has mounted, are slowly but surely altering the character of the Indian state.

With majoritarianism sweeping every aspect of the republic, the secular and plural idea of India is under great stress today.

4

The Indian Media's Role in Fuelling Communal Violence

Media Divides and Hates for Profit

MAYA MIRCHANDANI

Introduction

> *There was big propaganda in print media and electronic media against the foreigners who had come to Markaz Delhi and an attempt was made to create a picture that these foreigners were responsible for spreading COVID-19 virus in India. There was virtually persecution against these foreigners.*[1]
>
> —Justice T.V. Nalawade and Justice M.G. Sewlikar, Bombay High Court.

THEY WERE MADE SCAPEGOATS, SAID the two judges of the Aurangabad bench of the Bombay High Court as they dismissed the first information reports or FIRs filed by the Indian police against thirty-five men—twenty-nine of them foreigners. These men, members of the Tablighi Jamaat, a transnational, conservative, largely peaceful Muslim sect that was founded in India in 1926, had been charged with violations under the colonial-era Epidemics Act imposed across India as a stringent, nationwide lockdown was put in place virtually overnight in the third week of March 2020.

The men had arrived in Delhi for a congregation earlier that month, before the WHO declared a pandemic and countries like India closed their international and domestic borders in an effort to stop the spread of the deadly virus.

As it censured the media for skewed reporting, the term used by the court—scapegoat—was important. It recognized deliberate malice against a group of men who found themselves stuck in Delhi with no choice but to stay in cramped quarters in the tight lanes near the shrine of Sufi saint Hazrat Nizamuddin.

With COVID-19 cases detected among some of them, the entire group was accused of a dual crime: one, bringing the virus into India and two, deliberately concealing the intent of their travel, which was to gather for a religious meeting. All this, even though the congregation met in the heart of the national capital, under the administration's nose, and its foreign members entered India by air legally, with the legitimacy of passports, valid visas and immigration stamps as evidence of good faith.

Unfortunately, this group of Muslim men became the target of virulent hate and misinformation. They became the 'scapegoats' the court referred to, ones that allowed the Indian government to—at least for a time—deflect attention from the impact of the sudden lockdown on ordinary Indians who lost their jobs and livelihoods without notice.

As the Modi government sought global praise for its 'strong leadership' and tough action taken in the face of a pandemic, images of migrant labourers, who were forced to trudge home across state borders—some sprayed with disinfectant as they crossed district lines—were an inconvenient truth.[2] And therefore, an equal and opposite convenient scapegoat, the men of the Tablighi Jamaat, became easy targets. Daily attention on their culpability as 'super spreaders' of COVID-19 distracted the Indian public from stories of abject want and desperation as India witnessed one of its largest internal displacements in history.

The treatment of these men by the police, by ruling party politicians and especially by the media is a leitmotif of our polarized times. The court observed that the action of the central government against mainly Muslim individuals and no other foreigners from other faiths, who had also travelled to India at the same time, was questionable.

Yet the disproportionate coverage of their alleged culpability in the media underscored, once more, the power of the right-wing Hindu nationalist propaganda that seeks to create a narrative of blame even where none can be placed. The truth is that Islamophobia's deep roots have found the space to spread under a regime driven by a need to assert its strident Hindu nationalist (Hindutva) ideology over a constitutionally secular nation by pitting Hindus against Muslims and portraying them as a civilizational majority under threat from marauding invaders who entered these lands centuries ago.

In the case of the Tablighi Jamaat, the blame for the spread of an unfamiliar virus that wreaked havoc in the world was placed squarely on their shoulders, and they were painted as Muslims who deliberately plotted to spread a disease in Hindu-majority India. The shrillness and abuse were mitigated only slightly after the Bombay High Court's order.

Modi and the Media: A Propaganda Model

Propaganda wars that further Hindutva's political agenda—shaped and hardened over decades since the Partition of India in 1947—thrive on this 'fear of small numbers'.[3] The mass media, with its reliance on market forces, internalized assumptions and self-censorship 'manufactures consent' through a process of repeated representations of issues in a particular way.[4]

Shifting media narratives are representative of a symbiotic politico-media complex knit tightly by what Noam Chomsky and Edward Herman identified as the five filters of the propaganda model: i) ownership and orientation of media outlets, ii) advertising, iii) complicity between government and media managers in sourcing news, iv) generating flak or negative responses among a mass public and v) identifying a common enemy.

The intent of the fifth filter, particularly relevant to our times, is to stoke fear and exploit public animosity towards groups that pose potential threats, both real and imagined. Such a propaganda model creates a nexus between the state's political and ruling classes, its media and other agencies like law enforcement. It defines government interest as national interest, and political interest as public interest, in the face of a common enemy.

This nexus is responsible for 'manufacturing consent', with the media almost entirely following the state's line. The ruling BJP's Information Technology (IT) cell—that has been repeatedly accused of gathering support by trolling party critics online,[5] selectively editing videos and photographs and designing targeted disinformation campaigns—is tasked daily with ensuring its message goes out across all media platforms and drowns out any dissenting or critical voices, which attempt to provide context and address either misinformation or disinformation,[6] by distracting or discrediting them.

Hindutva's majoritarian identity only speaks for itself. The language of minority rights and the protection of fundamental civil liberties is absent entirely from its discourse, which depicts all that is Hindu as Indian and Indian as Hindu, and all that is supportive of the ruling BJP as patriotic. It is important to distinguish between the majority and majoritarian identity.

Political anthropologist Arjun Appadurai defines majoritarianism as the 'objectively larger group in a national polity' that seeks to close the gap between the majority and the 'purity of the national whole'. Foot soldiers of the government—paid trolls, blind bigots and sympathetic journalists—help the journey towards such an end by manufacturing a sense of offence based on past grievances and preying on and exaggerating a sense of fear among the majority.[7]

Bogeys about interfaith marriages as deliberate attempts by Muslim men to seduce and convert Hindu women in order to turn 'Hindu' India into a Muslim majority nation; the framing of political dissent, and calls for upholding human rights; or for dialogue in Kashmir as treason; criticism of the Modi government's economic policies as unpatriotic or 'anti-national'; and exaggerated accusations of 'jihadi' radicalization among Indian Muslims without any evidence to back up the claims, have all become lightning rods around which such hate blazes. And twenty-four-hour news television, which fans these nightly flames, has become a willing accomplice.

In the democratic backslide that India finds itself in today, the media's role as the fourth estate, tasked with the recording of history as it unfolds, mediating between power and the public, and holding governments accountable, has waned. Unlike the more overt tactics which authoritarian leaders use to usurp power, it is this more subtle backsliding that thrives, encouraged by populist leaders who win at the ballot, and perpetuated by both the co-option of mass media and the silencing of free speech and dissent.

It thrives among a populace that has bought into the propaganda of a majoritarian project not in spite of, but because of, the very institutions that are meant to act as checks on unbridled power, but do quite the obsequious opposite.

The Muslim as the Enemy

As India reeled under the lockdown's economic impact, TV networks ran nightly courts in their studios with news anchors acting as judge, jury and executioner. These were obvious efforts to shift attention away from the hardships and losses so many ordinary Indians suffered. For these media professionals, it was as though COVID-19 in India only had one cause for its spread. Primetime news debates fuelled the hate further with hashtags like #coronajihad[8] as the pandemic struck.

Many newspapers also played along by carrying separate columns of figures on their pages displaying COVID-19 cases across India—with one exclusively for cases that could be traced back to the men of the Tablighi Jamaat based on their travel and interaction records. But the focus on them did not remain only about them—it led to what is now called an 'infodemic' that raged against ordinary Muslims across the country and amplified everyday bigotry.[9]

Political majoritarianism[10] is another name for a supremacist project that defines ethnic or religious majorities as a nation's rightful owners, argues historian Mukul Kesavan. As alarming as the rhetoric against this group of religious Muslim men was, it was hardly surprising. The scene for such a hateful spin had already been set, especially in the weeks that preceded the explosion of the coronavirus pandemic in India.

Reportage on the alleged culpability of members of the Tablighi Jamaat, who met despite global concern over the spread of COVID-19, came on the back of virulently communal reportage by Indian TV channels on the widespread Hindu-Muslim riots in Delhi that left scores dead and thousands of families homeless, even as the union government cracked down on protests against the newly passed CAA.

Rhetoric painting all Indian Muslims as somehow 'un-Indian' at best, and completely 'anti-national' at worst, had reached a crescendo in the weeks before the lockdown. In fact, 'dog whistle' politics—where the BJP's message of Hindu primacy is often coded in seemingly neutral language—has become a hallmark [11]of the Modi era BJP's communications machine over the last seven years.

Dealing with this daily vilification and such tests of their pride in the Indian tricolour, Indian Muslims took to sit-ins and peaceful protests to defend their rights as natural-born citizens of India. They believe that the Act, enumerating conditions for asylum for non-Muslim religious minorities from neighbouring Pakistan, Bangladesh and Afghanistan—combined with calls by the Narendra Modi-led BJP national government for a national register of citizens, intending to distinguish between citizens and illegal immigrants—will unfairly target India's largest religious minority, especially in rural, impoverished and under-educated communities where many may or may not have adequate documentation (including evidence of land ownership or birth certificates of ancestors long deceased) to prove their citizenship.

The Nexus: Hate in the Media or a Hateful Media?

The images of Muslims sitting in peaceful protest, demanding their rights and protections as citizens under India's Constitution, even as the capital, Delhi, readied for local elections, were powerful in many ways. For those who have fought against discrimination and bigotry, the pictures exemplified the crossing of a Rubicon whereby Indian Muslims would no longer cower and fear the majoritarian state but assert their place as rightful Indians.

But for those who thrive on the manufacturing of offence, the images were manipulated to feed stereotypes that perpetuate fear. After all, the BJP's many lawmakers said that these protests were disruptive and showed how Muslims were 'organizing', and retaliated by shouting for these 'traitors' to be shot dead, in the middle of a heated electoral campaign in Delhi. [12]

Hate and polarization need vehicles of dissemination. Both, twenty-four-hour news television and unfiltered social media optimized by rabble-rousing politicians to spread propaganda and transmit opinion packaged as news, have normalized this 'othering' of the Indian Muslim and the desire to 'show them their place'. Television news debates have become the new reality TV, with a focus on sensationalism and shock value.

News anchors shout for 'answers' and panellists shout over them to be heard—everyone is party to the whipping up of frenzy. Religious conflicts are disguised as political differences and ideologically opposed political voices exhort action from those who support them. Social media has seen the generation of viral disinformation that gains traction among polarized echo chambers in the day and ends up making headlines on TV screens by the evening.

If mass media—television, and now social media—find such tropes easy, truncated news-gathering budgets in the industry have led to greater dependence on news agencies (including a prominent video news agency with close ties to the Indian state) that now heavily determine the input of footage, interviews and information to newsrooms, using which news content is packaged and presented.

During the anti-CAA agitation, this meant that almost all footage from the protest sites, with conservatively dressed Muslims daring to gather together in large numbers in public places, was framed as 'anti-national' and a threat to national security. In fact, in research on Muslim children in Delhi schools based on her own experience, author Nazia Erum highlights entrenched micro-aggressions that children either cause or are subject to—like the association among schoolchildren of Muslims with terrorism—as much a result of bias in their environment as it is a result of the media their elders consume and share.[13]

The role of the media in the spread of propaganda, sowing identity-based, tribalist divisions and propelling real violence, is neither new nor unique to India. Nazi Germany mastered political propaganda that enabled Hitler to rise to power and annihilate six million Jewish people in gas chambers during World War II. Radio Rwanda's anchors pitted Hutus and Tutsis against each other, and exhorted violence by fomenting fear and grievance and ascribing blame.

As the Indian media plays a wilful role in a similar exercise against Muslims, it is more important now than ever before to call out patterns of such propaganda, innocuous or neutral as they may seem, before it is too late.

It is not easy to measure the true impact of hateful, false and inflammatory text and visual content that perpetuates tropes and stereotypes by default, but Marshall McLuhan's definition of the media as an extension of ourselves is useful to consider.[14] In 1964, McLuhan argued that the phone extends our voice, the TV extends our eyes and ears, the computer extends our brain, and electronic media overall extends our central nervous system.

This extension of technology can allow us to detach ourselves from the world around us in a way that we are no longer actively culpable in the crimes and injustices committed around us. By removing the element of guilt in consumers' minds of such hateful or misleading content, it becomes easier for them to identify as victims of persecution by those gathering on their TV screens.

The distance TV creates between viewer and viewed, or a keyboard does between an online abuser and their victim, has empowered hate in a way that face-to-face social interaction censures or discourages. Repetitive and constant exposure to such ill-intentioned news coverage not only erodes an overall ethical standard and the quality of fact-based, constructive, informed journalism, but fuels biases and real violence.

Media houses are not just third-party observers but part of the narrative and 'info-wars' that dictate a majoritarian mindset. Under the garb of speaking for equal rights, they celebrate the dilution of minority rights.

For example, the Modi government's decision to ban the Muslim practice of triple talaq was lauded as a triumph, not only as a victory for oppressed Muslim women but as point scored over the Opposition Congress, which had, in the 1980s, overturned a Supreme Court verdict ensuring a divorced Muslim woman would be granted maintenance.[15]

More importantly, however, it was lauded as an affirmation of the BJP government's commitment to gender equality, even though the hypocrisy of that claim was on display barely days after the triple talaq decision in 2017, when the same government argued against criminalizing marital rape, saying it would 'destabilise the institution of marriage'[16] in the Delhi High Court. This, even though the Justice Verma commission, which revamped India's rape laws after the horrific Delhi gang rape of December 2012, recommended that marital rape be made a crime.

Or take the case of expansive, elaborate broadcast studio sets[17] for religious 'triumphs' like the Ram Janmabhoomi verdict by the Supreme Court, which has paved the way for the construction of a grand temple to the Hindu god Ram at the site of the demolished Babri Masjid in Ayodhya in Uttar Pradesh.

The News Broadcasting Standards Authority (NBSA), an autonomous, self-regulating broadcasters' body in which violations are adjudicated on by a retired Supreme Court judge, issued an advisory prior to the Ayodhya verdict, asking TV channels to cover the dispute and the verdict in a manner that refrains from inciting communal passion and upholds the values of secularism. It asked news channels to specifically avoid the impression of bias in favour of or against any one community and avoid speculation on the legal outcomes.

Nonetheless, prominent news anchors did exactly the opposite[18] and insisted Muslims should agree to the 'best possible solution'—that of a temple at the disputed site—criticized lawyers representing the 'Muslim side' and invited panellists who made inflammatory remarks against Muslims that the anchors themselves may not have had the courage to.

The foundation-laying ceremony for the temple in August 2020, presided over by the PM, was broadcast live across TV channels, once again as a celebration of Hindu identity and cultural nationalism, even as the pandemic raged.

No surprise, then, that reporting and analysis of the mass gathering of Hindu devotees at the earlier than originally scheduled[19] Maha Kumbh Mela[20] in March and April of 2021, saw extremely muted criticism—especially on mainstream news television—even as India found itself in the throes of a deadly second wave of the coronavirus pandemic, a year after the first cases. The event took place in violation of all established COVID-19 protocols of masking and distancing.[21] Reports later indicated over 90 per cent of the Kumbh Mela's attendees had tested positive for COVID-19[22] (making the event a super spreader), exposed weak tracing and isolating capabilities, and threw a poorly connected mountainous state like Uttarakhand's public health system into a major crisis.

Such coverage is in the same vein as the deliberate segregation of COVID-19 cases linked to the Tablighi Jamaat across news platforms, the breathless coverage of Muslim men testing positive at a time when overall testing rates were extremely low and the entire congregation was tested for the virus, or the generalized representation of terrorists as men in skullcaps and/or beards. If journalism moulds opinion and discourse, such selective messaging in the garb of journalism muddies the pond for independent and rational decision-making by viewers.

The intended meaning of such images, and their impact on our objective understanding or processing of the information we are bombarded with, are clearly motivated by a question of power.[23] In the digital age, where all information is online minutes after being aired on TV, or vice versa, headlines play the dual role of framing opinion as well as serving as anchor text. The words used in headlines, therefore, can become key triggers for the thought process that follows in activating relevant current or dormant associations in collective public memory.

An Existential Crisis in Indian Media

'The Sudarshan TV show on the infiltration of Muslims in Civil Services is insidious and rabid since it tends to target one particular community.'—Justice D.Y. Chandrachud, Supreme Court of India,[24] Sudarshan News case (WP(C) No.956/2020)

In the garb of 'investigative journalism', Suresh Chavhanke, the editor-in-chief of a Hindi TV news channel called Sudarshan TV, promoted nine episodes of a 'news' show titled 'UPSC Jihad' in August 2020. The intention of the 'investigation' was to prove that Muslim students of Jamia Millia Islamia University (which was at the forefront of protests against the CAA) were 'infiltrating' the Indian bureaucracy and police.

The discriminatory and provocative show made the claim that Muslim aspirants to the Union Public Services Commission (UPSC), which conducts exams for the various civil and police services, had risen exponentially and that the UPSC had relaxed age limits, reduced qualifying conditions and allowed them more attempts to sit the exam. It also made the charge that Muslim aspirants were receiving 'foreign funding' to 'infiltrate' the services. Even the twitter handle of the informal grouping of Indian Police Services, the (IPS) Association termed their show a 'communal and irresponsible piece of journalism'.[25]

In a landmark hearing that took place a few weeks after the TV promos were first aired, the Supreme Court of India stayed the telecast[26] of six out of nine episodes, even though the Ministry of Information and Broadcasting had cleared the show for airing the week before, as long as it didn't 'violate programme codes'.[27]

Yet, after four episodes were telecast, the government's own lawyers were forced to admit in court that the programming was offensive, in poor taste and could provoke communal attitudes. While Sudarshan TV's legal team argued for the right to free speech, the Supreme Court took a strong view against content that promoted hatred.[28]

Three judges of the Supreme Court of India maintained that while the channel was free to investigate the affairs of NGOs it claimed was funding the study of aspirants, it censured the editors for targeting an entire community as being part of a conspiracy. They also questioned the value of the NBSA and called it toothless. The censure addressed the elephant in the room: the need for the NBSA to strengthen its self-regulatory framework and ensure compliance from its members.

Even as the court asked whether NBSA had any value beyond its letterhead, it knew the answer to this rhetorical question. All the NBSA could do was ask the 'offenders' at Sudarshan TV to apologize during prime time. But it needed the Supreme Court to intervene, enforce the reprimand and ban the remaining incendiary episodes. The judgment also highlights an inherent contradiction in the media's own industry regulatory frameworks—that of 'falling foul of the standards' it prescribes for itself.

However, in instance after instance, conflating religion with culture, and support for the government with patriotism; TV channels continue to hype up coverage of previously innocuous religious festivals and imbue them with a nationalistic fervour, carry provocative images of processions outsides mosques; and the management looks benignly on as news anchors spread hate night after night by questioning the practice of Islam in public places, or Muslim participation in Hindu festivals.

Despite censure from the courts, television news media has barrelled along this path of hate and division. So much so, that a television news debate in which Nupur Sharma, a prominent BJP spokesperson made defamatory comments about the Prophet led to a diplomatic impasse[29] with several Muslim countries from Jordan to Indonesia. Iran, the UAE, and Kuwait summoning Indian envoys to register a protest, forcing the government to distance itself from both its spokesperson and her comments.

Nearly two-and-a-half years later, in September 2022, as the Supreme Court of India heard petitions challenging the rising levels of hate speech in the India media, it went a step further. In observations, Justices K.M. Joseph and Hrishikesh Roy observed that the role of television news anchors in ensuring their shows do not descend into hate speech, is critical,[30] especially in the absence of effective regulation. Calling visual media 'the chief medium of hate speech' it asked why the government was 'standing by as a mute witness when all this is happening'.

However, even though it has rightly, and consistently, raised concerns around the proliferation of hate speech in the media, and its subsequent impact on the spread and normalization of acts of violence in the real world, the Court's approach is largely regulatory and legal. While seeking effective, enforceable guidelines, it also needs to consider a major structural flaw— mainstream Indian broadcast media's business model. As this chapter illustrates, today's television news media thrives on hate; and it comes cheap. 'Hate drives TRPs, drives profit', Justice Roy observed. Therefore, at the heart of the Supreme Court's concerns must also lie the absence of any incentive for the business model to change and must always find a way to strike the balance between censuring hate speech while protecting and ensuring freedom of expression, in keeping with Article 19 of the Indian Constitution.

Today's newsrooms are hybrid and convergent, and use overlapping print, broadcast and digital formats. The pace of technological development in news gathering, production and dissemination, coupled with the spread of social media, means that editorial filters that would once have caught and removed inflammatory, discriminatory or bigoted content barely exist now.

Additionally, the proverbial worm, which democratized the media and information space and led to the creation of an 'interconnected estate'[31] in which mainstream print, broadcast and digital media cohabit with social media and reach global audiences, has turned.

Even a decade ago, social media was seen predominantly as an equalizing force, predominantly for good. It led to revolution, justice and change, from movements ranging from the Arab Spring to #MeToo internationally, from the Lokpal agitation against political corruption to the fight for gender justice after the 2012 Delhi gang rape in India.

Today, however, whether through easy-to-use social media apps or through 'clickbait' news and opinion on regular news websites, propaganda in the world's largest democracy is in overdrive. Aggressive anti-Muslim rhetoric plays out online in a 24/7 cycle, with little or no time or desire for accuracy or context.

And whether it is mainstream mass media bodies or social media platforms that lay down 'community standards' and 'user guidelines', each day brings new instances of the failure of these companies and organizations to uphold their own standards.

In fact, social media platforms have become regular battlegrounds for narrative warfare. Their algorithms foster abilities to profile users and curate targeted content that confirm and reinforce bias and prejudice, irrespective of which side of the divide the user may stand on. Needless to say, the formats all feed off each other in our technologically disrupted, interconnected information universe.

Hate for Profit

To ask why a robust media industry can succumb to the proliferation of hate in such a manner is not a rhetorical question. Much of it is also tied intrinsically to problematic ownership and revenue models, licencing and inadequate funding. The value of television channels as propaganda tools cannot be overstated, and rich politicians have used personal wealth to further political messaging through ownership controls.

Worse, as both economic constraints and cheaper online options drive corporate sector advertising away from the more expensive, big mainstream media organizations, the latter have come to depend disproportionately on government advertising in the form of both public relations and 'public service' messages paid for by different arms of the Union and state governments.

It is no wonder, then, that big news organizations, eager to access the only real source of money in the markets today, appear to fall in line with the regime of the day, even if that means becoming a willing accomplice in the propagation of hatred in society. Prime Time anchors are instructed to avoid overly critical commentary, or at the very least, avoid naming the PM directly when being critical of the BJP's communal agenda or policies. [32]

'Hate trackers', which gathered data on real crimes against minorities, were forced to shut down as they brought unwelcome global attention.[33] News organizations have been willing to participate in political propaganda for a price, and some, according to an investigative 'sting' operation by Cobrapost, even agreed to spread communal hate in return for cash from the ruling party.[34]

Those who have resisted have been at the receiving end of tax raids, police complaints, charges of treason and government-backed lawsuits, either against the journalists themselves, or against their financial backers. In fact, in few democracies has a government so brazenly brought pressure to bear on private-sector advertisers or used its own financial instruments and cut off access in order to ensure the media only tells those stories that it wants told.

The tragic irony of today's BJP government is that it has adopted all the tactics and media management toolkits of its earlier political opponents—the very systems that it claimed to fight against, in which bribery, intimidation and violence were the norm. Today, several people who experienced the lash of the Emergency first-hand are among the PM's cabinet colleagues.

Yet, they are only too willing to accuse any journalist not in agreement with their worldview of being biased and, worse, corrupt. The organized army of trolls often endorsed by the PM [35] and his cabinet colleagues have made abuse and invective the everyday currency of our political conversations.

The net result of these efforts is a wave of intimidation against smaller news organizations or independent journalists who try to swim against the tide, and a growing tendency to self-censor or seek 'balance' in the interest of preservation among bigger mass media organizations.

For example, media discourse in 2017, especially on news television and in social media, around a fresh exodus of Rohingya refugees from Myanmar, often skewed the narrative away from their plight as refugees fleeing a genocide to one that painted them as illegal immigrants seeking a better economic future or potential terrorists intending to threaten India's national security.

In the interests of balance and objectivity, both arguments were given nearly equal space on TV and in print, even though the humanitarian imperative demanded much more urgent attention. In this case, too, vitiated social media discourse led by 'influencers' with hundreds of thousands of followers, divisive hashtags and viral comments found their way into the nightly news cycle.

Conclusion

The Indian mass media landscape today comprises over 300 TV channels (reaching 112 million households), 50,000 newspapers and magazines (with a readership of over 250 million), around 300 radio stations, 1,000 feature films in eighteen languages made each year, and a plethora of print, electronic, digital and telecommunications media. Twitter and Facebook have some of their largest consumer bases in India.

Across platforms, writers, journalists and citizen journalists opine and reflect prevailing moods, especially against minorities, rather than fact-check their rationale. That job has been left to a new genre of journalists, the fact-checkers, who call out members of their own fraternity for hate speech and disinformation. The pressure on the few remaining advertisers to stop the sponsorship of such programming in the media has mounted.

Over the last year, as scandals of rigged TV ratings come to light, some have made public statements[36] against 'toxic media channels' that are creating a country which thrives on hate and withdrawn their advertising from such spaces.

While resuming office after winning again in 2019, Prime Minister Modi had repeatedly made clear his contempt for a media establishment he believes is biased—and worse, beholden to a corrupt elite. 'Today the masks are off all journalists,' he said, in an interview[37] to—ironically—a journalist. 'That is why your reputation is on the line.'

Modi's many voluble supporters applauded his sentiments then, without acknowledging that the very critiques they consistently make of past dispensations apply to them today. Riding a wave of 'anti-establishment' sentiment since he first arrived in the PMO, Narendra Modi has succeeded in creating the most pliant, cowering media any leader since Indira Gandhi[38] has enjoyed.

5

Islamophobia and Sinhalese Buddhist Nationalism in Sri Lanka

NEIL DEVOTTA

'Another Zahran is born.'

— A Sinhalese nurse, while holding up a newborn Muslim baby[1]

IN JUNE 2014, A SINHALESE mob attacked Muslim homes, businesses and mosques in and around Aluthgama, a town about 40 miles (over 64 km) south of Colombo, Sri Lanka. It was among the worst anti-Muslim violence to take place in the island since the first ever Sinhalese-Muslim riots of 1915. Many feared that the so-called 'Aluthgama riots' were a dry run geared to mark this sorry centennial the following year. For Muslims, the increasing Islamophobia leading up to the attacks in Aluthgama and its vicinity were terribly disconcerting, given that the community had consistently supported the country's Sinhalese-led governments against the LTTE, which had waged a nearly three decades-long war to create a separate state for the minority Tamils before being brutally defeated in May 2009.[2]

Indeed, as part of its war against the Sri Lankan state and in an act of ethnic cleansing, the LTTE forcibly evicted over 60,000 Muslims from Northern Province in October 1990 and also attacked Muslims in Eastern Province on multiple occasions.[3] By then, thanks to Muslims helping the state intelligence services against the LTTE and Muslim elites lobbying with Middle Eastern countries on the island's behalf, the community was branded the 'good minority'.[4] This appellation masked an eddy of anti-Muslim sentiment long present in the country, but the speed with which the anti-Muslim agitation took shape stunned Muslims, and caused them to feel used and abused.[5]

After the civil war, the first major anti-Muslim incident took place in September 2011, when Buddhist monks led a mob that destroyed a Muslim shrine in Anuradhapura. They claimed that Muslims planned to convert the shrine, which had endured for nearly 400 years, into a mosque, and this could not be allowed as Anuradhapura was sacred Buddhist land. The well-planned attack on the shrine saw its organizers claiming that the Sinhalese were a fast 'vanishing race' being threatened by Muslims who were 'breeding like pigs'.[6] No one disputes Anuradhapura's Buddhist credentials, but the fact that a Muslim shrine could endure for nearly 400 years also proves that Buddhism coexisted with Islam and other religions, a fact reinforced throughout much of the island's history.

In April 2012, another rabble led by monks attacked a mosque in Dambulla, a location that, like Anuradhapura, Buddhists consider a sacred area. Thereafter, hoodlums often accompanied by Buddhist monks associated with a radical group called the Bodu Bala Sena (a Buddhist power force, or BBS) took the lead in attacking various mosques as well as prominent and even not-so-prominent Muslim businesses. The BBS-inspired attack in Aluthgama and nearby

Muslim communities represented the worst post-civil war anti-Muslim violence.

The BBS enjoyed then President Mahinda Rajapaksa's and his brother and Defence Secretary Gotabaya Rajapaksa's imprimatur, since they appeared to believe the group could be used to manipulate Sinhalese Buddhist nationalist sentiment to further consolidate their power and institute a family dynasty.[7] While the island has fielded numerous Sinhalese Buddhist majoritarian organizations since its independence in 1948, the BBS's raison d'être seems to be the subjugation of Muslims (and Christians, especially evangelical Christians).

In doing so, it allied with the 969 Movement in Burma (Myanmar) that has targeted Rohingya Muslims and promised to work together to protect Buddhism across the world, and it clearly draws inspiration from the prevalent post-9/11 Islamophobia that has become a worldwide phenomenon. With the internet and globalization enabling 'emulative linkages',[8] whereby groups manipulating Islamophobic agitprop learn rhetoric, tactics and strategy from one another, the BBS evidences how an entity can appropriate a phenomenon trending globally and apply it locally. In that sense, the attacks on Sri Lanka's Muslims represent a microcosm of the Islamophobia zeitgeist the world is currently experiencing.[9]

This essay suggests that the renewed assertiveness among Sinhalese Buddhist nationalists and changing cultural dynamics among the island's Muslims has exacerbated the Islamophobia phenomenon in Sri Lanka. If the former feel emboldened thanks to the LTTE's defeat, the latter stems from the Wahabi–Salafi teachings that have made Sri Lanka's Muslims more conservative and insular in ways that culturally distance them from their Sri Lankan and South Asian heritage. This phenomenon of embracing greater piety and seeking greater religious authenticity by aping Middle Eastern customs is not unique to Sri Lanka or to South Asia.

But the socio-cultural and spiritual transformation it has induced in turn disrupts common spaces—and hitherto settled notions of habitus—in ways that make the dominant community (in Sri Lanka's case, the Sinhalese Buddhists) feel threatened. This sense of threat reinforces the majoritarian belief that minorities who do not recognize their subordinate place in a predominantly Buddhist society qualify to be put in their place, forcibly if necessary. Hence the silence accompanying anti-Muslim violence and the palpable satisfaction many feel when such attacks take place.

Sri Lanka has experienced varied nationalisms over the past century. If anti-colonial nationalism (even if it was not as strident as that evidenced in British India) led to independence in 1948, linguistic and religious nationalisms led to Sinhalese Buddhist superordination and Tamil separatism. While the Sinhalese understandably celebrated military victories over the LTTE, just as most Tamils appreciated LTTE military successes, the vast majority of Sinhalese and Buddhists maintained that they could easily get along with Tamils if not for LTTE terrorism.

The sentiment hardly acknowledged that Sinhalese Buddhist majoritarianism birthed LTTE terrorism and that the military too resorted to terrorist tactics against Tamils in the north-east. At the same time, the rhetoric about coexistence seemed related to Hindu-Buddhist syncretism and prior camaraderie. This sense of linkage appears lacking when it comes to the Muslim community. Indeed, the Islamophobia that Buddhist groups have fanned, coupled with Muslims' growing insularity thanks to the Salafi-Wahabi influence, have pushed the island's Muslims further apart.

Islamophobia amid Majoritarianism

While scholars have debated the merits and demerits of the term 'Islamophobia',[10] it is generally considered a 'shorthand way of referring to dread or hatred of Islam—and, therefore, to fear or dislike of all or most Muslims'.[11] The fear could stem from Islamist terrorism, which may make Islamophobia rational, but it is more often spread by depicting Islam as primitive, barbaric, misogynistic and inferior to other religions (especially Christianity), with Islam being treated more as an ideology than a genuine religion.[12] The latter, especially, helps justify the ethno-religious discrimination and violence generally associated with Islamophobia.

In the West, Islamophobia has led to fears that Europe is on the verge of becoming 'Eurabia'[13] as far-right and populist politicians—ranging from Marine Le Pen in France and Geert Wilders in Holland to Nigel Farage in the United Kingdom and Donald Trump in the United States—have used it to upend democratic politics in their respective countries.[14] Indeed, the issue played no small role in the UK's vote to leave the European Union (especially after rumours claimed voting against Brexit would allow thousands of Turks to enter Britain).

Islamophobia may get justified within the context of Islamist terrorism. For instance, Pakistan's willingness to use jihadi forces to destabilize India in disputed Kashmir[15] and the renascent Islamism in Bangladesh[16] cause anxiety and promote Islamophobia in India. In these instances, events abroad induce Islamophobia. But a nationalist ideology rooted in religion can also fan it and unleash massive violence. Indeed, nationalist ideologies make communal violence acceptable and even desirable, for nationalist narratives tend to promote communal violence by linking jeremiad and mytho-history with chauvinism to promote an exclusivist ideology, which individuals and parties manipulate and profit from. This is what the Hindu nationalist ideology in India and the Sinhalese Buddhist nationalist ideology in Sri Lanka do by framing Muslims as a dangerous, predatory and destabilizing 'other'.

In India, right-wing Hindus coalesce around Hindutva, the notion that all Indians, irrespective of their religious beliefs, ought to subscribe to a Hindu ethos.[17] This has partly led to an obsession with demographics, leading to claims that Muslims conspire to procreate at a faster rate and outnumber Hindus, and that Muslim men resort to 'love jihad' whereby they seduce and marry Hindu women so as to enrich Muslim numbers. It has also led to programmes designed to convert Muslims and others to Hinduism. The irony is that Islamophobia has made India's Muslims the most insecure and fearful,[18] with the pro-Hindutva BJP's election victories in 2014 and 2019 exacerbating these fears.

In Sri Lanka, too, an ideology similar to Hindutva predominates among the majority Sinhalese Buddhists. This nationalist ideology claims Sri Lanka is the island of the Sinhalese and the chosen repository of Buddhism; Sinhalese Buddhists have been ennobled to preserve and propagate Buddhism; minorities live there, thanks to Sinhalese Buddhist sufferance and must, hence, respect the majoritarian ethos.[19] It further argues that all those who challenge this hegemonic Sinhalese Buddhist position seek to diminish the pre-eminence of Buddhism and Sinhalese Buddhist predominance and are, therefore, traitors. Those branded traitors may include minorities, NGOs, civil society associations, journalists and any mediapersons who speak out on minorities' rights.

Foreign governments that criticize Sri Lankan policies or activities that threaten or marginalize ethnic and religious minorities are also castigated for supposedly loathing and seeking to undermine the island and its foremost faith. Such is the narrative within which the

BBS and similar organizations locate and propagate Islamophobia in Sri Lanka. And with the LTTE militarily vanquished and Tamils consequently marginalized, the island's Muslims are being targeted as the new insidious 'other' threatening Sinhalese Buddhist civilization.

Among the identities that fuel nationalism, religion and language are the most important. This is because both religion and language contribute to regionalism and culture in ways other identities may not, even as they influence historical narratives. If nations resort to nationalism to secure and propagate their unique attributes, the passions associated with nationalism are rooted in historical events (real or imagined) that combine notions of greatness with episodes of humiliation.

Religion and language often play a central role in the narratives that celebrate such greatness and bemoan national humiliation. This is certainly the case with Sinhalese Buddhist nationalism, which is rooted in a mytho-history that helps legitimize majoritarianism even as it fans past humiliations and present-day threats. In short, minorities must behave in a 'proper' manner by appreciating the established 'ethnic hierarchy' in which the majority community is assured of its 'legitimate' place and the minorities of their 'proper' place.[20]

The nationalist ideology in Sri Lanka is easy to promote given that the Sinhalese and Buddhists constitute large majorities within a constitutional order bereft of minority guarantees. Such demographics devoid of constitutional strictures led to an ethnocracy by the 1950s, when the Sinhala language was made the only official language. This allowed the majority community to arrogate positions associated with the state while especially marginalizing Tamil minorities.

While Tamils (both those identified as Sri Lankan Tamils and Indian Tamils) comprise over 15 per cent of the population and are the island's biggest minority group, Muslims represent nearly 10 per cent of the population. Slightly higher fertility has contributed to the increase in Muslim numbers, but so has Tamil migration. By some estimates, over a million Tamils fled Sri Lanka during the civil war (1983–2009) and this exodus has helped increase the percentage of other groups. Indeed, the groups that have made the most population gains in the island are Sinhalese and Buddhists. For instance, while the Sinhalese and Buddhists were 66.1 per cent and 60 per cent, respectively, in 1911, today the Sinhalese are around 75 per cent and Buddhists at over 70 per cent.[21] Nationalists obsess over demographics, so those among the Sinhalese Buddhists disregard the population gains of their community and instead harp on the slight increase in Muslim numbers.

Sri Lanka's Muslims

Muslims have lived in Sri Lanka for around 1,300 years, when Arab traders who had adopted the religion got to the island around the seventh century. As per 2012 census figures, Muslims number close to two million people and comprise 9.3 per cent of Sri Lanka's population.[22] The Portuguese called those of Arabian descent Moors, and this was how Muslims were classified in Sri Lanka during colonial times. The classification led to many claiming ties to countries in the Middle East—notwithstanding the community's matrilineal and matrilocal practices and use of the Tamil language, which suggests they are related to native Sri Lankans and people along the coastal areas of southern and western India.[23]

Tamil leaders like Ponnambalam Ramanathan first claimed publicly in 1885 that Sri Lankan Moors were of Tamil (and South Asian) ethnicity, which led to serious Muslim-Tamil disagreement. That the claim was made at a time when the British colonial authorities were considering nominating a Moor to the Legislative Council only aggravated the rift. Thirty years later, Ramanathan took the lead in defending prominent Sinhalese who were accused of participating in and supporting the 1915 anti-Muslim riots, and this further pushed the island's Muslims away from Tamils and contributed to the community emphasizing its religious identity over the common linguistic identity it shared with Tamils.

While most Muslims are of South Asian ancestry, a small Malay community continues to live in the island thanks to the Dutch bringing over Muslims from Java in the seventeenth and eighteenth centuries. Following independence from colonial rule, Muslims voted for the United National Party (UNP) and Sri Lanka Freedom Party (SLFP), the island's two main parties led by the Sinhalese. During presidential elections held over the past four decades, Muslims have mainly supported the UNP. During parliamentary elections, most Muslims choose between the Sri Lanka Muslim Congress (SLMC) and All Ceylon Muslim Congress (ACMC). Some among the community feel that establishing Muslim parties was a mistake, as this has helped split the community and added to the island's extant ethno-religious divisions.

Muslims in the Northern and Eastern Provinces rely on farming, while others engage in forms of trade that range from prominent clothing and electronic establishments to eateries and restaurants, hardware stores and butcher shops. Remittances from the Middle East and revenue from tea and garment exports comprise Sri Lanka's main foreign currency earnings, and Muslims play a leading role in all three areas.[24] Sinhalese Buddhists have monopolized employment within the military and bureaucracies, and Muslims have consequently used their community networks to engage in business. While the resulting conspicuous trading has led to a sense that Muslims are a relatively wealthy community, large numbers of them live in poverty, especially in Colombo's congested areas.

As noted above, the Muslim community has consistently supported the Sinhalese state against the Tamil separatist movements. The LTTE exacerbated the Muslim-Tamil divide by attacking mosques, murdering Muslims and extorting money from Muslim businesses. For instance, the LTTE's attempt to kidnap for ransom a Muslim trader's daughter sparked the 1985 Tamil-Muslim riots in Eastern Province, which led to scores of homes and businesses being destroyed, especially Muslim ones.

Successive government policies have also aggravated this Tamil-Muslim divide. For instance, the J.R. Jayewardene government encouraged Muslims to take up arms against Tamil militants in the 1980s, and after the civil war, some police and military personnel have pitted Tamils against Muslims and vice versa when dealing with land and water disputes, especially in Eastern Province.[25]

The fear that a Tamil-dominated north-east would lead to Muslim marginalization was the basis for the SLMC demanding an autonomous Muslim administrative enclave in Eastern Province. The demand, together with Muslim concerns and aspirations, was best captured by the so-called Oluvil Declaration of January 2003, which claimed Muslims were a separate nation; the north-east region constituted the community's traditional homeland; north-eastern Muslims were entitled to self-determination; majority Muslim areas in the north-east must be linked into a unit so as to enable political autonomy; and Muslims who live outside the north-east should also be guaranteed their basic rights.

The Oluvil Declaration is a clear indication of how Sinhalese Buddhist nationalism and Tamil nationalism pushed Muslims to also assert themselves along ethno-religious lines. The subsequent call to form a Muslim regiment within the Sri Lanka Army to protect predominantly Muslim areas in Eastern Province, a call some in the military seemed to support despite the SLMC and others opposing it, was also a manifestation of Muslim assertion.

Sri Lanka's Muslims are mainly Sunni, whose identity combined Islam and South Asian culture. Muslims speak Tamil, one of the oldest South Asian languages, although now many Muslims also speak Sinhala fluently. They mainly dressed in typical South Asian fashion (women in sari or the salwar kameez and men in shirt and sarong or pants). This changed after Muslims began migrating to the Middle East for employment. Many returned imbibed with Salafi and Wahabi teachings and began promoting an exclusivist and hyper-orthodox 'universal *umma*-consciousness'.[26]

The attendant austere, uncompromising and puritanical influence manifests itself in the activities promoted by groups such as Tablighi Jamaat, Jamiat-ul-Ulema, Jamaathi Islami, and Thawheed Jamaat, the increasing number of Muslim women who wear the burqa and *niqab*, and men who have adopted *jubba*-style Middle Eastern attire. And it has led to attacks on Sufi Muslims for being 'kafirs' (non-believers) who peddle Hindu ideas, their mosques being branded 'houses of Satan' and rigid codes of conduct being superimposed on the wider Muslim community.

It is possible that the attendant conspicuous performance of piety associated with such Middle Eastern accoutrements and fundamentalist forms of Islam are related to the island's civil war,[27] although the imbibing and aping of Salafi-Wahabi teachings and customs in recent times is not unique to Sri Lanka. In short, the so-called 'Saudization' of Islam is a phenomenon other South Asian states have also had to grapple with,[28] and the radical transformation taking place among the region's Muslims is connected to people working in the Middle East and Middle Eastern funds being channelled to mosques and schools to promote Salafi-Wahabi practices.[29] It appears piety is associated with respectability, even as Salafi-Wahabi practices are associated with Islamic authenticity.

The upshot is that all this has magnified the insularity within the community. The state is partly responsible for Muslim insularity in Sri Lanka. For instance, religious establishments can own and operate schools in the country, and this has prevented students from various communities commingling with each other. But Muslim insularity also stems from Muslims' proclivity for self-segregation, which helps buttress anti-Muslim stereotypes. The Salafi-Wahabi ideology has exacerbated this tendency by encouraging Muslims to disassociate themselves from non-Muslims. Indeed, as noted above, it has even promoted intra-Islamic violence by castigating Sufis and others as apostates.

This does not mean Muslims in general do not interact with those from other religions; it instead suggests Muslims' modus operandi are partly responsible for interreligious interaction not being more widespread. Associated with this insularity is the phenomenon of many Muslim youth cheering for the visiting Pakistani cricket team (which most recently took place right after the civil war ended). Some have indicated that this is due to Muslims feeling discriminated against, but such actions suggest that the community's loyalty to the global umma supersedes its loyalty to Sri Lanka and provides groups like the BBS ample fodder to question Muslim patriotism.

The Muslim-only town of Kattankudy, in the Batticaloa district, is a good example of this self-segregation. One of the most demographically dense areas in South Asia, Kattankudy comprises around 50,000 people and fifty mosques. Most of the town's women operate in purdah and outsiders are viewed with suspicion. This in turn has made it a haven for Islamic fundamentalism, which the likes of Tablighi Jamaat, especially, have promoted. The date palm trees that have been planted along the road at the entrance to the town gives it a Middle Eastern aura, although some Muslims themselves question the need for such stark differentiation.

The growth of Islamic fundamentalism has led to occasional violence, especially between Sufis and those who espouse Wahabi–Salafi tenets. Islamic teachers from India, Pakistan and Bangladesh visited Kattankudy and nearby towns and it led to claims that Muslims in the area were being radicalized. This was evidenced when it turned out that the leader of the 2019 Easter Sunday bombings was from Kattankudy.

Anti-Muslim Politicking

If Islamophobia refers to the irrational fear of Muslims, anti-Muslim politicking relates to manipulating such fears for political ends. And this is what has mainly transpired within Sri Lanka during the post-civil war period. The BBS and similar groups were at the forefront of this, but powerful politicians and certain business interests who stood to gain from eliminating Muslim competitors enabled their activities. This is why a number of extremist monks have called on people to boycott Muslim businesses and some now advertise their establishments as Sinhalese Buddhist businesses.[30]

The BBS first made a name for itself by campaigning against halal (permissible under Islamic law) products being marketed, claiming that the halal certification that was granted by a Muslim entity symbolized Islamist extremism taking root in the island. That was accompanied by protests against Muslim women wearing the burqa and niqab. Its outlandish claims designed to demonize the island's Muslims included accusations that Muslims were heavily involved in selling narcotics, Muslim proprietors were forcing Buddhist employees to work on Buddhist holidays (which are typically national holidays) and thus preventing them going to the temple, Muslim men were seducing Buddhist women and seeking to convert them to Islam, Muslim clothing stores were selling underwear with the Buddha's image, and such businesses were also handing out toffees and selling female foundation garments that made Sinhalese women infertile. Hardly any leading Sinhalese Buddhist politicians spoke against the group through all this. Their reluctance to do so meant the leading monks of the BBS were free to operate with impunity.

Humiliating and vilifying Muslims was crucial to the BBS's modus operandi, which is typified by the following screed by the monk Galagoda Aththe Gnanasara (here referring to a site called Kuragala that contains a Muslim shrine and evidence of ancient Buddhist monastic life):

> Kuragala is a historically important place where over 12,000 monks resided. Some consider this place the Diva Guhawa (God's Cave or God's Abode) because there is a beautiful plane there. But Sailani Muslims took over this place. Now this is a bloody problem. There is no God. This God doesn't even have a face. So we ask what testicles are they showing? If I put it simply, since we have to speak in 'pure Sinhala', which is understood by everyone. What is this religion? This place has a name given by the Whites. They've destroyed all the Buddhist countries like Afghanistan. They've come here now to pray saying they're praying to God. They say that this is close to our culture. They make us feel that their faith is like ours, that there is nothing wrong if they too pray there. This is a trick they're playing on us. This is how they caught Kuragala. During the season who comes there? Princes and princesses from the Middle East. They take over this place. Then they make a connection from Kuragala to Sri Pada (Adam's Peak). They will say this is Diva guhawa where

> God urinated. Then they'll say God kept His foot on Adam's Peak. Because, Allah is a big octopus. Allah is a big octopus. He urinates in one place. He defecates in another place. That's what they say. They say the whole world is Allah's. We cannot let this fairy tale continue. We say this has to stop. No matter which powerful person intervenes, we will go on. We ask the Government not to test the patience of our youth.[31]

The election of Gotabaya Rajapaksa as president in November 2019 saw groups like the BBS taking a back seat, because they feel comfortable with the current government's Buddhist supremacist agenda. This is evidenced by how some within the government have promoted policies that specifically target Muslims. These proposals range from banning cow slaughter, a profession mainly associated with Muslims, to banning the burqa. In March 2021, the government introduced a regulation on deradicalization that can be used to target detractors. The regulation, which is associated with the draconian 1979 Prevention of Terrorism Act, permits the Ministry of Defence to create reintegration centres, and Muslims fear it could be used against members of the community just as China has used camps to persecute Uighurs.[32] Thus far, the most prominent Muslim arrested is the leader of the ACMC, who also happens to be a Member of Parliament. But the government has also arrested and imprisoned others remotely linked to the 2019 Easter Sunday bombers,[33] which suggests it plans to use the bombings to further the anti-Muslim agenda of its most fervent nationalist supporters.

Easter Sunday Bombings

During the civil war, the LTTE, which perfected techniques associated with suicide bombings, carried out numerous attacks using its Black Tigers. Yet, not even the LTTE launched the sort of coordinated attacks that Islamist extremists carried out on Easter Sunday 2019, which killed 269 people (including forty-five foreign nationals and eight bombers). The attacks targeted three churches and three major hotels. The strong calls by the Catholic cardinal and other clergy against revenge attacks targeting the Muslim community prevented major rioting. But had a Buddhist place of worship been among those attacked, there would likely have been island-wide anti-Muslim violence comparable to the anti-Tamil pogrom of July 1983, which helped launch the civil war.

Sri Lankan authorities initially accused two groups of being responsible for the bombings. Very little was known of the first, Jammiyathul Millathu Ibrahim (JMI), even among Muslims. The second, called the National Thawheed Jamaat (NTJ), was clearly influenced by the Islamic State (IS). But while the IS claimed responsibility for organizing the attack, the Sri Lankan bombings were a home-grown affair and could have been easily prevented had intelligence sources followed through on information that Indian authorities especially provided them.

The Indian assistance aside, Sri Lankan Muslims who were upset over the extremist tones the NTJ leader Zahran Hashim embraced—going so far as to claim that Sri Lanka was a Muslim country—not only forced him out of Kattankudy but also reported his extremism to Sri Lankan authorities months before the bombings were conceived. The Sri Lankan government has hitherto delayed releasing a committee report on the bombings, which has caused many to wonder about the links those sympathetic to the NTJ may have had with political leaders and military officials.

The big question was why the NTJ targeted Christian churches when it was Buddhist radicals in groups like the BBS that were mostly responsible for the anti-Muslim violence. Initially, pro-

IS social media claimed that the attacks were in response to the Christchurch, New Zealand mosque shootings which killed fifty Muslims. The Sri Lankan government also initially sought to draw a link between the Christchurch shootings and the Easter Sunday attacks. This is a stretch, unless one appreciates the IS worldview rooted in a binary of 'believers' versus 'infidels'. If those who subscribe to IS ideology are believers, then westerners and Christians are crusaders whose lifestyles are antithetical to fundamental Islamic values. For an ideology that respects no borders and nationalities, Sri Lankan Christians, irrespective of their ethnicity, were worthy of being attacked because they fit into the crusader bracket.

Consequently, while it was IS ideology that influenced the likes of Zahran Hashim, the anti-Muslim agitprop and violence that Sinhalese Buddhist nationalism fanned was what likely helped radicalize so many to the NTJ cause.[34] Just as the violent Tamil nationalism the LTTE came to represent was a reaction to violent Sinhalese nationalism, the NTJ and the Easter Sunday bombings are most likely a violent Muslim reaction to Sri Lanka's recent anti-Muslim violence.[35] Sri Lankans must thus come to terms with how politicians and Buddhist leaders have enabled and manipulated Islamophobia for personal gain and thereby contributed to this disaster.

Conclusion

Sri Lanka's minorities are increasingly finding themselves besieged, thanks to uncompromising and extremist Sinhalese Buddhist nationalists in power. The Islamophobia that these nationalists fan when pursuing political and ideological goals place the island's Muslim community in an especially precarious position. While some government leaders speak in comforting tones, the state's actions when dealing with Muslims are anything but tolerant. This was clear when the government insisted on cremating Muslims who died from COVID-19 despite the island's Muslims, civil society and the international community pleading against the practice.

The WHO repeatedly noted how there was no danger from COVID-19 victims being buried, and yet, the Sri Lankan government pointed to the possibility of groundwater pollution to sanction cremation. It showed utter disregard for the angst this caused Muslims and only changed its policy in March 2021 when seeking support among predominantly Muslim countries to counter a United Nations Human Rights Council resolution that pressures the island to account for human rights abuses. This abrupt about-turn showed that the government's COVID-19 cremation policy was unrelated to scientific evidence and was instead based on a desire to torment and humiliate Muslims. Doing so was likely in retaliation for most Muslims voting against Mahinda Rajapaksa during the 2015 presidential election, which contributed to his defeat, and also for voting against President Gotabaya Rajapaksa in 2019. But this was also a policy that Sinhalese Buddhist nationalists championed and that was popular among most Buddhists, with many seeming to derive sadistic pleasure from seeing Muslims' torment when forced to cremate dead relatives.

When the current government headed by President Gotabaya Rajapaksa came to power, many feared imminent anti-Muslim violence, but the COVID-19 pandemic may have stymied this. Some government officials initially sought to blame Muslims for the spread of the coronavirus—since many among those first infected were from congested Muslim areas in Colombo—but subsequent clusters among soldiers, garment factory workers and others made it clear that government blunders were mostly to blame for the spread of COVID-19.[36] In any case, the economic costs associated with the coronavirus may be curtailing the government's anti-Muslim politicking, as it relies heavily on tourism, remittances—especially from the Middle East—and foreign direct investment, and will want to project a peaceful and stable environment.

Sri Lanka comprises various inter-religious groups that advocate pluralism across the country, so communal conflict is evitable.[37] Yet, Sri Lanka's post-independence history is rife with ethno-religious violence. And while the country is poorer for such carnage, there are many among the majority community who have profited handsomely from the violence. These include those currently in power, which is why the country's Muslims have reason to worry about their well-being.

6

Fear, Radicalism and Violence

Sri Lanka's Cyclical Crisis

GEHAN GUNATILLEKE

THE LAST DECADE HAS FEATURED several major episodes of anti-Muslim mob violence in Sri Lanka. The violence was often instigated by prominent Sinhala Buddhist militant groups and was accompanied by virulent anti-Muslim hate speech and propaganda permeating social media channels. Then on 21 April 2019, suicide bombers linked to a radical Islamist group launched coordinated attacks on three churches—in Colombo, Negombo and Batticaloa, respectively—and three hotels in Colombo.[1] The incident was the first of its kind in Sri Lanka and left over 250 civilians dead.

This chapter examines the cyclical relationship between majoritarian antagonism towards Sri Lankan Muslims, Islamist radicalism and anti-Muslim violence. It explores the hypothesis that the communal crisis confronting Sri Lanka is deeply connected to features of Sri Lanka's socio-political culture, which, to varying degrees, perpetuates Islamophobia, Islamist radicalism and anti-Muslim violence.

The chapter is presented in three sections. The first discusses post-war anti-Muslim and Islamist violence in Sri Lanka and sets up the inquiry into which socio-political factors drive the perpetuation of such violence under various governments. The second section explores these factors and examines the complex and mutually reinforcing relationship between Sinhala Buddhist majoritarianism, Islamist radicalism and anti-Muslim violence. The concluding section offers some thoughts on how the cycle of antagonism, militancy and violence might be broken through a process of cultural transformation.

Anti-Muslim and Islamist Violence

Sri Lankans identify themselves mainly along ethnic and religious lines. The Sinhalese make up around 75 per cent of the population. Over 70 per cent of the population is Buddhist, the majority of whom are Sinhalese.[2] Therefore, many people in Sri Lanka actually distinguish themselves under the ethno-religious label 'Sinhala-Buddhist'. Muslims (i.e., adherents of Islam), most of whom are Moors, constitute 9.7 per cent of the population.[3]

In view of these demographic complexities, the nature of post-war anti-Muslim violence may be better understood when the conflict behind such violence is conceptualized as 'ethno-religious' rather than purely 'religious'.

A significant number of anti-Muslim attacks took place in Sri Lanka in 2013 and 2014. There were 241 reported incidents of violence against Muslims in 2013, and at least 200 reported incidents in 2014.[4] Many of the attacks involved threats and intimidation against Muslim-owned businesses, and anti-Muslim propaganda and hate speech. Episodic violence featuring large-scale physical destruction of Muslim homes, businesses and places of worship also took place. In June 2014, for instance, anti-Muslim mob violence broke out in Aluthgama and neighbouring areas. The violence broke out following an incendiary speech by Ven. Galagoda Aththe Gnanasara Thera, the general secretary of the militant organization, Bodu Bala Sena (BBS).[5] The ensuing anti-Muslim violence led to the death of at least four persons, and damage or destruction of over a hundred Muslim homes and businesses.

Anti-Muslim violence continued throughout the period between 2015 and 2018. At least sixty-four attacks on Muslims were recorded during the period between November 2015 and June 2016.[6] In 2017, there was a spate of attacks on Muslim-owned businesses in April and May.[7] Then, on 17 November 2017, in Gintota in the Galle district, communal tensions following a traffic dispute erupted into anti-Muslim violence, resulting in damage to 'dozens of Muslim homes and businesses'.[8]

The violence continued into 2018 and in March that year, the worst anti-Muslim violent episode in Sri Lanka's postcolonial history took place in Digana, Teldeniya, and in surrounding areas in the district of Kandy. The violence followed a traffic incident that led to the death of a Sinhalese lorry driver and resulted in two deaths and damage to four mosques and over 400 Muslim-owned businesses and homes.[9]

A new dimension to inter-communal conflict then emerged on Easter Sunday, 21 April 2019. The Islamist group National Thowheed Jamaat (NTJ) launched simultaneous suicide bombings against three Christian places of worship and three hotels. The attacks claimed the lives of over 250 persons.[10] Up until that point, Islamist militant groups had hardly featured in Sri Lanka's inter-communal confrontations.[11]

Therefore, little was known about the motives of the group at the time. The nature of the targets—Christian places of worship and tourist buildings—did not fit well with any of the local pre-existing inter-communal contexts. There is no record of major Muslim-Christian tensions in any part of the country. In the next section of this chapter, I attempt to explain how socio-political phenomena in Sri Lanka may have contributed towards the recruitment efforts of Islamist groups.

Anti-Muslim violence occurred soon after the Easter Sunday attacks. In May 2019, mobs attacked Muslims in the Kurunegala and Gampaha districts.[12] The violence left scores of Muslim-owned homes and businesses destroyed. The timing of the violence suggests that these were acts of reprisal for, or at least opportunistically connected to, the Easter Sunday Attacks.

The Cycle of Fear, Radicalism and Violence

Mutually reinforcing phenomena contribute towards the perpetuation of anti-Muslim violence in Sri Lanka. In exploring these phenomena, I am cautious not to attribute a direct causal nexus between any of these phenomena and anti-Muslim violence. Instead, my aim is to illustrate the underlying socio-political environment that enables such violence.

Majoritarianism and Islamophobia

Many within the Sinhala Buddhist majority community believe that Sri Lanka is a Sinhala Buddhist country, and that the country *belongs* to them. Elsewhere, I have called this the Sinhala Buddhist 'entitlement complex'.[13] This entitlement complex stems from an expansive political project that gained currency from the latter half of the nineteenth century onwards. It relies heavily on the *Mahāvamsa* or 'Great Chronicle', which offers a powerful mythological basis for the belief that Sri Lanka is a Buddhist country, and that Sinhala Buddhists are divinely protected at the request of the Buddha himself.[14]

Early ideologues such as Hikkaduwe Sri Sumangala Thera,[15] Anagarika Dharmapala and Piyadasa Sirisena advanced this narrative during the late nineteenth and early twentieth centuries.[16] Contemporary ideologues such as Gunadasa Amarasekera and Nalin de Silva have continued this discourse, and have idealized a 'single, overarching Sinhala-Buddhist culture' wherein minorities were respected, provided they accepted 'the norms of the dominant culture as their own'.[17] The potency of this political project is evident in how it has captured the political imagination. Sinhala Buddhist nationalism has come to represent the ideological position of mainstream political parties such as the Sri Lanka Podujana Peramuna, which secured nearly two-thirds of parliamentary seats in the August 2020 general elections.[18]

Meanwhile, as a direct consequence of both the success of the ideological project, and Sinhala Buddhist nationalist control over policymaking, school history curricula unquestioningly incorporate narratives of Sinhala Buddhist entitlement to the country. For instance, chapter six of the government-issued history textbook for grade six students contains an account of Dutugemunu, a Sinhalese king, defeating Elara, a Tamil ruler.

The Tamil rival is described as 'foreign' and the Sinhalese king's military campaign is described as one that was meant to 'liberate the country from foreign rule', 'reunite the country' and 'protect Buddhism'.[19] This Mahāvamsian narrative has thus come to be accepted as 'indisputable history',[20] thereby embedding an entitlement complex into one of the primary means through which the Sinhala Buddhist community is educated and socialized.

The Sinhala Buddhist entitlement complex is accompanied by existential fears with respect to the perceived fragility of Sinhala Buddhist demographic, religious and cultural dominance. S.J. Tambiah describes the Sinhala Buddhist community as a 'majority with a minority complex'.[21] Many Sinhala Buddhists see their status as under threat due to the perception that Sinhala Buddhists, as a distinct identity group, have a majority status nowhere else in the world.

While Tamils, Muslims and Christians are numerical minorities in Sri Lanka, they are perceived as part of larger transnational communities. In essence, many Sinhala Buddhists see themselves as a national majority living among minorities that are part of *global* majorities. In this context, they remain highly sensitive to the activities of minorities.

Certain phenomena trigger Sinhala Buddhist existential fears. Some of these phenomena directly concern the Muslim community and have produced Islamophobia in Sri Lanka. First, there are fears that the Muslim population in Sri Lanka is growing faster than the Sinhala Buddhist population. The slight statistical increase in the overall population share of Sri Lankan Moors between 1981 and 2012—from 7 per cent to 9.2 per cent[22]—has contributed to this fear. Moreover, in recent times, some Muslim subgroups have resorted to more overt assertions of Muslim identity and piety. Such assertions have also increased the overall visibility of Muslim religious practices.[23] This visibility has 'created an illusion of an increase in the Muslim population, adding to the fear and suspicion of the majority towards the motives of the Muslim community'.[24]

Second, and connected to the first fear, is the apprehension that the Muslim community is becoming increasingly radicalized. This fear was largely reinforced by the Easter Sunday Attacks. I will return to this phenomenon in the next subsection of this chapter.

Third, there is a longstanding fear with respect to Muslim dominance over trade, which is often perceived as a major threat to the economic prosperity of the Sinhala Buddhist community. This antagonism towards Muslim economic activity dates back to the British colonial period; influential ideologues such as Anagarika Dharmapala emphasized the threat of Muslim traders to whip up anti-Muslim sentiment by calling them 'Shylockian' and accusing them of profiting off Sinhalese naivety in the economic realm.[25]

In more recent times, the economic condition of the country has underscored anti-Muslim sentiment. The failure of the state to deliver on the promises of economic prosperity following the end of the civil war in 2009 has led to the scapegoating of Muslims involved in trade and business.[26] Post-war governments were therefore able to deflect potential criticism of their policies by fostering a culture of paranoia about the Muslim community's monopolization of economic gains.

Islamophobic discourses in the economic domain are also connected to deeper general frustrations among the Sinhala Buddhist community with respect to unemployment and class stratification.[27] Therefore, entitlement complexes and existential fears interact with economic frustrations to incentivize anti-Muslim behaviour.

Regional and local economic associations formed on the basis of ethno-religious identity often draw from these frustrations and advance the practice of denying Muslims equal economic opportunities. For example, Sinhala Buddhist economic associations in localities such as Amparai Town and Kiribathgoda have attempted to exclude Muslim-owned enterprises from operating. Even organs of government at the local level occasionally engage in such practices. For example, in the aftermath of the Easter Sunday Attacks, the Wennappuwa Pradeshiya Sabha banned Muslim vendors from selling goods at the Dankotuwa public market citing 'security concerns'.[28] The decision was prompted by complaints received by Sinhalese residents and business groups following the Easter Sunday Attacks but were clearly motivated by economic competition and prejudice towards the Muslim community.

One of the most notable manifestations of both majoritarian entitlement and existential fears is the emergence of Sinhala Buddhist militant groups such as BBS, Sinhala Ravaya and the Mahason Balakaya. These groups are often fronted by Buddhist monks and are involved in advocating for legal reforms targeting Muslim activity such as the wearing of the burqa, the operation of Muslim madrasas, halal certification[29] and cattle slaughter.[30] They have also been at the forefront of anti-Muslim violence in Aluthgama in 2014, Gintota in 2017, Amparai, and Digana and Teldeniya in 2018, and Kurunegala and Gampaha in 2019.

Often, the propaganda of these groups is designed to play on and resonate with the deep existential fears within the Sinhala Buddhist community. For example, the false claim that Muslim restaurant owners mix 'sterilization pills' into the food consumed by Sinhala Buddhists is designed to resonate with fears that the Muslims are conspiring to out-populate the Sinhala Buddhist community.[31]

Islamist radicalism

The Muslim community in Sri Lanka is often incorrectly understood as a 'singular religious-cum-ethnic bloc'.[32] The Sri Lankan Muslim community is not homogeneous, and in fact comprises diverse subgroups, divided along ethnic, geographical and theological lines. Within this milieu, Sri Lanka has encountered a rise in Islamist radicalism. Several factors have contributed to this rise.

Economic liberalization in Sri Lanka during the late 1970s, and the growth of Saudi Arabian oil wealth, enabled greater scholarly interaction between Sri Lankan Muslim groups and Saudi Arabian thinkers. This interaction, over time, strengthened an Islamist movement in Sri Lanka. Following the general election of 1977, import and currency controls were removed in Sri Lanka, and soon Sri Lankan people and money were freely moving within the global economy. By the 1980s, a number of young Muslims migrated to the Middle East, possibly attracted by the prosperity in the region following the oil boom. Moreover, scholarships to study in religious universities in Saudi Arabia and Egypt were made widely available to Sri Lankan Muslims.[33] These migrants later returned to Sri Lanka with a view to 'purify' Islam. According to Islamic scholar Ash-Sheik Muneer Mulafer, since the late 1970s, such cross-fertilization of ideas has contributed to the emergence of militant strands of Islam in Sri Lanka.[34]

Socio-economic developments occurring due to remittances from Sri Lankans working in the Middle East, and the cross-fertilization of ideas, produced a new Muslim middle class in Sri Lanka that has adopted practices similar to the growing middle class in the Gulf. Such mimicry is often evident in forms of attire. For example, the number of middle-class women wearing hijab (various forms of head covering) and niqab (a veil that covers the face of a woman) has increased across Sri Lanka, leading to visible changes in the attire of Muslim women.

Similarly, a number of men who previously wore sarongs or trousers began to wear the white jubba, a form of dress that is regularly worn by Muslim men in the Middle East. Such attire has become a form of asserting both general Muslimness, and more specifically, Islamic piety.

On the one hand, as pointed out by Farzana Haniffa, 'Muslim women across class and region, unconnected to any piety group, now wear the *hijāb*'.[35] She observes that such a 'dress has become a marker of cultural difference; more a sign of Muslimness in a multi-ethnic polity and less of a newly and consciously embraced personal piety'.[36] M.A. Nuhman argues that the hijab is a classic 'symbol of Muslim identity'.[37] Therefore, overt religious manifestation—often in the form of appearance and attire—ought to be understood not merely as a means of signalling piety, but also as assertions of Muslim identity.

Meanwhile, Islamist groups have proliferated in some Muslim-inhabited parts of the country, particularly in the Eastern Province. Many of these groups receive funding from Middle Eastern, and specifically Saudi Arabian, sources.[38] According to Mohamed Faslan and Nadine Vanniasinkam, 'the increase in different groups and sub-groups within the Muslim community since the 1950s ... resulted in the splintering of the Muslim community'.[39] External manifestations of piety are then often advocated by these groups in their efforts to outbid each other and attract and sustain such funding.[40]

Dennis McGilvray observes that these 'sharp internal conflicts' regarding the practice of Islam have been manifested through symbolic 'Islamization' in the form of Arabic dress, public theological disputes and the erection of new places of worship.[41]

In this context, the Thawheed Jamaat is perhaps most strongly influenced by Saudi Arabian ideological thinking. The group has, over time, splintered into multiple subgroups, including the Colombo-based Dharus Salaf, All Ceylon Thawheed Jamaat (ACTJ) and the Sri Lanka Thawheed Jamaat (SLTJ). These Colombo-based subgroups exert ideological influence over the Muslim community at a national level. Meanwhile, subgroups such as the Batticaloa-based Dharul Adhar, and the Kattankudy-based NTJ, have had an impact at the subnational level.

Such competition has manifested in intra-Muslim violence. A number of scholars studying intra-Muslim conflict have observed that violence between Islamist groups and other Muslim groups since the early 2000s reflected the growing threat of Islamism in Sri

Lanka.[42] The NTJ was one of the first Thawheed Jamaat groups to actively adopt more militant strategies. For example, violent evictions of the Sufi Abdur Rauf group from Kattankudy in 2000 and 2006 are attributed to persons who eventually formed the NTJ.[43] Of course, the NTJ would be subsequently associated with the Easter Sunday attacks of 2019.

Connecting the dots

Majoritarianism, Islamophobia, Islamist radicalism, and violence in Sri Lanka are interconnected and mutually reinforcing. Islamophobic discourses feed off deeper majoritarian entitlement complexes and existential fears, in which the Muslim community comes to symbolize a 'threat' to the Sinhala Buddhist community. This status of being a 'threat' is then seemingly legitimized by intra-Muslim competition that ultimately incentivizes Islamist radicalism.

Groups such as the BBS have suggested that such Islamist radicalism vindicates their concerns with regard to the Muslim 'threat'. The ensuing public discourse is often filled with hate and antagonism and has directly contributed towards violence against the Muslim community.

Pre-existing economic and socio-political fault lines within a particular locality can interact with deeply held Islamophobic discourses to create the conditions for anti-Muslim violence. A 'trigger event' usually precedes the outbreak of the violence.[44] Such trigger events can include traffic accidents (e.g., in Aluthgama in 2014 and in Gintota in 2017), disputes at restaurants (e.g., in Amparai in 2018), and the death of a Sinhalese individual (e.g., Kandy in 2018). The 2018 violence in the Kandy district illustrates this interaction of factors.

First, some segments of the Sinhala Buddhist community in this area hold certain entitlement complexes and existential fears.

Many Sinhala Buddhists have long-standing and historically rooted beliefs that they are the 'hosts' of the area, and that minority communities, including Muslims, are 'guests'. Moreover, many Sinhala Buddhists possess certain existential fears with respect to the perceived population growth and economic prosperity of Muslims in the country. Perceptions of 'Muslim radicalization' can compound these fears.

Second, these majoritarian discourses interact with the fault lines that exist between competing groups in the district. For example, Sinhala Buddhist traders often compete for economic space with Muslim traders. Such competition can, over time, foster major antagonism between the two communities. The interaction between deeply entrenched majoritarianism and prevailing fault lines produces toxic conditions in which the rhetoric and propaganda of militant groups enjoy added resonance—particularly within social media spaces.

Finally, a trigger event that escalates the tensions to actual violence can take place. In Kandy, that trigger event was the death of a Sinhalese lorry driver following an altercation with a group of Muslims. The funeral of this person, and the incitement of violence that took place around the funeral, sparked mob violence that resulted in two deaths, and damage to four mosques and over 400 Muslim businesses and homes.[45] This incident reflects the manner in which a complex set of factors can come together to produce ethno-religious violence in a particular location.

Anti-Muslim violence can then circle back to reinforce incentives among some disenchanted members of the Muslim community to gravitate towards more radical forms of Islamism. The Easter Sunday Attacks of 2019 in some ways reflect the plausible connection between anti-Muslim violence and Islamist radicalism. It is plausible that experiences of anti-Muslim violence, and outrage over such violence, motivate young Muslims to gravitate towards militant Islamist groups seeking to recruit disenchanted young followers.[46]

However, once they join such groups, agendas that are not particularly connected to or interested in local contexts may be prioritized. This prioritization may explain why the chosen targets of the Easter Sunday Attacks were Christian places of worship rather than Buddhist places of worship—despite the perception that Sinhala Buddhist militant groups perpetrated violence against Muslims. The choice of Christian places of worship is much more aligned with global radical Islamist agendas.[47]

The Easter Sunday attacks have, then, become a watershed event likely to create new waves of majoritarian existential fears that underlie prejudice towards the Muslim community in Sri Lanka. Perceptions concerning the Muslim community that are already shaped by deep-seated prejudice are likely to be compounded by these attacks. Therefore, the attacks themselves add to the cycle of fear, radicalism and violence.

Conclusion: Breaking the Cycle

Since the end of the armed conflict in 2009, majoritarian entitlement and existential fears have underscored the rise of Islamophobia in Sri Lanka. Within these toxic conditions, and owing to other socio-economic and political phenomena, Islamist radicalism has also grown in the country. Such radicalism has incubated violent groups, one of which perpetrated the first major Islamist attack on Sri Lankan soil on Easter Sunday in 2019.

Islamophobia has, meanwhile, remained a precursor to anti-Muslim violence, which in turn has fuelled Islamist radicalism. The cycle is then completed, as such radicalism has provided further impetus to majoritarian fears. Sri Lanka then appears to be trapped in a perpetual cycle of fear, radicalism and violence.

I conclude this chapter with some reflections on how this cycle might be broken. Admittedly, symbiotic discourses are difficult to end. It is difficult to see which discourse needs to be, or can be, ended first. I am inclined to think legal and institutional reform has limited currency in this regard. What is needed instead is a cultural transformative project that effectively replaces majoritarian entitlement and existential fears with ideas of coexistence and equal citizenship.

Yet, the obvious question remains: how are such entrenched phenomena, which have become rooted in a majority community's collective psyche, ever reversed and replaced? Two ideas come to mind. These must not be understood as a panacea, but instead as domains of intervention through which, over time, change might take place.

First, Sri Lanka's educational curricula must be radically reformed. The current secondary school history curricula contain 'strong explicit stereotypes' of minorities, and history textbooks are largely confined to a 'Sinhalese-centric history of the country'.[48] These textbooks must be revised to enable students to learn about the multicultural historical legacy of Sri Lanka. A meaningful and consultative process must be undertaken to reform Sri Lanka's history curricula to replace a majoritarian narrative with one of a shared history of all the peoples of the country.

Second, a broader discourse that draws from 'resonant' vocabularies should be undertaken to mainstream ideas of coexistence and equal citizenship in Sri Lanka. By 'resonant', I simply mean that the language of reform must be authentic and must draw from relatable norms found in the dominant culture of the country. Such discourse could adopt what Michael Ignatieff calls 'ordinary virtues'. He observes that virtues such as 'compassion', 'mutual recognition' and 'forgiveness' can form a vital vocabulary for convincing individuals and communities to recognize and respect the 'other'.[49]

Moreover, Abdullahi An-Na'im suggests the use of 'arguments (that) are likely to be persuasive to the specific community, or able to address their apprehensions and concerns, in relation to whatever frame of reference that is accepted by that community as authoritative or applicable'.[50] Therefore, transformative discourse cannot simply evade the real and imagined existential fears of the Sinhala Buddhist community in Sri Lanka. In this regard, Buddhist values such as *mettā* (loving kindness) and *karuṇā* (compassion) could be invoked to advance a discourse of coexistence and equal citizenship.

These values must be meaningfully explored and mainstreamed among the Sinhala Buddhist majority if Islamophobia is to be addressed. In essence, cultural transformation cannot be achieved by attempting to cause a rupture in Sinhala Buddhist culture. It must instead come from an *evolution* of the very norms that undergird this culture. It is estimated that if overarching majoritarianism is eventually replaced with ideals of coexistence and equal citizenship, Islamist ideological movements will be starved of the 'victim narrative' vital for their legitimacy and sustenance.

Admittedly, such a radical shift may seem extremely difficult to achieve. Yet, if the cycle of fear, radicalism and violence is the result of a long-discursive process, breaking such a cycle through a similar inter-generational project is worth imagining.

7

Christians in Pakistan

Retrospect and Prospect

MICHAEL NAZIR-ALI

THE CHRISTIAN STORY IN PAKISTAN is a long one but it is also discontinuous and disrupted. Archaeological discoveries in Taxila have provided some support for the late second century claim in the *Acts of Thomas*, written in what is now south-eastern Turkey, that the Apostle Thomas went to India in the service of an Indian king called Gondaphares. He preached the gospel and ministered to the poor there, eventually converting Gondaphares and his court.

He then went on to work in other parts of the country and, in the end, was martyred by being pierced with spears. Until the nineteenth century, all of this was regarded as 'Apostolic romance', that is, legends about the Apostles sent out by Jesus. In the nineteenth and twentieth centuries, however, coins and steles were discovered featuring a king called Gondaphares, who ruled an Indo-Bactrian kingdom which covered the area known as Gandhara. The coins are in both Greek and a Prakrit vernacular.

The Greek on the coins, moreover, is of a form used only between 20 and 60 CE! It is well known that this area had been under the influence of the Achaemenids, and the Seleucids and thus Aramaic influence also cannot be discounted. Knowledge of Greek and Aramaic in the region meets the objection that if St Thomas went to India, in which language did he preach to the people? The main question, however, is: how did a romancer, writing in the second or third centuries in what is now Turkey, know that there was a king called Gondaphares in what is now north-west Pakistan in the first century?

There seems to be knowledge of Indian culture in the *Acts* and behind the *Acts*' romancing there lies an even older historical work, the *Passio Thomae*, which has been suitably embellished, in the light of his interests, by the author of the *Acts*. These hard facts are supported by others, like an accurate description of Gondaphares' palace in Taxila by the author of *Acts* and the discovery of the Taxila Cross, an ancient cross, which resembles other such Indian crosses, and is now in the custody of Lahore Cathedral.[1]

Whatever we may say of the 'Northern Theory' about St Thomas' arrival in the subcontinent, we cannot ignore the fact that the ancient St Thomas churches of south India, which also claim that they were established by him, have a long and continuous history. Just as there are points of connection with the north, so there are with the south. It seems that there was a Jewish presence and this would have made communication possible between St Thomas and the local populace.

It is possible that Thomas went on to other parts of India (the *Acts* explicitly states this) and Rooney tells us that we must entertain the probability of Thomas making more than one journey to the subcontinent.[2] As Bishop Young of Sialkot has shown, there continued to be bishops in Afghanistan, Baluchistan and Kashgar until the fourteenth century and, no doubt, they would have had a concern for missionary work in the areas that now constitute northern and western Pakistan.[3]

Whatever we may say of the earliest times, the next 'window' into a Christian presence does not occur until the sixteenth century. Christian presence was of two types: there seems to have been a significant 'oriental' Christian component in the Mughal armies. These Christians were often termed 'Armenians' but, in fact, this term covered all types of Eastern Christians: Copts, Syrians, Greeks as well as Armenian.

There seems to have been a Christian quarter in cities like Lahore both for these expatriates and for local Christians. There was an 'oriental' Christian presence at the courts of both the emperors, Akbar and Jehangir: one of Akbar's wives, Maryam Begum, had a Christian background and he seems to have had a Christian adopted son.

Although no church building, of an Eastern type, has been found, the well-known wall paintings in the *zenana* at Lahore Fort, although badly damaged, suggest an Eastern origin, showing a bishop with a patriarchal cross, Jesus praying in Gethsemane, someone reading from the Bible or a service book, sacraments being administered, etc.

It is known that the orientals wished to present Akbar with a Persian translation of the New Testament but the Jesuits, at the court, suppressed this because they wished to check it for consistency with the Latin Vulgate, a task not completed until Akbar's son, Jehangir, was on the throne! We know also that bishops of the Eastern tradition came to Mughal India to minister to their people there.[4]

The second type is, of course, related to the arrival of Western missionaries. Among the first of these were the Jesuit missions to the

Mughals. There were three such missions during Akbar's time, all at the emperor's express invitation. The first consisted of an Italian, a Spaniard and a Persian. They engaged enthusiastically in the interfaith dialogue and debate which Akbar was encouraging. They were also given permission to preach and to make converts.

Although they established schools and hospitals, the mission was ordered back to Goa, just as Akbar was appearing to be more receptive to their message. The second mission was specifically directed at Lahore, where the missionaries began a school for the sons of the nobility. Once again, the mission was withdrawn because it was felt that the emperor had no intention of becoming a Christian and the opposition of the ulema was growing. The superiors of the mission seem not to have understood the value of presence and of service and were fixated on the emperor's conversion, hoping that this would lead to mass conversions in the population.

The third mission was led by a relative of St Francis Xavier and had much more success in planting a church among the poor in Lahore, as well as maintaining a presence at the royal court. Akbar gave them permission to build a church and Prince Salim (later to be the Emperor Jehangir) funded its construction in the last decade of the sixteenth century. This church was destroyed several times, but a church still stands on the site provided by the Mughals and has been identified as such by the distinguished Pakistani archaeologist, Dr Majeed Sheikh.[5]

The mission continued under Jehangir, who even had the sons of his deceased brother baptized! A story is told that the Jesuits wanted all Christian converts to be paraded through the streets of Lahore on elephants, as the princes had been, and as it was the custom to parade converts to Islam on elephants. Jehangir seems to have had no objection but asked why they should not be paraded on donkeys in imitation of Jesus, who had entered Jerusalem on one. Eventually, a compromise was reached: the converts would parade on elephants but the priest, baptizing them, would come on a donkey!

The church in Lahore continued to function until after Jehangir's death. The emperor himself attended often and, it was claimed, that he either asked for baptism on his deathbed or even that he was baptized.[6] While the mission in Lahore is of the utmost importance, we should not neglect the Carmelite mission based in Thatta in the south. Thatta, and its sister port of Lahri Bandar, was an important Mughal city in those days and may well have retained vestiges of an ancient Christian presence. The Carmelites served both the expatriate European and Eurasian population, as well as the local people. The mission seems to have been well-contextualized in the culture and provided educational and other services to the local community. Like other Christian places of worship, the church was destroyed under Shah Jahan and the educational work closed under Aurangzeb.[7]

The Jesuit commitment to inculturation is shown in their mastering of both Persian, the language of the court, and Urdu or Hindustani, the emerging vernacular of northern India. Some of the work they did on the geography, government and languages of India remained the standard for many years.

They also produced fine manuscripts of Christian apologetics, the most famous being the *Mir'atu'l Quds* or The Mirror of the Sacred, being an account of the life of Jesus Christ. There are several surviving manuscripts, but the oldest of them is in Lahore Museum. Both in these manuscripts and separately, they produced a tradition of Christian miniatures in the Mughal style, with themes from the Bible, the birth, life, death and resurrection of Christ, the Blessed Virgin Mary, the apostles and saints and much else.[8]

Although the fortunes of the Jesuit and Carmelite missionaries waned after the accession of Shah Jahan, and even further under Aurangzeb, we know that a Christian presence continued in Lahore well into the eighteenth century—that is to say, just before the advent of Protestant missionaries like William Carey and his companions in northern India.

There had been an Anglican presence, in the form of chaplains to the East India Company, since the seventeenth century, but the company was hostile to missionary work among the indigenous population until it was forced to yield by an act of the British Parliament. In spite of its hostility, there were some remarkable chaplains who were interested in reaching out to the people in the land. Among them was Henry Martyn, the great translator of the New Testament into Urdu, who carried out a thorough revision of the Persian New Testament and Psalms and began the work in Arabic before his tragic death in 1812 at the age of just thirty-one.

Carey's involvement in the newly founded Fort William College was crucial in the development of vernaculars like Urdu and Bengali which had, hitherto, been neglected in favour of classical languages like Persian and Sanskrit. Alexander Duff arrived from Scotland, and with the support of reform-minded Indians, initiated a programme of liberal arts education for the young.

This model of mission as education was to become very popular throughout the subcontinent and to it we owe the existence of Forman Christian University, Kinnaird College for Women, Lahore; Murray College, Sialkot; Gordon College, Rawalpindi and Edwardes College, Peshawar. Numerous schools were also established with the aim of both providing the best education for children and also witnessing sensitively to the Christian faith.

It is true that much of this effort was, at first, directed towards the Hindu and Muslim elite and succeeded in its aim of creating a class of those open to modern knowledge. To a lesser extent, it also created small groups of Christian leaders who were crucial to the growth and development of the nascent church in northern India and what is now Pakistan.[9]

Although the Eastern Rite Catholic Churches in south India have had a hierarchy for long, and so also the church in Goa, in what is now Pakistan, Roman Catholic missionary work began again after 1830. In Sindh, it was resumed after the British conquest of 1842 and a hierarchy of sorts was created in the Punjab from 1880. Once again, there has been heavy involvement in education and health work, much of which continues.

As with other churches, while a number of institutions have catered to the elite, there has also been considerable educational, social care and health work among the poor, especially, but not only, those from the Christian community. Both indigenous and foreign religious orders have played a major part in the missionary work of the Catholic church.[10]

At first, in the nineteenth century, missionaries gave much attention to Muslims, Sikhs and caste Hindus. Except in one or two cases, such as that of the Narowal Khojas, this did not result in mass conversions, though there were some outstanding individuals who contributed a great deal to scholarship and the development of a theological tradition.

As the Indian scholar James Massey has pointed out, in the middle period of the nineteenth century, the missionaries, as well as Indian Christians, were very wary of reaching out to the lower castes, in case this jeopardized the church's work among Muslims, Sikhs and caste Hindus. It was only in 1870 that a lower-caste man, named Ditt, was brought by another convert to a missionary for baptism.

The missionary refused to baptize such unpromising material but Ditt persisted and was eventually baptized. He then became a missionary among his own people, which resulted in the mass movement of lower-caste people in that area into the Christian faith.[11] It was not only among this group that there was a response to the Christian mission. Other groups such as Balmikis, Mazhabi Sikhs, Faqirs and Scheduled Castes in the Sindh have continued to be evangelized and brought into the churches.

In the areas in the subcontinent under consideration, the so-called Scheduled Castes and Scheduled Tribes constitute around a third of the population as a whole. If other 'lower castes' are included, the majority of people are from there. It should not be a surprise that religions like Islam, Sikhism and Christianity, which reject caste, should attract those who have experienced discrimination and rejection. There have been many examples of low-caste groups converting to Islam, sometimes in the very locations like Sialkot, which have seen Christian mass movements. The point is that it is unremarkable to say that the majority of Christians are from these backgrounds, because the population as a whole has very substantial numbers of such people and, in suitable circumstances, some are inevitably attracted to an egalitarian faith like Christianity.[12]

The New Zealand sociologist Wayne McLintock has divided the ethnic background of Christians into a number of categories: those from caste Hindu or Muslim family backgrounds (although many have emigrated because of persecution and discrimination), Goans and south Indians, especially in Karachi (again much depleted because of emigration), Anglo-Indians (many have left Pakistan), tribal background Christians, mainly in the Sindh and south Punjab, and Punjabi Christians of varying backgrounds but mainly from the mass movements among the Scheduled Castes.

To these we can add a few from the ancient churches of South India, Armenia etc. The distribution is uneven, with the vast majority in the Punjab but substantial numbers in cities like Karachi and among nomadic groups in the Sindh.[13]

We have noted already the contribution of Christians, both local and foreign, to education and health. Generations of Pakistanis, of all faiths, have been taught by Punjabi, Goan and other Christians. Until quite recently, nursing, as a profession, was virtually a Christian monopoly.

It is most encouraging that there are now many more Muslim nurses. Christian hospitals and clinics continue to deliver medical care, sometimes in the most remote locations. Apart from the health and education sectors, Christians are to be found in banking, journalism and a host of other professions. The already creaky sanitation system of the country would collapse completely without the thousands of Christians who work to keep the land of the pure clean. In law and in the judiciary, Christians have played a significant role, when they have been given the opportunity.

Chief Justice A.R. Cornelius, a devout Roman Catholic, was hugely influential in the framing of both the 1962 and the draft 1971 Constitution. The latter was accepted even by the Islamist parties but rejected by the leader of the secular Pakistan People's Party, Z.A. Bhutto, on the grounds that it had been drafted by a *dhimmi*, that is, a non-Muslim second-class citizen.

In the armed forces also, Christian officers and soldiers have played a distinguished role in the defence of the country and have been recognized as such by successive governments.[14] Most of the above is often acknowledged by political and other leaders in Pakistan. What is, perhaps, less well-known is the part played by Christians in the movement for Pakistan and in its creation. At the gathering in Minto Park (now Allama Iqbal Park) in Lahore, where the 'Pakistan Resolution' was passed in 1940, a distinguished Christian delegation, consisting of Dewan Bahadur S.P. Singha, Joshua Fazal Din, C.E. Gibbon, F.E. Chaudhry, S.S.S. Albert, Rajkumari Amrit Kaur and others, was present.

Chaudhri Chandu Lal, a member of the Muslim League's executive, made an impassioned speech asking that the equal rights of Christians and other groups be embodied in any constitution of the new state. This was warmly endorsed by the Quaid-E-Azam and the Muslim League.

In November 1942, the Christian members of the Punjab Provincial Assembly held a reception in honour of the Quaid, which was also attended by his sisters and by leaders of the Muslim League. At the reception, S.P. Singha, on behalf of the Christians present, promised to support the creation of Pakistan. In reply, Mr Jinnah said that if the Christians joined them, 'we will forever be grateful to you'.

The Christian members went on to support the Muslim League in its opposition to the partition of the Punjab. When this particular aim was not achieved, the Christians met the Quaid and his sister to assure them that they would support the inclusion of West Punjab in the state of Pakistan. When it came to a vote in the Assembly, the numbers for and against were tied at 88–88.

The Christian members Singha, Gibbon and Fazal Elahi then cast their votes with the Muslim League, thus ensuring the inclusion of West Punjab in the new state. One can only imagine what Pakistan would have been like without its Punjab! The same day, S.P. Singha used his casting vote, as the Speaker, to prevent India and Pakistan having a common National Assembly by voting for a new National Assembly for Pakistan. For such acts of courage, these members were threatened with death and grievous bodily harm by their opponents.

Not to be deterred by these, the Christian members appeared before the Punjab Boundary Commission, under Sir Cyril Radcliffe, and voiced the Christian community's preference for Pakistan.[15]

Having made such a signal contribution to the creation of Pakistan, we can see why Christians have such a grievance about what has happened since. From the very beginning, when the Hindu and Sikh zamindars (or landowners) fled to India after Partition, their Christian landless labour began to migrate to the cities and towns to take up sweeping as a living and, like many other refugees, building makeshift homes for themselves in the *bustis* (slums) that were emerging at the time.

Many of these areas have become disadvantaged ghettos, with minimal public amenities and services. They have also had the effect of segregating the communities from the mainstream of national life and creating an inward-looking and self-regarding mentality.

The Objectives Resolution of 1949, now attached to the Constitution, is quite general in tone but declares that the polity of Pakistan is to be based on Islamic principles, while giving full freedom to non-Muslims to profess and practice their faith. It also echoes Article 18 of the UN Declaration on Human Rights in safeguarding freedom of thought, expression and belief.

Liaquat Ali Khan, the prime minister, declared at the time that the Objectives Resolution was not a charter for theocracy, and it seems to echo the Quaid's desire for a polity based on Islamic 'ideals and principles'. It has been taken, nevertheless, by those who wish to impose an Islamist ideology on the country as a point of departure for the inexorable 'Islamization' of the laws and policies of the nation. Many of those wanting an ideological state were the very ones who had opposed its creation in the first place on the grounds that it would divide the Muslim strength in India and because they did not believe that Jinnah was a suitable person to lead the umma.

The Objectives Resolution has been followed by waves of Islamization: successive declarations of Pakistan as an Islamic republic, the increasing limiting of official positions to Muslims (under President Zia the reason given was that the head of a department also has to be the imam in leading prayers and, therefore, a pious Muslim), the enforcement of Sharia on Muslims and non-Muslims alike and much else besides.

For Christians, this has meant increasing marginalization and a feeling of unjust victimization. The system of separate electorates increased this sense of marginalization because local members of Parliament knew that Christians and other minorities could only vote for their candidates on a national slate and so had no relevance to local politicians and their electoral fortunes.

Its reversal to joint electorates, with special seats for minorities, in addition, on the basis of party strength in the assemblies, is not perfect but, at least, gives minorities a stake in local democracy and in the election of representatives to national and provincial legislatures.

The enforcement of Sharia, with Hudud penal law, has further disadvantaged non-Muslims. A non-Muslim lawyer cannot appear in a Sharia court but a non-Muslim can be punished by it. Where Hudud crimes are concerned, non-Muslims cannot be witnesses, even where the crime has been committed against a non-Muslim.

The bête noire, however, of all these are surely the blasphemy laws. It is often claimed that these laws date from the time of the Raj and have not been invented by Pakistan. It is true that there have been laws since then against outraging religious sentiment, desecrating a place of worship or insulting a religion.

The laws were carefully drafted, and the maximum prison sentence was two years. They were hardly ever used. What has made Pakistan's laws notorious are the amendments which first introduced life imprisonment or death for desecrating the Qur'an or insulting the Prophet of Islam and then made the death sentence mandatory for insulting the Prophet.

Quite apart from questions, asked by Muslims, about whether these laws correctly reflect the Sunnah or practice of the one they believe to have forgiven those who insulted him, the capacity of these laws to be misused to settle personal scores, to whip up mob hysteria against individuals or communities and to induce fear in non-Muslims is beyond dispute.

Since their implementation in the 1980s and 1990s, people of all faiths and of none have been charged with the offence of blasphemy, but Christians and other minorities have been charged in numbers quite disproportionate to their actual population, according to the government's own figures. Once they are charged, the local police comes under huge pressure to prosecute and the local, and sometimes higher, courts are intimidated to convict.

The need surely is to return to laws which protect all religions from gratuitous insult, though not criticism, and where the punishment is proportionate to the offence. In the meantime, there is an urgent need, first of all, to make sure that everything has been done to conciliate the parties involved and to avoid bringing a charge.

Some enlightened police officers are trying to do this. Secondly, if a charge has been registered, for the matter to be removed from local jurisdiction and referred to some central body for investigation and the decision to prosecute or not. If a decision is made to prosecute, although I am generally not in favour of special courts sitting in camera but if ever there is a case for these, this is it. The decisions of such courts should, of course, be appealable in the higher courts.

I believe that some such simple administrative steps would make it more difficult to misuse this law while other solutions are being sought. Such steps would greatly reassure minorities that their people will not be plunged into life-threatening situations on the whims of those who have an ulterior motive or wish to stir up hatred against a person, a family or a community.[16]

The nationalizing of Christian and other schools and colleges in 1972 was, however, carried out by the secular and socialist

Pakistan People's Party under Mr Bhutto. Not only were most such institutions ruined by this action, it deprived the Christian community, in particular, of an important means of upward social mobility. The partial return of some, and their renewal, has created some hope that the churches will, once again, be able to contribute significantly to national education and to the development of their own community as well as others. It is urgent that the remaining institutions are also returned promptly and this grave injustice is put right.

The churches have also been at the forefront of protecting workers from exploitation. The establishment of the Pakistan Christian Industrial Service was for the sake of serving all disadvantaged workers, regardless of creed. The Commission for Justice and Peace of the Catholic Bishops' Conference, similarly, has contributed significantly to raising awareness of social issues and suggesting solutions for them. Its workers have sometimes paid for their courageous work with their lives.

What then are the prospects for a community ravaged by emigration, poverty and, in spite of its services to the wider community, the temptation to look inwards and concentrate on internal issues, conflicts and dissensions? Both vocational education—technical training, for example—and conventional education hold the key to social mobility.

Organizations like Starfish are helping in the education of the poor but we need many more such initiatives. Not only the government, but large national and multinational businesses need to be held to pledges to recruit minorities at every level in the organization.

Assistance for entering and operating small businesses will create mobility not just for the owner, but for those employed in the business. This is happening already, but the scale needs to be increased. Unless Christians and others feel they have a stake in the country they helped to create, the situation will not change significantly.

The question of numbers remains a thorny issue. Official censuses put the number of Christians at less than 2 per cent but I know from personal experience that this is a significant underestimate: the official figures show that Karachi, the largest city in Pakistan, had 1,00,000 Christians.

When I mentioned this to the clergy there, they laughed and said that just one area where Christians live had that number! There are more than 1,000 churches in Lahore district alone.[17] The World Christian Encyclopaedia, a highly respected source, puts the number of Christians in Pakistan at 7.5 million by 2025, or around 3 per cent of the population.[18]

The UK Home Office's Country Policy and Information Note on Pakistan's Christians and Christian converts sets out a number of figures, but the most reliable of them puts the number in 2018 at more than 6 million.[19]

The only way the exact figure could be settled is by a census conducted by the churches themselves, but they lack the resources to do so. I understand that the Hindu community has conducted some kind of census and this has greatly strengthened their hand in negotiating with the government and local authorities regarding services, access to education and jobs and development grants.

In the end, what we need in Pakistan is a change in mindset which recognizes all citizens as equal, with equal responsibilities and rights. The contribution of all those who have contributed to its creation and welfare should be acknowledged. Christians need to emerge from their ghettos to take their rightful place in society and to continue working for the well-being of all their fellow citizens.

Freedom of expression, belief and worship are a sine qua non in a democratic society and Christians and others need to be free from the fear of sudden allegations of blasphemy, mob violence and terrorist attacks. The future of Christians in Pakistan depends on whether the country chooses to follow the path of its founders and to become an open, democratic society, or to follow those who opposed its creation and now wish to turn it into a theocratic state where only one kind of narrative is allowed to prevail.

8

Genesis of the Shia Predicament in Pakistan

MOHAMMAD TAQI

THE RISE AND DEMISE OF three non-Arab Muslim empires, viz. the Ottoman, the Safavid and the Mughal, and that of western colonial rule in the Middle East and South Asia, has had an incredible influence not only on the geographical concentration of the major sects of Islam but also on the religio-political identity of their followers, which in many ways has lasted till date.

The Ottomans and the Mughals were Sunni and patronized the Hanafi school of Sunni Islam, and the Safavids established a Shia order in greater Persia and made the Ithna Ashari (Twelver) Shiism its state religion. Assorted Sufi orders originating in Central Asia, Afghanistan and Persia, which share many spiritual elements of the Shia faith, had already arrived in the Indian subcontinent, but it was not until the arrival of the Shia émigré from Safavid Persia in the sixteenth century that the creed's evolving temporal and political overlay made its way to India as well.

These early interactions, which started in the Indian south, led to conversions from both the Muslim and non-Muslim communities into the Ithna Ashari faith and eventually culminated in the establishment of several princely states like Golconda, Bijapur and Ahmednagar, ruled by Shia dynasties. The might of the Mughals, however, not only kept the south Indian Shia political dispensations from expanding northwards beyond the Deccan plateau, but eventually subsumed them as well. Depending upon which Mughal king was at the helm, the Shias were accommodated, tolerated or persecuted in the realm.

When the Delhi-based Mughal power started declining in the early eighteenth century, assorted princely states and fiefdoms started emerging all over India with local strongmen asserting their authority independently or under a titular association with the waning empire. One of the largest and richest among these successor states was Awadh, which roughly corresponded to the central regions of India's present-day Uttar Pradesh (northern province).[1]

The Awadh state, founded in 1722 by a Mughal court-affiliated Iranian pioneer, Saadat Khan,[2] went on to become a powerhouse of Shia political power, theology[3] and culture[4] under his successor nawabs. The Shia polity that flourished in these successor states, principalities[5] and fiefdoms was a function of the official patronage to the local clergy and the elite; the direct links of the ruling dynasties with, and financial support[6] to, the theological establishment of the Shia holy cities in Iraq and Iran; and the relative prosperity of the masses at a time when the Delhi empire was crumbling.

The evolution of the Shia Awadh under 135 years of nawabi rule moulded a Shia religio-cultural identity which transcended that state and influenced not only other Shia communities across the subcontinent, but also the competitive Sunni and the synergistic Sufi co-religionists. The Shia communal identity among the Muslims of

India was thus fairly well-defined and distinct from the other sects, yet fairly syncretic with them as well as with the Hindus.

This, however, does not discount the proselytizing efforts and polemic by, and a low-intensity sectarian friction between, the various sects. What perhaps was not at play yet was the overarching Muslim political identity as both the Sunnis and Shia still remained in the relative comfort zones of their existing, albeit rapidly declining, power centres in various states and regions.

After the British completely overpowered the Mughal dynasty, the princely states, including the ones ruled by Shia dynasties, either fell to them outright or accepted their overlordship. Awadh was no exception and bore the brunt of the colonial wrath for its last ruler, Nawab Wajid Ali Shah, had joined the 1857 War of Independence against the British.

After the debacle, the nawab was exiled to Calcutta, the British fury was unleashed on the Awadh court—just like it was against the Delhi court—and its institutions were literally trampled upon. For example, the mosques and *imambaras*—Shia centres for Muharram and other commemorations—in the capital Lucknow were turned into army barracks and garrison:

> No restraining conscience or voice of moderation spoke out on the unnecessary occupation of the most important mosque in the city after the revolt. The implications of using the Asafi Imambara, which was also the tomb of one of the best-loved nawabs of Oudh, deeply riled the Shiite. British troops ate pork, swilled alcohol, trampled the sacred hall in regimental boots, and manifested every other kind of contempt for the religion of old rulers of the province.[7]

As the shock of the colonial power upending the Muslim rule over India gradually subsided, a political and doctrinal assessment and introspection commenced within the vanquished community. As is evident, the Muslim population of India was as heterodox as any other community of the subcontinent, if not more.

It comprised not just assorted sects, including the Sunni and the Shia, which in turn included an array of sub-sectarian denominations, but assorted socio-economic and ethno-cultural stratifications. Both the analyses of the great debacle and the proposed remedies, therefore, were as diverse as the sections of the community.

The resulting *weltanschauung* or worldview could be broadly categorized into traditional or conformist, fundamentalist or orthodox, and a modernist political interpretation of Islam and its role in the recovery of dwindling Muslim fortunes.

The fourth approach was a secularist orientation of assorted varieties, ranging from liberal and/or Marxist to nationalist and militant. There was considerable overlap, exchange and also friction and outright confrontation among these religious and areligious paradigms. The first three approaches essentially collaborated or competed with each other to shape Muslim identity politics in colonial India, and eventually in Pakistan.

A series of revivalist movements among the Indian Sunni Muslims had, however, antedated complete colonial control, the post-1857 Sunni modernist religio-political activism and the Shia awakening.

The Deoband seminary, for example, which was founded in 1867, sought to 'purify' the subcontinental Muslims of what it perceived as the heretical practices that they had adopted over a millennium of interface with the native religions. It represented the fundamentalist vision of restoring the austere Islam of the Prophet Muhammad's era.

The Barelvi revivalist movement was a response to this Deobandi revivalism, and was pioneered by Ahmad Riza Khan in Bareilly, Uttar Pradesh. While both the Deobandi and Barelvi schools of thought *(masalik)* subscribed to the Sunni Hanafi denomination of Islam, they differed enough in creed and in practice to go on to virtually become adversarial subsects apostatizing each other and the Shia.

After 1857, the Barelvi and Deobandi movements represented, respectively, the traditional or conformist versus the fundamentalist or orthodox approaches to Muslim identity politics. While they were not overtly opposed to British rule at the outset, they subsequently took different trajectories.

The Deobandis eventually developed a formidable nationalist and anti-colonial bent that resulted in the formation of the religio-political party, Jamiat-e-Ulama-e-Hind (JUH). It joined hands with the Congress in the freedom struggle. The Barelvis, on the other hand, maintained a collaborative relationship with the British. Ahmad Riza Khan even pronounced British India the Dar-ul-Islam or a land safe for Islam and the Muslims. They were not able to or desirous of organizing into a single political party either.

The Barelvi pirs and sheikhs (holy men and saints) preferred to maintain their local and regional political pre-eminence by collaboration with the colonial rulers, and later, the postcolonial ones as well. They opted to join outfits like the All India Muslim League (AIML) or, before that, the Punjab-based Unionist Party.

On the other hand, the Aligarh movement, pioneered by Sir Syed Ahmed Khan, a Sunni Muslim, became the key vehicle for the modernist reform agenda, and was geared towards a cross-confessional Muslim political identity as against the Indian national identity at home, and a pan-Islamist approach beyond the subcontinent's borders. It tried to position itself as, and has largely been perceived as, non-sectarian and class-, status- and ethnicity-neutral.

The idea ostensibly was to encourage and form a unified Muslim political identity and put it up against the British colonial entity on one hand, and the Hindu majority on the other. Sir Syed was indeed joined in his effort by towering personalities from across India. A coterie of prominent Shia individuals were members of the founding committee of the Aligarh College.[8]

Some of them, like S. Amir Ali, Raja Amir Ahmed Khan of Mahmudabad, Nawab Mushtaq Ali Khan of Rampur, Sir Salar Jang, et al were Ithna Ashari, while others like Sir Agha Khan III belonged to the smaller Ismaili Shia community. Scores of Shias, like the Rajas of Mahmudabad and Rampur and Sir Agha Khan, made huge financial contributions to the college ab initio and also on an ongoing basis.

Sir Agha Khan was among the key proponents and financiers of the movement's crown jewel, the Aligarh Muslim University, and of course, the AIML a few years later, and became its first permanent president. Perhaps the most prominent Shia associated with both the Aligarh movement and the AIML was the Ismaili-turned-Ithna Ashari lawyer from Bombay, Muhammad Ali Jinnah. Originally a member of the INC and a secularist proponent of Hindu-Muslim unity, Jinnah joined Muslim identity politics a little later but with a vengeance.

Many other Shias from across India gravitated towards Aligarh and Jinnah's AIML, which were to become the Pakistan movement in due course. But while Aligarh and the AIML captured the imagination of a sizeable section of the Sunni and Shia elite, there were competing trends in both communities that were trying to negotiate both the Muslim political identity and its relationship with the Indian national identity and polity.

With the state power and patronage apparatus gone, as in the case of Awadh, the Shia communities of the subcontinent essentially went back to the drawing board. With the Deobandis looking back to the austere practices of the early Islamic society and the Barelvis trying to maintain a spiritual status quo, the Shias placed themselves somewhat in the middle of that spectrum.

They focused on reinforcing the creed and perpetuating the ritual practice under a newly evolving clergy and civic leaders, both as a function of self-preservation and a confessional statement. Curiously, while the Twelver Shia belief system includes faith in the return of their twelfth Imam Muhammad al-Mahdi as the promised Messiah, the Shia renaissance did not have a messianic foundation or message.

Instead, the community sought to organize itself through guilds, associations, charitable foundations and endowments, for religious, missionary, cultural, social and educational purposes. The traditional ulema (clergy), the *umara* (elite) and the emerging middle-class intelligentsia, each contributed to the efforts, and

> all of these initiated the construction of a novel form of associational Shi'ism, one framed within an equally original discourse of modern Muslim respectability, and carrying within itself an implicit critique of the former aristocratic elitism of north Indian Shi'ism ... In Lucknow from the 1880s, such *anjumans* (organizations) played an important role in the formation of a new, literate middle class, one tied together by aspects of social and occupational commonality and contrasted with the city's 'old' nobility and aristocracy.[9]

This evolution of a perceived Shia political identity necessitated an organizational vehicle to liaise with fraternal entities beyond northern India and, more importantly, to represent the community at the national level, where assorted non-Shia parties and groups were jockeying to assert their pre-eminence. After a clerics-led outfit, Anjuman-e-Sadr-us-Sudoor (Council or Assembly of the Central Minister) floundered and failed in 1905, an All India Shia Conference was launched in 1907,[10] a year after the founding of AIML.

The Shia Conference met annually in the following years and its membership rose and included the clerics, the landed elite, professionals and the middle-class intelligentsia. It eventually allied with the INC, but the importance of the Shia Conference was not just in numbers, outreach or its stance on the Pakistan project, but in helping develop a Shia political identity and in a devotion to 'defending the specificity and interests of the Shia community'[11], its qualitative difference from the Aligarh movement and AIML.

The Shia conference negotiated and proclaimed a modernist Shia political identity without compromise on or concealment of faith in a highly communal Indian political milieu. The Aligarh movement and the AIML, on the other hand, included scores of Shia leaders and cadres, who downplayed their Shia identity and preferred the veneer of being non-denominational Muslims. This ended up having critical, and eventually devastating, implications for the Shia, especially after the creation of Pakistan. Jinnah and other Shia elite in the AIML fold consciously downplayed their Shia confessional identity:

> Shi'a individuals from across India, ranging from late nineteenth-century Muslim modernist intellectuals such as Chiragh Ali, Badr-ud-din Tyabji or Sayyid Ameer Ali to major Muslim nationalist politicians of the early twentieth century such as the Raja of Mahmudabad, Sayyid Wazir Hasan and Muhammad Ali Jinnah are just a few examples of spokesmen from the Shi'a minority who crafted themselves as generic Indian Muslim leaders in order to consolidate wider representative roles. Concomitantly, academic treatments of their political biographies have overwhelmingly emphasized their legacies as Muslims, rather than as Shi'as.[12]

Whereas the obvious and altruistic explanation for these leaders suppressing their confessional identity at the political fora is that they wished to present a united Muslim front against the British and the INC, as well as to keep doctrinal differences out of the temporal realm. Wilfred Cantwell Smith had written:

> Some of the greatest leaders of Islamic modernism have been Shi'i in the technical sense: Amir Ali, Sayyidayn, and others. Jinnah, also, is a Shi'i, and many of the League's least dispensable figures: e.g., the Rajahs of Mahmudabad and Pirpur. But these men have functioned not *qua* Shi'i but *qua* Muslim. In so far as a Shi'i is Shi'ah-community conscious, he is *ipso facto* less advanced.[13]

Smith, however, was only partially right. Concealment of faith does not automatically qualify a person as 'more advanced', especially if they happen to be actively courting, enlisting and defending avowedly sectarian clergymen to an ostensibly non-denominational but avowedly communal political party. It was even more dangerous since Jinnah, a non-practising Muslim himself, had a barely rudimentary understanding of the doctrinal differences between assorted sects of Islam and no desire to identify, discuss and address those before shoving them under the rug of a generic Muslim identity.

His failure to foresee and pre-empt the sectarianism that would eventually befall the state he had founded was at least partly a function of his personal vanity and zeal to outmanoeuvre his adversaries in the INC, to achieve what he wanted for himself rather than for Muslims. In that, his motives and tactics were more self-serving than altruistic.

Much like the father of Muslim reformism, Jamal al-Din al-Afghani, Jinnah had for much of his life cultivated ambiguity as to his sectarian membership. He had always taken pains to avoid publicly presenting himself as a Shia and dodged any questions he was asked in this regard. As chief of state, he did not want to be identified with a minority Muslim denomination, but aligned himself with a generic Muslim identity.[14]

Jinnah's approach was dangerous at multiple levels. Whereas some pan-Islamist Indian Muslim leaders and ideologues, like Muhammad Ali Jauhar and the poet-philosopher Allama Sir Mohammad Iqbal, tried to negotiate a doctrinal via media between the Sunni and the Shia, Jinnah made no attempt of the sort.

While those leaders left alone the issue of the Prophet Muhammad's rightful succession, which forms the basis of the Shia-Sunni schism, they consciously attempted to find common ground at least over certain issues like the tragedy of Karbala by acknowledging the event and accommodating the Shia sensibilities over it. Jinnah, however, simply lacked both the intellectual wherewithal and the political will to do so.

> Unlike Jinnah's silent treatment of Karbala, an event the recollection and ritual commemoration of which is integral to the Shia beliefs: 'Iqbal constitutes Karbala as a political project to unite and mobilize Muslims, especially the Muslim minorities of the South Asian subcontinent. For Iqbal, Karbala is also a move away from the ritualistic-symbolic realm toward the spiritual-active one.[15]

On the flip side, Jinnah made a conscious effort towards, and succeeded in, recruiting to his cause the fundamentalist radicals of the Deoband variety. But in the process, he made no effort to temper their anti-Shia zeal or work on constitutional guarantees for the Shia or other numerically smaller sects such as the Ahmadiyya in his new state, before or after it was created.

He opted to ignore the fact that anti-Shia zealotry in the subcontinent not only antedated colonial rule but had taken on a peculiar urgency and virulence in its aftermath:

> All Indian Sunni Muslim revivalist movements were at one time or another involved in anti-Shi'a polemics. It was as if colonization had provoked introspection, inciting ulama and (certain radical) Sufi masters to embark on a quest for authentic Islam. This, in turn, led them to reject the religious syncretism that had been central to South Asian Islam.[16]

As early as 1939, Jinnah was assuring Deobandi cleric Ashraf Ali Thanvi that 'religion could not be divorced from politics in Islam'.[17] The AIML's recruitment drive brought into its fold radical Deobandis like Maulana Zafar Ahmed Ansari, Maulana Shabbir Ahmed Usmani, and even the school's founder Qasim Nanautavi's grandson, Zahir Qasmi. Through the agency of these clerics, Jinnah was able to turn the tables on the Congress-allied JUH.

Shabbir Ahmed Usmani et al carved the Jamiat-e-Ulama-e-Islam (JUI) out of the JUH. The JUI would declare at its 1945 Calcutta conference that Jinnah's two-nation theory—that the Muslims of India weren't merely a religious entity but also a national entity distinct from their Hindu compatriots—had its origin in the proclamation of the Quran, and was not the invention of any man:

> On this ground this conference declares that the 100 million Muslims in the subcontinent of India are a distinct and independent nationality and a nationality of peculiar constitution which is grounded on the righteous principles of the Islamic millant and Shariat and not on the basis of race, colour, geography ... This session wholeheartedly supports the demand for Pakistan and the division of India.[18]

Similarly, the AIML recruited dozens of Barelvi pirs and sheikhs from the Northwest Frontier, from Sindh, and above all, from the Punjab provinces. Pirs of Manki, Zakori, Makhad, Golra, Taunsa, Sial, Multan and so on filled the ranks of the AIML. The Barelvi umbrella group, All India Sunni Conference, unlike the Deobandis, did not transform into a political party until after the creation of Pakistan, when the group became Jamiat-e-Ulama-e-Pakistan (JUP) in 1948.

When some of the fundamentalist clerics whom Jinnah had recruited to his cause started asserting their Sunni creed and went as far as apostatizing and otherizing the Shia—even the ones within the AIML's fold—he failed to take any disciplinary action. The emboldened Sunni clergymen in the AIML were already making a case for which brand of Islam would hold sway in matters of state in the proposed new country. Jinnah, on his part, perhaps felt that while he needed the agency of these clerics for the creation of Pakistan, he would be able to curtail their power and ambition in the new state. Regardless, he failed to curb the rising fundamentalist sectarianism:

> While Shia candidates, eager to please the Sunni voters, tried their best to obscure all doctrinal differences and acute conflicts between Shias and Sunnis,189 Sunni "ulamâ" within the Muslim League became more outspoken. For example, Maulana Zafar Ahmad 'Usmani published a fatwâ in the League daily al-Manshûr (Delhi), justifying the inclusion of Shias in the League with the argument that Sunnis could cooperate with *khawârij* heretics during their confrontation with idolaters (i.e. the Hindus), because even khawârij would fight for Islam and against kufr. His colleague Maulana S. Nasîr ul-Haqq was quoted in Nawâ-i Waqt on 3 November 1945 with the verdict that

> according to the Prophet only those who followed the path of the *khulafâ'-i-râshidûn* were on the right path, whereas all other groups, parties or sects would be "a work of Satan".[19]

Various Shia organizations and individuals had become increasingly wary of the trajectory taken by both the Aligarh movement and the AIML under Jinnah. They feared that a non-denominational modern Muslim identity project run by the majority sect had the potential to obliterate the Shia religio-political identity. That assorted Shia elite were affiliated with both entities did little to assuage this concern, since those very individuals, in their public persona, were the prime examples of the loss of such identity.

These deepening concerns led to various Shia outfits calling upon certain financiers like the Raja of Mahmudabad to stop funding the Aligarh College, which he complied with. But that was not the end of it:

> Suspicion of Aligarh College among many Shi'a culminated in the 1910s, with an organized lambasting of what was assumed to be a nascent Sunnification of the college. This story of the descent of Aligarh from a space where a Muslim qaum was constructed into one of sectarian controversy has been almost entirely sidelined in a body of scholarship more preoccupied with Aligarh's unitary qualities. But in 1913 the Shi'a Conference issued a pamphlet which outlined a number of Shi'a grievances within the college.[20]

Ultimately, in 1917, a Shia College was founded in Lucknow which was purported to be not in competition with Aligarh, but it pried away virtually all the major Shia members and donors of that institution's parent body, the Muhammadan Educational

Conference.[21] Be that as it may, Jinnah retained and gained the support and financing of a large number of the Shia elite for his AIML, ranging from the mercantile magnates of Bengal, Bombay and Karachi to the landed aristocracy of north India and the Punjab, especially after the 1937 reorganization of the party.

However, as had been the case earlier, the stalwarts were there not qua Shia but qua Muslim or even qua politicians who had an eye on their mostly Sunni-dominated constituencies: '(In) colonial India specifically, the realm of Muslim politics has been widely understood as a climate in which the interests of many Shi'a public figures were best served by abrogating their Shi'a status and framing themselves as Muslim representatives.'[22]

The landmark 1940 Lahore Resolution, which paved the way for the creation of Pakistan, had pledged guarantees to protect the rights of minorities in the Muslim majority units it had proposed, but Jinnah spurned demands for similar safeguards by the Shia as sectarian. Within days of the Lahore Resolution, the younger brother of Jinnah's most allied Shia ally and biggest financier, Raja of Mahmud, the Maharajkumar Amir Haidar Khan of Mahmudabad, felt compelled to write Jinnah a letter outlining those demands:

> 1) Shias should have a say in elected bodies and governmental institutions, which should work according to the principles of justice (*insâf aur adâlat*) instead of prevalence of the majority; 2) freedom for Shia beliefs and customs; 3) the governors of all provinces and the Governor General of India should have special powers to protect the Shias in case of injustice done to them by other groups; 4) all Shia *auqâf* must be under exclusive Shia control; 5) if any law was passed according to Hanafi *fiqh*, the special fiqh of the Shias must be observed in their cases[23]. – Is this a quotation, kindly clarify?

Jinnah wrote back,[24] chastising the Maharajkumar of Mahmudabad, who, unlike his older brother, had always steered clear of the AIML, that

> his (Maharajkumar's) mind is still working in the direction which is not likely to benefit the Shias ... You will forgive me if I do not see eye to eye with you ...the proper policy for the Shias is to join the League whole-heartedly. The League is now able to enforce justice and fair play between Mussalman and Mussalman whatever be his sect or section. The one thing alone that matters is that we are all Mussalmans.'[25]

While rejecting nearly all the demands, Jinnah tried to assuage the Maharajkumar on the issue of Shia endowments (auqâf) and that 'if law is passed in accordance with the Muslim Hanafi Law, the special principles of Shia Shariat must also be taken into consideration'. He went on to dissuade the Maharajkumar from participating in the All-Parties Shia Conference, which he did none the less. The Maharajkumar also chose to stay in India after the Partition in 1947.

The older brother, however, remained a devoted follower of Jinnah and continued to organize and finance the AIML, but not for too long:

> Not even the faithful stalwart of the Muslim League, Amir Ahmad Khan of Mahmudabad, could get satisfaction of his persistent demand that the League should nominate at least one Shia *âlim* (scholar) for the Constituent Assembly of India; he therefore tendered his resignation from that body in early August 1946.[26]

The Raja of Mahmudabad also resigned from the presidency of the All India Muslim Students Federation, the AIML's highly active student wing he himself had founded. He too chose not to migrate to Pakistan in 1947, instead crossing over from Quetta to Iran on his way to the Shia holy city of Karbala in Iraq, where he then settled.[27] He eventually moved to Britain but briefly came to Pakistan later, only to return to London, where he died. He was buried in the Shia holy city of Mashhad in Iran.

While the Shia religio-cultural identity in the Indian subcontinent was shaped over some 400 years, the development of a distinct Shia political identity paralleled that of a broader Indian Muslim identity in the wake of British colonization. The Shia organized themselves with varying degrees of success as a distinct confessional community, albeit in a modernist fashion, without harking back to medieval Islam or evoking messianic revivalist themes.

They mobilized and participated in the anti-colonial struggle of both the communal and Indian nationalist varieties, a la the AIML and INC, respectively, and played a huge part in the Indian Marxist movement as well. Contrary to the common perception, especially in Pakistan, the Shia did not act as a monolith even within the realm of separatist Muslim politics of colonial India.

While a plurality, if not majority, of the subcontinental Shia ended up subscribing to Jinnah and his AIML's message, there were sizeable sections that disagreed with the notion of heading into a state conceived on the basis of religion, as mere generic Muslims. The vociferous calls and demands for Jinnah to clearly define the place and protections for the Shia in the new state were incredibly prescient.

Jinnah, on his part, had a terribly reductionist approach and a cavalier solution to the complex problem of inter and intra-faith relations in the country he founded. Hailed as the touchstone of his ostensibly secular creed, Jinnah's first presidential address to the

Constituent Assembly of Pakistan on 11 August 1947 was reassuring but woefully simplistic:

> 'We should begin to work in that spirit, and in course of time all these angularities of the majority and minority communities, the Hindu community and the Muslim community—because even as regards Muslims you have Pathans, Punjabis, Shias, Sunnis and so on, and among the Hindus you have Brahmins, Vashnavas, Khatris, also Bengalees, Madrasis and so on—will vanish ... You are free; you are free to go to your temples, you are free to go to your mosques or to any other place or worship in this State of Pakistan. You may belong to any religion or caste or creed—that has nothing to do with the business of the State.'[28]

Whether Jinnah's massive enlisting of the clerics, theologians and pirs was just realpolitik on Jinnah's part and he actually intended to stick to his 11 August 1947 speech, we shall never know; he died a year after that speech. He was not much of a writer and didn't leave any written treatise about the orientation of the state he founded.

It is quite perplexing that for a man who spent his life practicing law and was virtually a fixture in the colonial Indian constitutional fora, Jinnah had not prepared a template for his new country's constitution. His thoughts and vision were expressed mostly in his speeches and correspondence and have been meticulously archived by him and his associates, but are interpreted, unsurprisingly, by his detractors and admirers according to their own political, religious or ideological leanings.

One thing is certain that the outcome of assembling such a massive religio-political contingent could only be each one of them jockeying for their brand of Islam to become the new state's *grundnorm*. And this is exactly what happened from the day the country's first constituent assembly went to work.

The fundamentalist associates of Jinnah in the Constituent Assembly of Pakistan, led by Maulana Shabbir Ahmed Usmani, aggressively pushed for the character of the constitution to be Islamic and successfully inducted a series of Islamic provisions in the Objectives Resolution of 1949, which was the guiding document to establish a framework for constitution-making in the country.[29] Some of the verbiage and its premise were alarming:

- 'Whereas sovereignty over the entire universe belongs to Allah Almighty alone and the authority which He has delegated to the State of Pakistan, through its people for being exercised within the limits prescribed by Him is a sacred trust;
- Wherein the principles of democracy, freedom, equality, tolerance and social justice as enunciated by Islam shall be fully observed;
- Wherein the Muslims shall be enabled to order their lives in the individual and collective spheres in accordance with the teachings and requirements of Islam as set out in the Holy Quran and the Sunnah.'

The fundamentalist leaders were a double-edged sword that Jinnah had carried in his scabbard, and after his demise, they were out in full force. The Objectives Resolution was the handywork of Jinnah's handpicked clergymen and set the stage for the transformation of Pakistan from ostensibly being a state for Muslims to a confessional Islamic state. Presenting the Resolution, then Prime Minister Liaquat Ali Khan said:

> 'Islam is not just a matter of private beliefs and conduct. It expects its followers to build up a society for the purpose of good life—as the Greeks would have called it, with this difference, that Islamic "good life" is essentially based upon spiritual values. For the purpose of emphasizing these values and to give them validity, it will be necessary for the State to direct and guide the activities of the Muslims in such a manner as to bring about a new social order based upon the essential principles of Islam including the principles of democracy, freedom, tolerance and social justice.'[30]

Both the Resolution's religious contours and Liaquat Ali Khan's endorsement of them were in tune with Jinnah's notion of a generic Muslim identity that would be benevolent and just in inter- and intra-faith matters. The problem, however, was that these were not lay documents and words but the building blocks of the social contract and constitutional compact that the peoples of Pakistan would end up living under. The mischief in the Objectives Resolution, and the potential for future mischief based upon it, was instantly identified by several Opposition politicians in the constituent assembly.

Bhupendra Kumar Datta, a Congress leader from East Pakistan, delivered a prophetic speech that foretold the disaster that the Objectives Resolution eventually entailed. He moved that the 'paragraph beginning with the words "whereas sovereignty over the entire universe" and ending with the words "is a sacred trust" be omitted', saying that such explicit inclusion would inevitably lead to mixing of religion and politics and potential for abuse.[31]

Datta's apprehension was that mingling the divine, which may not be critiqued, with temporal politics, which thrives on criticism, would create a tripwire that triggers charges of disrespect and put whatever is done in the name of religion beyond reproach. He said:

> Politics belongs to the domain of reason. But as you intermingle it with religion, as this Preamble to this nobly conceived Resolution does, you pass into the other sphere of faith … on the one hand, you run the risk of subjecting religion to criticism, which will rightly be resented as sacrilegious; on the other, so far as the State and State policies are concerned, you cripple reason, curb criticism. Political institutions, particularly modern democratic institutions, as we all know, Sir, grow and progress by criticism from broader to still broader basis.[32]

Datta's apprehension was that the Constitution and its preamble are supposed to outlast the framers and might become a tool in the hands of usurping adventurists. He pleaded:

> 'Let us not do anything here today that may consign our future generations to the furies of a blind destiny. Maybe, may God forbid it, but some day, perhaps even within our lifetime, extremely troublous times as we live in a political adventurer, a Yanshikai, or a Bachcha-i-Saka [*sic*] may find a chance to impose his will and authority on this State. He may find a justification for it in this Preamble.'[33]

Those concerns were prescient. While the Objectives Resolution was not supposed to become the substantive and operative part of the Constitution, and in fact remained merely as a preamble to the country's various constitutions, an army dictator, General Zia-ul-Haq, did make it a formal operative part of the country's 1973 Constitution,[34] and it remains so.

Within merely a couple of years after the Partition, the stage had thus been set for a Pakistani national identity which essentially was an extension of the generic Muslim identity that Jinnah had professed and practised. But with Jinnah himself gone without leaving any guidelines or safeguards behind, that generic identity, de facto, was Sunni in character.

But the problem with this extremely oversimplified proposition for the national identity was that the country was home not only to Bengalis, Sindhis, Baloch, Pashtun, Punjabis and others with distinctive ethno-national characters, but also to the world's second largest Shia population after Iran. The proposed and imposed one size was not going to fit all.

A review of the ethno-national conundrum is beyond the scope of this discussion, but suffice it to say that the secular ethno-nationalist movements were countered and crushed by force[35] from the get-go.

The Shia communities of the newly independent Pakistan tried to organize in a fashion somewhat similar to the pre-Partition era. An All-Pakistan Shia Conference and similar other entities came into being to advocate for and protect the religious rights of the Shia community in the developing corpus of laws and curricula, as well strategizing to cope with the increasingly menacing attacks on Shia ritual commemorations of Muharram or *azadari*.

The Shia politicians, by and large, continued their pre-1947 trend of participation in the political parties not qua Shia but qua Muslim. While they may have patronized the Shia rituals at a local level in individual capacities, they never did speak out in or as members of their respective political parties. While the Sunni politicians in mainstream parties like (what was by then called) the Pakistan Muslim League (PML) did not profess their confessional identity either, the demands from the clergy, both allied with their parties or agitating from the street, were not incongruent with their set of beliefs and posed little threat to the way they practised it.

While the Shia, numbering anywhere from 15 per cent to 25 per cent of the country's population, could not be wished away, they certainly were under threat from the hardline Sunni zealotry militating against Shia practices. The ostensibly non-denominational Islamization of the state was to have detrimental consequences for the Shia way of life.

While many politicians, like Prime Minister Huseyn Shaheed Suhrawardy, proposed[36] for Pakistan to become a democratic, pluralist nation state, the country's first military dictator, Field Marshal Ayub Khan, though secular in personal outlook and outwardly anti-clergy, pushed[37] for and transformed it into an ideological national security state.

While the Ayub Khan era initially brought some respite for the Shia, it also saw aggressive anti-Shia rioting and the Shia organizational response to defend their religious rights. But two ominous projects undertaken by Ayub Khan had far-reaching consequences for pluralism in Pakistan in general, and for the Shia in particular.

Firstly, in the name of educational reforms, he established complete control over academic curricula and introduced Islamic studies or Islamiyat—a reductionist version of religious education that promoted the idea of the generic Muslim at the expense of highlighting and studying diversity within Islam.

Under the same reforms, revisionist texts were introduced under an umbrella subject called the 'social studies', which subsumed history, geography and civic studies as individual subjects and framed, in anti-Indian terms, the existence of Pakistan and the generic Muslim identity therein.[38] This same subject and its curricula came to be known as the infamous Pakistan Studies, which for decades since have inculcated the warped notions of religion, nation and state in successive generations of students.

Additionally, Ayub Khan also institutionalized the use of jihadist proxies to prosecute war, by introducing the Mujahideen or holy warriors into Indian-held Kashmir, leading to an all-out war in 1965.[39] Ironically, Field Marshal Ayub Khan's army chief at the time was a Shia, General Muhammad Musa Khan. A secularist on first impression, Ayub Khan was anything but one.

Paradoxically, Ayub Khan, in his 1962 Constitution, got the adjective 'Islamic' removed and described the country as the Republic of Pakistan, but on the other hand, constitutionally mandated the teaching of Islamiyat in the school curricula. The Shia organizations, alarmed at the prospect of a sanitized version of Islam being taught, demanded the option of a Shia Islamiyat curriculum, with not much success.

The word Islamic was reinstated in the country's official name within a year after the Sunni religious parties agitated against the Ayub regime. Ayub Khan did not care for the unruly and bickering clergymen. Like Jinnah, he had only an elementary understanding of the nuances in Islam but had great fondness for a simplified version of Islam that he, as the military ruler, could easily manipulate.

He created an Advisory Council for Islamic Ideology, which later became the Council of Islamic Ideology, which exists till date, 'to make recommendations to the Central Government and the Provincial Governments as to means of enabling and encouraging the Muslims of Pakistan to order their lives in all respects in accordance with the principles and concepts of Islam'. The members of this council, though drawn from various sects and technocracy, were state-appointed and thus relatively pliable.

Ayub Khan thus ushered in what has been described as the statization of Islam,[40] whereby 'the nation-state started to discipline Islam in order not only to instrumentalize it, but also to neutralize potential rivals among the religious leaders' as well as smear secular ethno-national political rivals. While the Ayub regime tolerated or was indifferent to diversity within the various schools of Islam, it effectively laid the foundation of a generic Islamic identity becoming the state-sanctioned Pakistani national identity.

Ayub Khan added a highly jingoistic dimension to the two-nation theory, to create a supra-ethnic Pakistani identity that was Islamic in ideology, militarily oriented against India, and imposed by the state. And even more ominously, the army anointed itself as the custodian of the nebulous 'ideological frontiers', in addition to defending the physical frontiers. This state-sponsored religio-political identity sought to create homogeneity at the expense of both the diverse ethno-national spectrum of peoples comprising Pakistan, as well as their myriad religious persuasions.

Those who did not subscribe to this official formulation of identity ran the risk of becoming the outliers. The stage had been set for otherizing the non-conformist entities, whether political or religious.

In 1963, Shia commemorations of Muharram were violently attacked in Khairpur, Sindh and Narowal and Lahore in Punjab: 'Worst affected was Theri in the Khairpur District, where an imâmbârgâh was set on fire killing dozens of Shia worshippers. The overall death toll on 10 Muharram reached 120 according to official reports.'[41]

Assorted Shia organizations and both religious and political leaders protested with the Ayub regime and even met the dictator, presenting various demands, but did not make much headway. It eventually would take mass mobilization, street protests and several years to get their demands, which merely sought protections for ritual commemorations, endowments, and separate religious curricula where applicable, accepted.

This cycle of violence, followed by protests and demands for protection, were to become a recurring theme for the Shia in Pakistan. However, each successive military regime took up from where the previous one had left off and kept pouring more statist Islam and jingoism into the Ayub Khan formula. The ideology deck was also stacked against democratic forces, which were now bound in the straitjacket of the supra-ethnic Pakistani-Islamic identity.

Ayub Khan was eased out in another martial law by General Agha Muhammad Yahya Khan, who, though a Shia himself, followed his predecessor's Islamo-nationalist policies to the tee. While engaging with the Shia community and honouring the commitments made to them by Ayub Khan, Yahya Khan introduced a particularly virulent strain of religio-political indoctrination within the armed forces and the society at large. A hard-drinking man himself,[42] Yahya Khan appointed Major General (retired) Sher Ali Khan as his minister for information and national affairs. Sher Ali Khan, a self-described ideological man,[43] went to town with his mandate, from co-opting religio-political outfits like the Jamat-e-Islami to ratcheting up Islamist rhetoric and jargon:

> 'Expressions like the "ideology of Pakistan" and the "glory of Islam" used by the military high command were becoming stock phrases. Messages issued by the service chiefs and the President on the occasion of Defense Day reflected the ideological overtones. They sounded more like high priests than soldiers ... Sher Ali took the regime to the point of no return on the road to ideological involvement. He went from place to place preaching and pontificating about the Islamic ideology.'[44]

Another dangerous development of the Yahya Khan era was the army's use of the Jamat-e-Islami's Razakar (volunteer) death squads, the al-Badr and al-Shams, in suppressing the Bengali freedom struggle in East Pakistan.[45] This was not the first use of non-state jihadi actors by the army, as it had used them in the

Kashmir wars of 1947 and 1965, and certainly didn't turn out to be the last one.

The army provided patronage, arms and instructions to these jihadi vigilante gangs, who targeted the partisans of the secular secessionist movement, including the members of the Bengali intelligentsia. The ideological indoctrination unleashed on the country and absorbed by the army itself, as manifest in the army's increasing use of religious symbolism and slogans,[46] and ultimately the use of jihadist collaborators as force-multipliers, were the lasting legacies of Yahya Khan's three-year stint.

After the independence of Bangladesh, Yahya Khan was replaced by another Shia, Zulfikar Ali Bhutto, whose PPP had won a majority in the rump Pakistan. Bhutto became the country's prime minister after getting a new Constitution hammered out with the help of secularist and Islamist parties. The PPP itself was secular in outlook but pandering to religious elements, it had termed its economic creed 'Islamic Socialism'.

The country's new Constitution too was somewhat of a similar compromise and consolidated Islam as the state religion and included a slew of Islamic provisions. In an ominous development, however, the Bhutto government—with the help of secularists as well as the clergy, including the Shia—amended the Constitution to declare the Ahmadiyya sect as non-Muslim.

While the Shia were not impacted by this state-sponsored ostracizing of a religious community, it contributed to the intellectual and social milieu in which unofficial excommunication of smaller Muslim communities became acceptable. While Bhutto was hugely popular among the general Shia population, his government's handling of the separate curricula for Islamiyat or Dinyat (Islamic or religious studies) and the Shia endowment issues was not very different from that of his two predecessors, and eventually precipitated mass protests organized by the Shia clerical outfits.

A lesser known but highly pernicious move by the Bhutto government, which had far-reaching consequences for the Shia, was his adoption of the army's jihadist project in Afghanistan. Both the army and Bhutto were of the view that his opponents, the National Awami Party (NAP), and its overwhelmingly Pashtun and Baloch leadership, were backed by Afghanistan in their separatist designs.

The army plotted and Bhutto signed off on countering the Kabul government by harbouring the Islamist Afghan opposition leaders. The army-Bhutto combine financed, armed, trained and unleashed these Sunni Afghan jihadists against the Kabul government in 1973–74. From using domestic jihadi collaborators in Kashmir and Bengal, Pakistan had graduated to transnational jihadism, a project that would continue to grow and end in a devastating blowback for the country in general, and its Shia population in particular.

In 1977, Bhutto was ousted in a bloodless coup by an avowedly austere Muslim, General Muhammad Zia-ul-Haq, who first abrogated the Constitution but introduced virulent mutations when he restored it later in 1985 after a prolonged pro-democracy movement. Zia co-opted the Sunni clergy and political parties like the Jamat-e-Islami in his Islamization plan.

Two world events consolidated Zia's domestic position and project by getting him incredible international support. First, the 1978 communist revolution in Afghanistan, which was quite friendly to the Pashtun and Baloch nationalists and leftists in Pakistan, disconcerted the army. Subsequently, the Shia Islamic revolution in Iran in 1979, and the prospect of the ayatollahs exporting it, had alarmed the Sunni Arab world, led by Saudi Arabia as well as Pakistan's military and Sunni religious establishment.

The 1979 Soviet invasion of Afghanistan, in defence of the communist regime, reinforced these concerns. The transnational jihadist project sired by Bhutto and the army went big, overnight. The United States and Saudi Arabia jumped in to bankroll and arm the Afghan Mujahideen insurgency midwifed by Pakistan. In addition, the Saudis exported their puritanical Wahabi brand of Islam to pre-empt any Iranian expansion, and in the process strengthened Zia's hand:

> Under Zia ul-Haq, the law was Islamized, prohibiting the adoption of any law that contravened Islam as it had been defined by commissions of ulama. The domain of education suffered the same fate, with among other things the creation of a large network of religious schools. While many of these schools were state funded, others were financed by Saudi Arabia, including all of those associated with the Salafist current of Ahl-i Hadith, or the People of Hadith. The policy of Islamization gave rise to the first major conflicts with the Shi'a[47]. – is this a quotation, kindly clarify?

Zia's Islamization led to a major standoff with the Shia community when the latter resisted his 1979 decree that the *zakat*—a voluntary religious charitable contribution to be given to a deserving person or cause of one's choice—would be collected and used by the state as a tax. In 1980, thousands of Shias, led by a religious scholar Mufti Jaffar Hussain, marched to Islamabad.

The Zia regime eventually relented and allowed an exemption for the Shia. But apprehensive of the Shia mobilization, the Zia regime enabled the formation of a militant Deobandi Sunni outfit named the Sipah-e-Sahaba or the army of the Prophet's companions.

Founded in 1985, the Sipah-e-Sahaba unleashed a reign of terror against the Shia across Pakistan.

The Shia initially responded by forming their own militant group, Sipah-e-Muhammad, but were no match for the entity they were up against. The Sipah-e-Sahaba and its subsequent reincarnation, the Lashkar-e-Jhangvi, were allied with the Afghan Mujahideen and later the Afghan Taliban, as well as the al-Qaeda. Pakistan's Sunni religious parties, like the modernist Jamat-e-Islami and the orthodox Deobandi JUI, provided political support as well as manpower to this jihadi conglomerate.

The Pakistan army's project of using Sunni militants as force-multipliers, which had started in the killing fields of East Pakistan, had bloomed into a fully-fledged jihadist ecosystem by the mid-1980s. Zia's demise in an airplane crash in 1988 did not put a damper on this jihadist enterprise, for it was an institutional venture, not an individual one. Just as the army's jihadist project turned out to be permanent, its consequences for the Shia of Pakistan were perpetual.

The quasi-democratic governments in Pakistan from 1988 to 1999, and then since 2008, neither had the will nor the capacity to roll back the army's jihadist project. The country's fourth military dictator, General Pervez Musharraf, who ruled for nearly a decade from 1999 onwards, had claimed to usher in what he called the 'enlightened moderation', wherein he pledged to curb radicalization at home and the use of jihadist proxies across borders. But like Ayub Khan's ostensible secularization, the Musharraf era was anything but enlightened or moderate. Force into cooperating with the United States in the post-9/11 War on Terror, Musharraf opted to play a double game.

The army under him continued its jihadist intervention in Afghanistan and patronage of Sunni sectarian and militant outfits at home, while helping the US pick off certain al-Qaeda elements. This duplicitous policy of picking and choosing between the so-called 'good jihadists', who attack only others, versus the 'bad jihadists', who targeted Pakistani interests, had devastating consequences for the Shia of Pakistan.

The good and the bad jihadists shared the same hardline Sunni sectarian ideology, sanctuaries and training camps, madrasas and money-transferring network. Starting in the second phase of Musharraf's rule, these groups, like the Tehrik-e-Taliban Pakistan (TTP) and the Lashkar-e-Jhangvi, unleashed a reign of terror against the Pakistani population in general, and the Shia in particular. The mass murders reached genocidal proportions during the post-Musharraf era.

While the army eventually acted against the TTP in a circumscribed manner, it never dismantled its jihadist project. In fact, when the civilian political leadership called for cleaning up its jihadist mess, the army orchestrated to undermine and topple them.

The Shia predicament in Pakistan today is the result of framing, ab initio, the national identity in terms of a generic Muslim persona at the expense of doctrinal diversity, to which layers of jingoistic Islamic chauvinism were added under successive army regimes. The state's policies of Islamization of the Constitution, laws and curricula on one hand, and co-option of Sunni sectarian forces and siring of jihadist proxies on the other, have imperilled not just the Shia political and religious identity, but their very existence, in many cases.

The army's continuous control over the state's political structures, its national security and foreign policies, and its active undermining of democratic forces, perpetuates the conformist identity and vitiates diversity. The political leadership, including those from among the Shia, on their part have been lacking in formulating a coherent understanding of and a response to these challenges.

Nevertheless, the Shia, though butchered, bruised and battered over the past decade and a half, have survived and stood firm in the face of all odds. They remain a sizeable portion of Pakistan's population and an integral part of the society and would continue to be so without jettisoning their distinct religio-cultural identity.

9

Pakistan's Legal Framework and Treatment of Religious Minorities

FARAHNAZ ISPAHANI

ADDRESSING THE NATION IN MARCH 2022, then prime minister, Imran Khan, declared that 'our Pakistan was built on the ideology of Islamic welfare state' and its constitutional and legal order should approximate 'Riyasat-e-Madina'—the state ostensibly founded by Prophet Muhammad in the city of Madina in the seventh century.[1] Khan had earlier argued in his memoirs, published a decade earlier, that 'Pakistan came into existence as a country because of Islam and the Islamic beliefs of its founders and citizens.'[2]

Khan's rhetoric was not new to Pakistanis. Since its foundation in 1947, successive Pakistani leaders have declared Islam as their country's raison d'etre and have claimed that they are trying to build an Islamic state based on principles laid down centuries earlier. 'Islamization', as the process has often been called, has entailed ceding power to extreme Islamist clerics. The greatest brunt of accepting extremist demands has been borne by Pakistan's religious minorities. During Khan's three-and-a half-years in power, attacks on Pakistan's minorities increased.

'It's been a tough time for religious minorities in Pakistan, and observers warn of even tougher times ahead as Prime Minister Imran Khan vacillates between trying to forge a pluralistic nation and his conservative Islamic beliefs,' reported Kathy Gannon of the Associated Press in 2020.[3] She cited several incidents targeting Christians, Hindus and Ahmadis. These included gunning down of a Christian 'because he rented in a Muslim neighbourhood in northwest Peshawar',[4] the beating up of a Christian pastor, Haroon Sadiq Cheeda, his wife, and twelve-year-old son, who were told by their Muslim neighbours in eastern Punjab to leave their village, and the charging of an Opposition politician with blasphemy after his declaration that all religions are equal.

A senior political figure, allied with Khan's government and backed by Islamist extremists, stopped construction of a Hindu temple in the capital, Islamabad, while Prime Minister Khan turned to the Council of Islamic Ideology to decide if public money could be used in an Islamic state for construction of a non-Muslim place of worship.[5]

The executive branch of Pakistan's government is not alone in promoting religious intolerance or discrimination against minority communities. Pakistan's judiciary also has a track record of supporting extremists in denying rights of religious minorities. When the parents of a fourteen-year-old Christian girl, Huma Younus, pleaded that their daughter had been abducted from Karachi to be converted to Islam and married to her abductor, Abdul Jabbar, the Sindh High Court ruled that the conversion and marriage were 'valid under Islamic Sharia law.' According to the Court's ruling, definitions under Sharia law trumped modern notions of maturity and, therefore, the fourteen-year-old must be deemed to have given consent to her forced marriage and religious conversion. [6] In a separate case, the Lahore High Court granted custody of a thirteen-year Christian girl to a Muslim accused of kidnapping her, forcibly marrying her, and converting her to Islam. The judge in this case rejected an earlier High Court ruling that children under the age of fifteen lacked the mental capacity to change their religion.[7]

Ironically, the minimum age for marriage in Sindh, where the first case was decided, is eighteen, whereas it is sixteen in Punjab, where Lahore High Court has jurisdiction. But in Pakistan, religious arguments take precedence over legal ones. Rape and abduction of a minor girl would be considered a serious crime in most countries. In case of Pakistan's more than one thousand forced marriage and conversion cases a year,[8] the conversion of underage girls from Christianity or Hinduism to Islam makes it unlikely that the perpetrator of the crime would face charges. The conversion of the victim to Islam bolsters support for the abductor within Pakistan's legal system where Sharia law often overrides other aspects of criminality in most cases. Despite attempts to do so, especially in provincial assemblies, liberal Pakistani legislators have been unable to pass legislation against forced conversions and further amending Pakistan's child marriage laws.

These, more recent, instances of excesses against religious minorities reflect a problem that stems from Pakistan's Constitution declaring it an Islamic republic and saying that all legislation will be subject to Islamic injunctions. Although various leaders have interpreted what it means to be an Islamic republic differently at different times during Pakistan's seventy-five-year history, there has been consistency in Pakistan failing to fulfil its obligations towards its minorities under the Universal Declaration of Human Rights. Pakistan's non-Muslims account for 3 per cent of the country's total population today though when Pakistan was created in August 1947, its territory was to include 23 per cent non-Muslims.[9]

Pakistan's descent to its current state of religious intolerance is the result of a series of political choices made by its leaders after the death of Pakistan's founder, Muhammad Ali Jinnah. It began in 1949, when the constituent assembly declared that the objective of Pakistan's Constitution was the creation of an Islamic state. General Zia-ul-Haq's 'Islamization' drive during the 1980s represented the high point of concerted efforts to transform constitutional and legal structures according to Islam. Imran Khan's more recent pronouncements reflect the continuing aspiration of many in Pakistan to recreate an Islamist utopia.

It is important to point out that Jinnah never signed off on Islamization. His address before the constituent assembly on 11 August 1947 laid out a comprehensive statement of secular principles for Pakistan's future constitution.[10] That speech declared that religion would have nothing to do with the business of the state. But over the years that speech has been suppressed in Pakistan's public discourse and it is now assumed widely in Pakistan that Pakistan has no alternative conceptualization except as an Islamic state.

In March 1949, Prime Minister Liaquat Ali Khan moved in the constituent assembly what came to be known as the 'Objectives Resolution': a declaration of the goals of the new state that would form the basis of its future constitution and laws. The resolution described a vision for Pakistan diametrically opposed to the secular one Jinnah had offered in his 11 August 1947 speech.

'The Objectives Resolution accepted the premise that "sovereignty over the entire universe belongs to God Almighty alone" and that the State of Pakistan would exercise authority "within the limit prescribed by Him".' The resolution declared that 'Muslims shall be enabled to order their lives in the individual and collective spheres in accord with the teachings and requirements of Islam as set out in the Holy Quran and the Sunna' and 'adequate provision shall be made to safeguard the legitimate interests of minorities and backward and depressed classes'.[11]

The net effect of the Objectives Resolution was to define the state in Islamic terms, opening the door for further legislation based on the interpretation of Islam by a parliamentary majority. In the ensuing decades, however, democracy in Pakistan became intermittent, leaving the authority of inferring the Quran and Sunna (practices of the Prophet Muhammad) for long intervals in the hands of military dictators. With this began the denial of minorities' rights, along with the official denial of atrocities committed against them.

Within the first few months of Independence, Pakistan's leaders scrambled to define Pakistani nationhood, distinct from the ethnic identities of its various peoples. Hindus began to be described as 'the other' and non-Muslim members of Pakistan's first constituent assembly expressed concern about what they described as the mass expulsion of Hindus from Pakistan. In 1950, soon after the adoption of the Objectives Resolution, thirty-one Muslim clerics issued a twenty-two-point plan for implementing Sharia in the country. The ulema insisted that the state should be run only under Islamic laws and should be headed by a Muslim male as its president. Included in the twenty-two points was the notion that the freedom of non-Muslim citizens would be subject to 'prescribed boundaries and law', a clear reference to the dhimmi tradition that allowed non-Muslims to live within an Islamic state on condition of paying jizya (a poll tax). The Islamists thus made it clear that they did not aspire to modern notions of equal citizenship regardless of religion. For them, the most non-Muslims in Pakistan could expect were the protections traditionally afforded to dhimmis and that too only on the sufferance of the majority.

By 1953, the officially sponsored resentment against Hindus—handed down from Partition—was supplanted by antagonism towards the Ahmadiyya sect, also referred to pejoratively as 'Qadianis' or 'Mirzais.' Members of the Punjab-based sect deemed themselves Muslim, but their belief in a nineteenth-century prophet or messiah, Mirza Ghulam Ahmad, led to their excommunication by clerics of other Muslim sects. The Ahmadis had actively supported Jinnah and the demand for Pakistan and one of the sect's members, Sir Zafrulla Khan, served as Pakistan's first foreign minister.

The demands of the anti-Ahmadi agitators were unusual for a modern, democratic state. Not only was the state being asked to decide who was or was not part of a specific religion, it was being called upon to officially discriminate against members of a religious sect. The anti-Ahmadiyya campaign called itself the Tehrik-e-Tahaffuz-e-Khatm-e-Nabbuwat (Movement for the Protection of the Finality of the Prophet). Its appeal to mainstream Sunni Muslims was emotive. The believers had to defend the Prophet Muhammad's status as the final prophet of God, and this could only be done by legislation declaring Ahmadis non-Muslims and by restricting their role in government.

The problems with conceding these demands were manifold. At the most fundamental level, it would set the dangerous precedent of involving the state in determining which sects were acceptably Muslim. Once the Ahmadis were officially declared non-Muslim in 1974, a new campaign started with the intent to subject the Shias to similar proscriptions. That the protestors resorted to violence against a minority religious sect pointed to the likelihood that such campaigns might become the norm—a fear that has since been realized in the form of sectarian terrorism.

With the anti-Ahmadiyya protests, Pakistan had moved from purging non-Muslims to an extended period of bitter fighting over who may be deemed Muslim and how to make the state more Islamic. That debate continues to the present day, with grave consequences for religious minorities.

In 1956, when the second constituent assembly was finally able to arrive at some sort of consensus, it named Pakistan 'the Islamic Republic of Pakistan' and included the Objectives Resolution as the preamble to the Constitution. Part 3 of that Constitution laid down several 'Directive Principles of State Policy'. These included Islamic provisions such as 'steps shall be taken to enable the Muslims of Pakistan individually and collectively to order their lives in accordance with the Holy Quran and Sunna' and 'to promote unity and the observance of Islamic moral standards'. The Pakistani state was now committed to securing 'the proper organization of zakat, wakfs (religious endowments) and mosques', to 'prevent the consumption of alcoholic liquor' and to 'eliminate *riba* (usury or interest) as early as possible'.[12]

The 1956 Pakistan Constitution barred non-Muslims from holding the office of head of state. As if that were not enough, Part 12 of the Constitution was titled 'Islamic Provisions'. It included Article 197, which said that 'the president shall set up an organization for Islamic research and instruction in advanced studies to assist in the reconstruction of Muslim society on a truly Islamic basis'. Article 198 declared, 'No law shall be enacted which is repugnant to the Injunctions of Islam as laid down in the Holy Quran and Sunna, hereinafter referred to as Injunctions of Islam, and existing law shall be brought into conformity with such Injunctions.'[13]

Although Article 198 was qualified by the words 'Nothing in this Article shall affect the personal laws of non-Muslim citizens, or their status as citizens, or any provision of the Constitution',[14] it was enough for the Islamists to continue pressing for further Islamization, including limiting the rights of non-Muslims according to the various orthodox interpretations of Islam.

After imposing martial law, Pakistan's first military ruler, General Ayub Khan, arbitrarily framed a new Constitution for Pakistan in 1962. His only secular gesture was to initially refer to the country as the 'Republic of Pakistan', though later he reverted to the nomenclature of 'Islamic Republic of Pakistan'. Like the 1956 Constitution, the new basic law also included several 'Islamic provisions' and restricted the office of president to Muslims. A Council of Islamic Ideology was assigned the task of recommending to the government how to bring all laws 'in conformity with (the) Quran and Sunna'.[15]

From the perspective of Pakistan's religious minorities, Ayub's self-styled benevolent authoritarianism offered little relief against the tide of intolerance that had engulfed the country since Partition. The minorities' treatment now depended on the dictator's view of each community. Circumstances improved somewhat for Christians, whom Ayub did not view as a threat to the state, resulting in some of their co-religionists gaining senior positions in government. Anti-Ahmadi agitation was also contained because the field marshal chose not to exclude groups from the fold of believers that deemed themselves Muslims. Pakistan's Hindus bore the brunt of Ayub's particular variety of prejudice.

The loss of East Pakistan in 1971 drastically reduced the number and influence of religious minorities in the country. But the reduction in territory and population did not end the drive for Islamization. On the contrary, Pakistan's leaders persisted in nation-building through religion, rather than embracing inclusive civic nationalism. Pakistan's religious minorities were now more beleaguered than ever. The 1973 Constitution not only retained the Islamic provisions from earlier versions but also added new ones.

Islam was declared the 'State religion of Pakistan' and a promise was made to ensure that 'all existing laws' conform 'with the Injunctions of Islam as laid down in the Holy Quran and Sunnah'. The Constitution declared that 'no law shall be enacted which is repugnant to such Injunctions.'[16]

In addition to appealing to the Islamists with constitutional provisions, the civilian government led by Zulfikar Ali Bhutto also created a Ministry for Religious and Minorities Affairs, which was to undertake programmes appealing to the religious sentiments of the populace. Over the next four years, the imams of Islam's holiest shrines in Mecca and Medina were invited to tour the country in well-publicized religious ceremonies that were telecast live on state television; the printing of the Quran was standardized, and religious schools began to receive government funding. The government also provided subsidies for Hajj pilgrims. The result was that the number of Pakistani Hajj travellers increased from a few thousand to tens of thousands annually.

The Ahmadi controversy also resurfaced and in September 1974, both houses of Pakistan's Parliament passed the second amendment to Pakistan's Constitution, pronouncing Ahmadis non-Muslims.[17] The second amendment of the Pakistani Constitution altered Article 106, Clause 3, which lists religious minority communities, to include 'persons of Qadiani group or the Lahori group (who call themselves "Ahmadis")'. The Ahmadis were the only religious minority who were listed in the Constitution not by the name they use but by pejoratives applied to them by their detractors. It was akin to a predominantly Protestant Christian country describing Catholics as 'Papists' in its fundamental law.

Moreover, a new clause that attempted to define 'Muslim' was added to Article 260 of the Constitution, transforming a purely religious question into a matter of law. 'A person who does not believe in the absolute and unqualified finality of The Prophethood of Muhammad (Peace be upon him), the last of the Prophets,' it read, 'or claims to be a Prophet, in any sense of the word or of any description whatsoever, after Muhammad (Peace be upon him), or recognizes such a claimant as a Prophet or religious reformer, is not a Muslim for the purposes of the Constitution or law.'[18]

But the constitutional amendment created a religious dilemma for the Ahmadis and effectively took away their freedom of religion. Their faith required them to insist that they were Muslims, albeit with some beliefs that departed from those of other Islamic denominations. The law, however, would now deem them non-Muslims. Now, if they stated Islam as their religion on government documents, as their faith dictated, they would be breaking the law.

The government made things even more complicated by requiring all applicants for passports and mandatory national identity cards to sign a declaration if they wanted to be identified as Muslims. The language of the declaration made it impossible for Ahmadis to get a passport or national identity card as a Muslim without denouncing their denomination's founder as an imposter. On the other hand, accepting a passport or national identity card that described them as non-Muslim also ran against the Ahmadi religion.

For the first thirty years after Independence, Pakistanis at least debated the role of Islam in matters of state, even as the political balance gradually shifted against secular and pluralist ideas. Once General Muhammad Zia-ul-Haq seized power through a military coup in 1977, debate was terminated and replaced by arbitrary and forced Islamization. Zia changed laws by decree, imposed draconian punishments based on medieval interpretations of Islam, silenced secular critics, and changed school curricula to pass on his bigoted worldview to the next generation.

From the first weeks of his martial law regime, Zia imposed laws, which he described as reforms, designed to create a Nizam-i-Islam (Islamic system of government) in Pakistan.

Zia's lack of tolerance for other faiths was particularly evident in his general disregard for the concerns of Pakistan's minorities. On 7 February 1979, marking the Prophet Muhammad's birthday, Zia amended the Constitution through a military decree to change the concept of judicial review. Instead of merely judging laws in the light of the Constitution, the higher courts were now given jurisdiction to establish sharia benches to determine whether a law was repugnant to Islam.[19]

Zia's decision to allow the judicial review of laws on the grounds of their lack of conformity with Islam led to a plethora of litigation, with various groups and individuals challenging different aspects of the legal structure. Non-Muslims' standing as citizens was reduced before the courts, and the power of their franchise was also diluted by shrewd alterations to the electoral laws. Although Zia did not hold legislative elections until 1985, he changed the Representation of the People's Act of 1976 to reintroduce separate communal electorates.

Non-Muslim minorities could no longer vote along with Muslims to elect officials to local councils or provincial and federal legislatures. A fixed number of non-Muslim seats were to be allocated in each elected body and non-Muslims could vote for members only of their own religious community. This measure diminished the political influence of non-Muslims, as their representatives in elected bodies did not carry any weight within the major political parties. The Ahmadis, who did not accept their designation as non-Muslims, refused to accept electoral representation as a minority and therefore were effectively disenfranchised.

Using his sweeping powers under martial law, Zia issued a presidential ordinance in 1984 that barred Ahmadis from performing azan (the call to prayer) and from describing their places of worship as a mosque or a masjid. Zia's ordinance went further than the 1974 constitutional amendment in defining the terms 'Muslim' and 'non-Muslim'. The new definition described a 'Muslim' as someone who believed 'in the unity and oneness of Almighty Allah, in the absolute and unqualified finality of the Prophethood of Mohammad (PBUH: peace be upon him), and who does not believe in or recognize as, a prophet or religious reformer to be a prophet, in any sense of the word or of any description whatsoever, after Mohammad (PBUH)'.[20]

'Non-Muslim' was now defined by law to mean 'a person who is not a Muslim and includes a person belonging to the Christian, Hindu, Sikh, Buddhist or Parsi community, a person of the Qadiani group or the Lahori group (who call themselves "Ahmadiyas" or by other name), or a Bahai, and a person belonging to any of the scheduled castes (of Hinduism)'. A second decree, the Prohibition and Punishment Ordinance of 26 April 1984, inserted two new sections (298-B and 298-C) in the Pakistan Penal Code. The new section 298-B prescribed punishments for 'misuse of epithets, descriptions and titles, etc., reserved for certain holy personages or places'.[21]

The new 298-C was even more sweeping. Under this provision, 'Any person of the Qadiani or the Lahori group, who directly or indirectly, poses himself as a "Muslim" or calls, or refers to, his faith as Islam, or preaches or propagates his faith, or invites others to accept his faith, by words, either spoken or written, or by visible representation, or in any manner whatsoever outrages the religious feelings of Muslims, shall be punished with imprisonment of either description for a term which may extend to three years, and shall also be liable to fine'.[22]

The provisions of Ordinance XX made it virtually impossible for Ahmadis to practise their faith publicly in Pakistan. It was a law reminiscent of the Middle Ages, when public profession of faith by a sect other than that of the ruler elicited state retribution. Moreover, the ordinance allowed an Ahmadi to be subjected to criminal proceedings based on little more than the whim of a member of the religious majority. An orthodox Muslim could go to the police and simply complain that an Ahmadi had outraged his religious feelings, and the Ahmadi in question could be arrested.

It should be remembered here that several sects around the world use religious terminology for their leaders that is similar to the words used to describe holy figures of other religions. The Church of Jesus Christ of Latter-Day Saints (Mormons), for example, call the head of their church a 'prophet' and his closest advisers are 'apostles'. Yet the state of Israel does not forbid them to do so for fear of offending Jewish orthodoxy, nor do any of the world's Christian majority states have laws that provide imprisonment and fines for the use of such terminology.

Even though there was no precedent for such legislation in Islamic juridical history, Pakistan's superior judiciary upheld the ordinance in its entirety on grounds that Ahmadis needed to be prohibited from 'posing as Muslims' because they had not accepted the obligation to call themselves non-Muslims, which had been created by the amendment to Article 260 of the Constitution in 1974. The judges of the federal court, later supported by the Supreme Court, reasoned that a threat to law and order had been created by the hostility of Muslims to Ahmadis.[23]

Under Zia's rule, Pakistan's legal system was methodically stacked against religious minorities, and legislation was passed that gravely impinged upon their right to maintain or openly profess their beliefs. Furthermore, the Pakistan Penal Code (PPC) and the

Criminal Procedure Code were amended under Zia's rule, through ordinances in 1980, 1982 and 1986. These criminalized any act that could cause dishonour to the Holy Prophet (SAW), Ahle Bait (the family of the Prophet [SAW]), Sahaba (companions of the Prophet [SAW]) and Sha'ar-i-Islam (Islamic symbols). A simple complaint to the police about any action that may constitute a crime under the dubiously wide-ranging provisions of these ordinances could result in an arrest and trial, leading to punishments of imprisonment or a fine—or both.

It would perhaps be an understatement to describe these amendments and other related legislation as draconian. Article 295A of PPC states that a deliberate and malicious act to outrage the religious feelings of any class by insulting its religion or religious beliefs will be punishable by up to ten years' imprisonment or a fine or with both; 295B makes the defiling of the Holy Quran punishable by imprisonment for life; 295C mandates that the use of derogatory remarks in respect of the Holy Prophet be punished by death and a fine; 298A makes the use of insulting remarks in respect of holy personages punishable by three years' imprisonment or a fine or with both; 298B prescribes a punishment of three years' imprisonment and a fine for the misuse of epithets, description and titles reserved for certain holy personages or places of Islam by Ahmadis; and 298C makes an Ahmadi calling himself Muslim or preaching or propagating his faith or outraging the religious feeling of Muslims or posing himself as a Muslim a punishable crime attracting three years' imprisonment and a fine.[24]

These legal changes enabled bigoted Muslims to persecute, settle scores or otherwise seek advantage against non-Muslims and Ahmadis by bringing false cases against them under the vaguely worded blasphemy law. The march towards Islamization was not slowed by Zia's death and return to civilian rule. One of the legacies of Zia-ul-Haq that found special resonance in this period related to blasphemy laws. In October 1990, the federal Sharia court had determined that 'the penalty for contempt of the Holy Prophet . . . is death and nothing else'. The court directed the government of Pakistan to change the law to reflect its determination and added 'in case this is not done by 30 April 1991 the words "or punishment for life" in section 295-C, PPC, shall cease to have effect on that date'.

Decisions by the federal Sharia court are binding on the government under Article 203-D (3) of the Constitution. The government could have appealed the decision to the Sharia appellate bench of the Supreme Court but chose not to do so. In July 1991, it announced that it had decided to amend section 295-C as directed.[25] Once it became known that the death penalty was the only punishment in cases involving blasphemy or insult to Islam's Prophet, the floodgates opened for the abuse of the relevant provisions. And rampant abuse of these laws was by no means restricted to the authorities, though the police as well as political and sectarian organizations were most often involved.

In Pakistan, bail is restricted in cases involving the death penalty; a person accused under section 295-C would therefore face immediate imprisonment before the case was heard in court. The blasphemy statute thus became a convenient tool for retribution or to gain an advantage against anyone with whom one might have a dispute—regardless of the nature of the dispute.

Soon, there were instances of blasphemy complaints being lodged to force the hand of business rivals or even to exact revenge against someone who had spurned an unwanted sexual advance. Following the directive of the federal Sharia court of 1990, the alternative punishment of imprisonment for life contained in section 295-C became void. The death penalty is the mandatory punishment for blasphemy. No relief seems to be in sight for those charged with blasphemy, who face hostility from a society ever more preoccupied with enforcing religious homogeneity.[26]

Not to be outdone by the federal Sharia court in pronouncing legal sanctions against heterodoxy, the government introduced Ordinance XXI of 1991 on 7 July 1991 to increase the maximum punishment for outraging the religious feelings of any group from two years to ten years. As was the case with Zia's Ordinance XX, this new law was primarily directed against the Ahmadis.[27]

Pakistan's fourth military ruler, General Pervez Musharraf (1999–2008) described his policies as 'enlightened moderation' and often announced reforms that were diluted after initial publicity. For example, he announced his intention to change the procedure for initiating criminal proceedings under blasphemy laws, making it difficult to file false charges.[28] The announcement fell far short of ending blasphemy laws but was nonetheless welcomed by minorities as an improvement. Eventually, however, Musharraf failed to introduce the promised changes after protests from Islamist groups.

Similarly, he ended the separate electorates, allowing non-Muslims to vote and run for office alongside Muslims in general elections. Some seats in Parliament and provincial legislatures were still reserved for non-Muslims and for that purpose a non-Muslim voter register was created. Ahmadis still could not vote because they refused to put their names in the non-Muslim register of voters, insisting that they were Muslims notwithstanding what Pakistan's law declared them to be. Musharraf initially also expressed sympathy for Christians and Hindus and promised the end of religious militancy.[29] But overall, the situation did not improve for Pakistan's minorities during his decade in power.

In the years after Musharraf's removal from office in 2008, Pakistani laws, especially ones that deal with blasphemy, continue to deny, or interfere with the practice of minority faiths. Religious minorities are targets of legal as well as social discrimination. Pakistan has also witnessed periodic organized violence against religious minorities. Instead of developing a constitutional and legal framework that protects minorities, Pakistan's constitutional and legal structures help perpetuate their persecution and discrimination.

10

Understanding the Radicalization of Bangladeshi Society and Politics

ALI RIAZ

AN AUDACIOUS ATTACK ON A café in an upscale neighbourhood in the capital, Dhaka, on 1 July 2016 catapulted Bangladesh into the headlines in the international media. The Islamic State of Iraq and the Levant (ISIL) claimed responsibility for the attack, which cost twenty-nine lives, mostly foreigners.[1] This was followed by a suicide attack outside Dhaka.[2] Although the scale and nature of the café attack were unprecedented, it was not the first time that Bangladesh witnessed an attack by a militant group. Between February 2013 and June 2016, there were at least forty-eight attacks on religious and ethnic minorities, foreigners, liberal activists, authors and publishers reported in the press, some with several fatalities.[3]

Militant groups affiliated with al-Qaeda in the Indian Subcontinent (AQIS) claimed responsibility for twelve of those attacks while ISIL claimed responsibility for twenty-one. These incidents demonstrated that violent extremist organizations have found a foothold in the country; consequently, it was argued in the media and in public discourse that Bangladeshi society was encountering religious radicalism.

Notwithstanding the growing number of violent extremist groups, particularly violent Islamist groups, both local and global, available discussions tend to ignore the rise of extremism of other variants, and other sources of radicalization in Bangladesh. This chapter intends to address this lacuna and calls for an examination of other sources of radicalization of Bangladeshi society and politics.

Adopting a broader approach to radicalism and the radicalization process, I argue that the nature of radicalization in Bangladesh is multilayered. The phenomenon is a result of several related processes, including highly contentious rivalry among two political parties, growing authoritarianism, a constructed binary on national identity and emergence of two contesting social movements in 2013. These have created the space for radicalism, violent and non-violent, in mainstream discourse. While this chapter focuses on various factors, I will analyse two contesting social movements to show the relational dimension of the radicalization process.

Defining Radicalization

Despite a growing body of literature over the past decades on violent extremism and radicalization, particularly after the terrorist attacks on the United States on 11 September 2001, there is yet to be established a universal definition of radicalization. Research on radicalization emerges from the study of two different fields—terrorism and social movements—but these studies seldom interact with each other.[4] Besides, there has been a significant historical shift in the notion of radicalization in the past centuries. In the nineteenth century, for example, 'radical' referred primarily to liberal, anti-clerical, pro-democratic, progressive political positions'.[5]

Donatella della Porta reminded us that 'radicalization historically indicated movements and parties advocating democratic and republican institutions, mostly to be promoted through peaceful means'.[6] But both Schmid and della Porta noted, in recent years, particularly in the discussions on the emergence of 'radical Islamism' in a post 9/11 environment, scholars 'tend to point in the opposite direction: embracing an antiliberal, fundamentalist, anti-democratic and regressive agenda'.[7] According to della Porta, 'recently, radicalization has acquired an ambivalent meaning, denoting in some cases the presence of "nonmoderate" ideologies, in others the use of violent means.'[8]

The growing insistence on the connection, often as a phased progression between radicalization and terrorism, is questioned by several researchers, like Tore Bjørgo and John Horgan,[9] Randy Borum[10] and Peter Neumann.[11] They have demonstrated that there is neither a linear progression between these two, nor are they sequential.

As such, the relationship between radicalization and terrorism is ambiguous at its best; these two phenomena need to be understood individually and identification of the key characteristics of both are necessary. Neumann argues that the study of the causes of cognitive radicalization should not be considered as unrelated to the study of behavioural radicalization.[12]

For our discussion, I will focus on the radicalization distinct from terrorism. In agreement with Schmid, I argue that radicalism has two domains: thought/attitudinal and action/behavioural. In Schmid's formulation, cognitive aspect means advocating sweeping political change, based on a conviction that the status quo is unacceptable, while at the same time a fundamentally different alternative appears to be available. As for the behavioural aspect, the means advocated to bring about the system-transforming radical solution for government and society can be non-violent and democratic (through persuasion and reform) or violent and non-democratic (through coercion and revolution).[13]

Radicalization can be considered as adoption of either and/or both aspects of radicalism. As such, Sinai describes the process 'by which individuals—on their own or as part of a group—begin to be exposed to, and then accept, extremist ideologies'.[14] This is further explicated by Trip et al., who suggest that 'radicalization is a process of developing extremist beliefs, emotions, and behaviours'.

The extremist beliefs are profound convictions that oppose the fundamental values of society, the laws of democracy and universal human rights by advocating the supremacy of a particular group (racial, religious, political, economic, social etc.). The extremist emotions and behaviour can be expressed both in non-violent pressure and coercion and in actions that deviate from the norm and show contempt for life, freedom, and human rights.'[15] In this chapter, I draw on Sinai and Trip et al. in exploring the radicalization process in Bangladesh and underscore the cognitive element of the radicalization.

Radicalization is both a gradual and a relational process; seldom do individuals experience cognitive changes without interactions with other individuals and/or groups. The structural factors, like relative deprivation and social inequality, often serve as an enabling environment rather than the proximate cause of radicalization.' Della Porta aptly insists that 'radicalization stems from complex and contingent sets of interactions among individuals, groups, and institutional actors'.[16] Among the institutional actors, the state remains the most prominent one.

Radicalism on the Margin: 1972–1990

Bangladesh, which emerged through a bloody war and experienced a genocide, is not unaccustomed to radical ideologies and organizations. It inherited radical left political parties dating back to the British colonial era.[17] Some of these left-wing parties (for example, East Bengal Communist Party) espoused Marxist and Maoist ideologies and waged war against the state and civilians whom they described as enemies of the proletariat class. Their appeal gradually waned despite a severe economic crisis and the failure of the ruling Bangladesh Awami League (AL) to address this crisis.

The country also saw the rise of two radical political parties; one was clandestine while another grew out of a schism within the ruling Bangladesh Awami League. The clandestine group, Sorobohara Party (Party of the Proletariat), was dealt with severe state power and extrajudicial measures. The rising popularity of Jatiya Samajtantrik Dal (JSD, National Socialist Party) was met with repression and intimidation, which in turn led the JSD to adopt a violent path. As radicalism gained traction among the younger population, the state responded with force and repression. In January 1975, the ruling Awami League opted to turn the country into a one-party state.[18]

The one-party authoritarian regime of Sheikh Mujibur Rahman (commonly referred to as Mujib) ended in a violent military coup and the brutal murder of Mujib, his associates and family members (except two daughters who were away at the time of the coup) in 1975.[19] Over time, the clandestine left-wing movement fractured into several smaller parties, becoming fringe groups. As the country experienced military rule and pseudo-civilian rule between 1975 and 1990, mainstream politics focused on restoration of democracy through popular uprisings. As is the case with any military regime, the Bangladeshi state became predatory and increasingly repressive. Coercive state apparatuses gained resources and power.

By the time Bangladesh entered the new democratic era in 1991, the Bangladeshi political landscape was dominated by two political parties, the Bangladesh Awami League (AL) and the Bangladesh Nationalist Party (BNP). But various Islamist political parties, especially the Jamaat-i-Islami (JI), also emerged.

Smaller left political parties continued to maintain their presence, like the Communist Party of Bangladesh (CPB), various factions of the JSD, Bangladesher Samajtantrik Dal (BSD), Workers Party (WP), though with little electoral support. Some of them had the ability of popular mobilization. They had made substantial contributions to the restoration of democracy.[20] Despite ideological differences among these political parties, all shunned radical ideas and paths.

Radicalization post-1991

In 1991, as Bangladesh embarked on a democratic process, two political parties, BNP and the AL, emerged as the main contenders for power. Regular elections, the reintroduction of the parliamentary system, the presence of a vibrant civil society and a relatively free media marked positive developments, but there were few efforts to strengthen democratic institutions such as the election commission.

The independence of the judiciary remains elusive, and the horizontal accountability mechanism was not built as the independent anti-corruption commission never got off the ground. More importantly, the rivalry between these parties became increasingly acrimonious. Tolerance towards ethnic and religious minorities and political opponents began to decline, and the absence of good governance allowed economic growth to be disproportionately distributed, resulting in disparity.

Differences between political parties on fundamental issues are not unique to Bangladesh, but these debates began to be framed in absolutist terms. Questioning the bona fides of opponents, and their patriotism and commitment to the country, became the hallmark of political discourse. A political 'zero-sum game' culture took hold and opponents were labelled as 'mortal enemies'. These are markers of the radicalization of social and political discourses.

The rivalry between the two parties, the AL and the BNP, remained not only limited to electoral contestation, but descended into revenge politics. When in power, both used law enforcement agencies and the judiciary to persecute their opponents, with the goal being to annihilate the opponents. The assassination attempt on Opposition leader Sheikh Hasina in 2004 by a militant group which reportedly had connections with the ruling party leaders, and the cover-up by the BNP government, testifies to this attitude.[21]

The AL, on the other hand, framed politics as a struggle between 'pro-liberation' forces and 'anti-liberation' forces, the BNP being the latter. This characterization brought BNP's claim of being a legitimate party in Bangladesh into question, although it was established by a freedom fighter. This framing of the other in polar opposites was being practised even before the 1990s.

For example, 'the Mujib regime had branded its opponents anti-patriotic, anti-secular, and pro-Pakistani ...the BNP painted AL supporters as pro-Hindu, pro-India and anti-Islamic'.[22] The attitude that equates political rival with mortal enemy or an existential threat has proliferated at the grassroots level over the years.

The 2014 election, boycotted by the Opposition, accentuated this mindset among ruling party activists. Aided by the state machinery, they have been engaged in heightened violence against the Opposition activists, particularly the BNP. Events leading to the 2018 election, which was open season for violence against the Opposition by the state machinery and party activists, cemented this attitude.[23]

This political environment of intolerance has created the space for non-state actors, that is, clandestine Islamist militants, both local and global, to emerge within the country. Although the rise of militant groups in Bangladesh has an international dimension (for example, the Afghan war between 1979 and 1989),[24] it has been accelerated by poor governance on the one hand and the growing strengths of radical Islamist parties and groups in mainstream politics on the other.

The intolerant discourse in mainstream politics has naturalized and pushed the boundary further into more radical and extremist discourses in the daily lives and behaviour of political activists and common people alike. It is well to bear in mind the relational aspect of radicalization and underscore the cascade effect of these discursive practices.

Until recently, there was very little examination of the state as a potent source of radicalization of society, particularly in influencing the mindset of citizens. Schmid has noted,

> radicalisation [*sic*] is not necessarily a one-sided phenomenon, it is equally important to examine the role of state actors and their potential for radicalisation. The use of torture techniques and extra-judicial renditions in recent years, has been a drastic departure from democratic rule of law procedures and international human rights standards. These are indicative of the fact that in a polarised (sic) political situation not only non-state actors but also state actors can radicalize.[25]

There is sufficient evidence showing that how the state treats its citizens influences whether a violent group will get any support or sympathy. 'In many historical cases, everyday experiences of physical confrontation with police brought about an image of an unfair state, ready to use brutal force against its citizens. The more the repression was perceived as indiscriminate, the more the solidarity with—or at least the tolerance of—the militant groups increased'.[26]

In the case of Bangladesh, support for militant groups has remined very low,[27] but the growing phenomenon of extrajudicial killings and enforced disappearances has become a potential source of radicalization of mindsets. Between 2001 and 2019, at least 3,844 people have been killed by law enforcement agencies,[28] and between 2009 and 2019, 553 people have been victims of enforced disappearances.[29] The normalization of these killings, disappearances and unlawful, secret detentions provides an opportunity for those who offer radical alternatives to the current political scene and governance.

These developments are reflective of the growing authoritarian tendency of the incumbent since 2011. With the removal of the caretaker government provision of the Constitution, which allowed holding elections under a non-partisan government, the country has started to descend towards authoritarianism. Since the controversial election of 2014, which was boycotted by Opposition parties, the democratic space has shrunk remarkably.

Bangladesh's current state of governance is described as 'authoritarian', where the government 'hounding of the opposition' and 'a pervasive feeling that the ruling AL government has assiduously subverted democratic norms and institutions'.[30]

According to the Bertelsmann Foundation, 'Due to the worsened quality of elections, the formerly sixth largest democracy is classified as an autocracy again.'[31] The ruling party and the government have cultivated intolerance towards dissent and supporters of the ruling party have used draconian laws, like the Digital Security Act,[32] to silence the critics of government. The amplification of unfounded allegations against government critics, vilification of any dissenting voice in the media, including social media, by supporters of the government, which includes journalists, has been normalized. This shows how radicalism has permeated into the society and extremist rhetoric and actions have been normalized.

The Opposition, on the other hand, adopted violence as a means to settle political differences. For example, in the wake of the 2014 elections, the BNP was engaged in violence to halt the election, and in 2015, for more than ninety days, the country was paralysed by a general strike and blockade imposed by the BNP which cost 138 lives.[33]

Similarly, the JI perpetrated wanton violence on several occasions in 2013, when its leaders were sentenced by the International Crimes Tribunal (ICT), a national tribunal established in 2010. The ICT was established to try those who committed war crimes and crimes against humanity during the country's war of independence in 1971. The incidents of political violence between 2013 and 2017—a staggering total of 3,540—and the acceptance of these as normal politics, shows how extremism has become the mainstay of politics.[34]

Relational Radicalization: A Case Study

Two contending social movements that emerged between February and May of 2013, referred to as the Shahbag movement and the Hefazat-e-Islam (HI, Protector of Islam), demonstrate how radicalization takes place in a reciprocal manner, influences the other, and how radical ideas and intolerance can be mainstreamed and consequently influence the rhetoric and actions of various social and political forces.

Daniella della Porta, drawing on the works of Bosi and Davis,[35] informs, 'Within a relational field, the interactions between different groups and organizations can trigger processes of escalation, as groups attempt to outbid each other by the adoption of more radical positions or the use of more militant forms of action.'

These two movements appeared on the Bangladeshi political scene against the background of a tense political environment and serious contention between the ruling AL and the Opposition alliance, led by the BNP, on the modus operandi of the forthcoming general election. The ICT in February began delivering verdicts on cases against those charged with perpetrating crimes against humanity and war crimes during the war of independence in 1971.

On 5 February 2013, one of the JI leaders, Abdul Quader Mollah, was sentenced to a life term. Alleging that the verdict was lenient and reflected a secret deal between the ruling AL and the JI, bloggers and online activists started a sit-in demonstration at a square called Shahbag in Dhaka. They demanded that those accused of war crimes be given capital punishment; they demanded that all convicted be 'hanged'.

Within days, as the protests gained strength, the organizers added further demands, such as the proscription of the JI and confiscating the properties of JI-affiliated business enterprises, banks and other institutions to reinstate secularism as a state principle.

The government moved quickly to coopt the movement, with the prime minister extending support to the participants. The BNP, on the other hand, initially vacillated, then opposed the movement. Ten days later, when the movement seemed to start losing steam,[36] one of the participants of the demonstration, Rajib Haider, was hacked to death near his home. This reenergized the demonstrators, who alleged that the Islamists, especially the JI, had killed him.

However, subsequent 'discovery' by an Opposition newspaper called the *Amar Desh*, that Rajib Haider had previously made 'blasphemous statements' in his blogs, changed the narrative about the demonstration. By the following month, the HI, an alliance of various Islamic organizations, was resuscitated and demanded the introduction of an anti-blasphemy law and capital punishment for the 'atheist bloggers' who spearheaded the Shahbag demonstration. Islamists labelled the uprising and its organizers as anti-Islamic and branded the government as 'atheist' due to its support for the movement.

The political situation descended into violence after another JI leader was sentenced to death later in the month, the JI and its student wing, Bangladesh Chattra Shibir (BCS), unleashed violent protests throughout the country, and the government resorted to unprecedented heavy-handed measures.

The BNP described the police actions as 'genocide', launched scathing criticisms of the government for corruption, misrule and oppression; alleged that vested interests had been engaged in a campaign against Islam, the Almighty Allah and the Prophet Muhammad in the name of the spirit of Liberation War; and questioned the motives of the Shahbag movement and the neutrality of the war crimes tribunal. The reciprocal escalation of rhetoric to outbid each other became evident.

By the time the HI organized a massive demonstration in Dhaka on 4 April, not only had the situation became volatile, but the government had also started to appease the HI by arresting some of the bloggers for allegedly insulting Islam and the Prophet. The government's position shifted from being sympathetic to the Shahbag demonstrators to accommodative of the HI. The HI issued a thirteen-point list of demands, set a deadline of 5 May, and declared the intention of blockading the capital if their demands were not met.

These demands included the introduction of an anti-blasphemy law carrying the death penalty for anyone who 'insults' Islam and the Prophet. Other demands were for an end to the pro-women development policy; a ban on men and women mixing in public; an end to 'shameless behaviour and dresses'; and a call for the Ahmadiyya sect to be declared non-Muslim.

The movement, which was resuscitated to oppose the Shahbag movement, became the self-proclaimed standard-bearer of Islamic values and morality. Ignoring the repeated pleas of the government to cancel the rally and the pro-government activists' threat that they would confront them with force, hundreds and thousands of HI activists, mostly from madrasas, gathered in downtown Dhaka.

The rally itself remained peaceful, but violence broke out nearby throughout the day. The government forces, such as the police, the Rapid Action Battalion (RAB) and the Border Guard Bangladesh (BGB), launched a late-night 'clean up' operation and forced the demonstrators out of the square within less than an hour. The number of casualties remain unknown but were reported to be at least forty-one, which the government denied.[37]

The events that took place between 5 February and 5 May, marked by physical violence and death, perpetrated by the state and the HI activists, began as verbal assaults. But it also generated two contending radical narratives, which brought two conflicting notions of identity and nationhood to the fore.

As the Shahbag demonstrators occupied the city square, for weeks, they continued relentless chants demanding hanging ('*fashi chai*') of the war criminals, which essentially transcended the question of 'justice' and became an obvious attempt to pressure the tribunal to give a specific verdict. The demonstrators also chanted a slogan which openly called for violence against the student wing of the JI: '*Ekta duita shibir dhor, dhoira dhoira jobai kor* (catch one or two Shibir supporters, and slaughter them one by one)'.

Among others was a slogan with an explicit majoritarian element—'*Ami ke, tumi ke? Bangali, Bangali* (Who are you, who am I? Bangali, Bangali)—which insisted on a single national identity based on the ethnic identity of Bengaliness, ignoring the other ethnic nationalities.[38]

These tend to draw a line in the sand on questions of history and identity, contributing to the already polarized political and social landscape. The movement portrayed itself as the 'soul' of the nation. This portrayal bears the mark of exclusivity in the sense that it implies a singular soul of the nation, of a singular narrative of history. By the admission of the Shahbagh activists and global media representations, the Shahbag movement was reclaiming the 'secular soul of the nation',[39] and their demand for 'capital punishment' was to correct the wrongs of the past forty-four years of politics.

On the other hand, during the demonstrations on 4 April and 5 May, the activists of the Hefazat also displayed signs which said, 'The Bloggers is Atheist & Bisbeliver so Kill Him (sic).'[40] Islamists' (especially the Hefazat's) insistence that the existence and actions of Shahbag were un-Islamic, that Shahbag was a representation of atheism, was their explicit claim as the authority on Islam.

Despite Islam being practiced by a majority of the citizens of the country for centuries, despite the fact that various social practices are wrapped up with religious symbols and that there is a growing religiosity among Bangladeshis, the word and concept of 'atheism' was almost non-existent in the public lexicon in Bangladesh. A schism in society based on distinctions of 'believer' and 'atheist' was inconceivable even in 2012.

Granted, a perceived contestation between ethnicity-based identity and territory-based identity, between a 'secular identity' and a 'religion-informed identity', has been a crucial element of Bangladeshi politics, but they never presented themselves as existential threats to each other and it was never insisted by the proponents of these identities that the other must be shunned altogether, as if there could not be an accommodation between the two.

These two movements constructed the 'other' through discourses. Othering 'is the process of casting a group, an individual or an object into the role of the "other" and establishing one's own identity through opposition to and, frequently, vilification of this Other'.[41] The process of 'othering' does not stop at vilification but in some instances, extends to demonization, the threat of physical annihilation and even to physical annihilation.

As discourses intensify the 'othering' and consequent vilification and demonization, groups tend to engage in radical actions. The nature of these radical actions varies—from campaign to demonstration to physical intimidation to assault to war—depending on the perceived nature of threats, the benefits and the strengths, to name a few. In case of both Shahbag and Hefazat, it became obvious, because both intended to do so as a precursor to radical actions. The environment in which the murders of a number of bloggers took place in the subsequent months can be traced back to this extreme rhetoric.

Through selective history and memory, a single interpretation of events from 1971 to 2013 was created and seamlessly woven into narratives. For example, the memories of the activists of the Shahbag movement only had selective points of references—1971, 1992 and 2013—which exclude the expedient moves of the political parties, both the ruling AL and the BNP, which allowed war criminals to be rehabilitated and legitimated in politics.

In an equal manner, the Hefazat-i-Islam's narrative excludes 1971, the war and the heinous crimes, as if the war and genocide never took place. Their point of departure is conveniently post-5 February 2013, only after the Shahbag demonstration emerged. This is more than selectivity as it completely erases the foundational element of the nation.

Reductionism and essentialism are the principal markers of such constructions: for the Shahbag movement, it is the interpretation of 1971, what is summarized as 'the spirit of liberation'. The activists and their supporters have not explained what it means. How a single interpretation of 'the spirit of liberation' has emerged and how the proponents have arrived at that specific interpretation remains an open question.

In the view of the organizers of the Shahbag demonstration, there can be no different reading of 1971. Naeem Mohaimen, previously a strong supporter of the movement, pointed to this issue within two weeks of the start of the uprising:

> A …flattening in the Shahbag discourse happened with Lubna Marium …In a blog post, she had narrated the story of her brother Nadeem, who had fought in the war and never recovered from that trauma. The man who read Marx and Sartre could not handle brutality against a Pakistani soldier that he had witnessed, and eventually committed suicide. But, in the crucible of Shahbag, there is little space for any complexity. To speak even slightly sympathetically about the torture of a Pakistani soldier was to be a "rajakar" (collaborator). As I read harsh comments directed against her online (including a brutal poem by an author I used to admire), I wondered if anyone remembered that the film playing in the background of Shahbag's giant screen was *Muktir Gaan*, and the two women in the singing troupe were Lubna Marium and her sister? History no longer belongs to those who lived it.[42]

Similar points have been made by another activist:

> A large number of the Shahbag supporters have been quite intolerant to anyone who voiced any opinions—whether about the legitimacy of capital punishment, or the banning of Jamaat, or about including other issues in the demands.[43]

A reductionist and monolithic interpretation of a phenomenon and a concept was equally on display in the narratives of the Islamists in Bangladesh, particularly the HI. The literalist interpretation of Islam by the HI disavows the diversity, the syncretistic tradition in the country. Its demands include declaring the Ahmadiyya community non-Muslim. This clearly reveals the unwillingness to accept any variations within its frame of Islam.

The binary frames adopted by the participants of Shahbag and Hefazat were magnified and mainstreamed by the media and normalized by the actions of the political parties. It is this narrative of 'us' versus 'them' which allowed both groups to articulate their demands in extreme terms and create a radical, absolutist narrative.

The Shahbag protestors' insistence on 'hanging' as opposed to underscoring 'justice' represent 'a convoluted emotion that demands "an eye for an eye" or better "death for a death" without critically thinking through the consequences.'[44] One of the consequences is that it creates a mirror image that also demanded 'hanging'—but of the 'bloggers'/ 'atheist bloggers' by the supporters of the Hefazat.

Conclusion

Taking a broader view of radicalism and radicalization, this chapter has focused on various dimensions of radicalism and sources of radicalization of Bangladeshi politics and society. The chapter demonstrated that although violent Islamist extremist organizations, which have proliferated in the recent years, deserve to be closely analysed as examples of the prevalence of radicalism in Bangladesh, they are not the only sources of radicalization. The actors of mainstream politics matter, as does the style of governance.

Our discussion has also shown that not only has radical rhetoric gained prominence in politics, but radicalism has also been normalized and mainstreamed, as demonstrated by the two social movements of 2013. I have also argued that radicalization is not an exclusive preserve of non-state actors. In the available literature, the role of non-state actors, be they Islamists or not, has received attention while seldom has the role of the state been explored.

11

Religious Intolerance in Bangladesh[1]

C. CHRISTINE FAIR AND PARINA PATEL

Introduction

BANGLADESH, WITH AN ESTIMATED POPULATION of 162 million, 90 per cent of which is Muslim, is the eighth most populous country in the world and is home to about 10 per cent of the world's Muslim population.[2] While Bangladesh entered the comity of nations under the leadership of Sheikh Mujibur Rahman (known as Mujib) and his Awami League party as a secular democracy with sharp curbs on Islamist politics, these features were short-lived. In 1975, a group of disgruntled army officers murdered Mujib. After this coup, Bangladesh suffered various coups and counter-coups, ultimately resulting in the seizure of power by Major Ziaur Rahman in 1977.

Zia's government reinvigorated religion-based politics and struck secularism from the 1972 Constitution, replacing it with 'Absolute trust and faith in the Almighty Allah shall be the basis of all actions'. Zia's military regime revised the Constitution to conform with Islamic notions of social justice and introduced '*Bismillahir Rahmanir Rahim* (in the name of Allah, Most Gracious, Most Merciful)' in the Constitution's preamble.[3] Zia withdrew the ban on religion-based political parties, which resumed their activities.

Lt General Ershad, who led the second military regime (1981–1990), continued with Zia's Islamization efforts. In 1988, his government established Islam as the state religion. While democracy was restored in 1990, there were no efforts to restore secularism or restrict religion-based politics until Mujib's daughter, Sheikh Hasina, became the prime minister for a second time in 2008. Three years later, in 2011, her government restored secularism but retained Islam as the state religion and *Bismillahir Rahmanir Rahim.*[4]

Under Hasina's leadership, the quality of Bangladesh's democracy continues to deteriorate. Freedom House currently assesses Bangladeshi democracy at a score of 39 out of 100, which means that Bangladesh is only 'partly free'.[5] Scholars of Bangladesh have been even more critical, arguing that Sheikh Hasina's consolidated seizure of power has rendered Bangladesh an autocratic kleptocracy.[6]

Bangladesh is important for less salubrious reasons as well: it has been a site of al-Qaeda–Indian Subcontinent (AQ-IS), and later Islamic State (IS), competition, both of which have perpetrated several attacks in Bangladesh using local cadres. Additionally, several domestic and Pakistani Islamist militant groups have long operated in and from Bangladesh.[7] At the same time, communal tensions between Muslims and non-Muslims persist, as do conflicts between Muslims of different sectarian backgrounds. We include Ahmadis as a Muslim sect, both to respect their self-identification as Muslim and to align with Bangladeshi law, which has not declared them to be non-Muslim.[8] Nonetheless, the United States still 'generally views Bangladesh as a moderate voice in the Islamic world'.[9]

In this chapter, we explore sectarian and communal intolerance in Bangladesh using a unique dataset derived from a 2017 nationally representative survey of Bangladeshi respondents, which included numerous survey items germane to this study. We find deep support for Sharia among Bangladeshi respondents, including its draconian physical punishments, as well as a strong preference for upon non-Muslims. Bangladeshi Muslims not only register high levels of communal intolerance, but they also evince significance sectarian intolerance.

We organize the remainder of this chapter as follows. In the next section, we provide a brief history of democracy and secularism in Bangladesh. In the third section, we describe Bangladesh's contemporary challenges with both sectarian as well as communal intolerance and violence. In the fourth section, we describe the data and methodologies we have used to assess communal and sectarian intolerance in Bangladesh. Fifth, we discuss our findings. We conclude with a discussion of the implications of this study.

Islam and Democracy: Uneasy Partners in Bangladesh

In 1947, the British divided the erstwhile Raj into India and Pakistan after Muslim League activists demanded a separate Muslim state based upon the so-called 'Two Nation Theory', which held that Muslims could not live with security and dignity in a Hindu-dominated democratic India. The Pakistan that emerged had two wings, East and West, separated by the expanse of India. East Pakistan was ethnically homogeneous, dominated by a Bengali ethnic majority; nearly a quarter of the population was Hindu. In contrast, West Pakistan was ethnically diverse but had less religious diversity.

West Pakistan deployed political Islam to suppress ethnic aspirations in both wings of the nascent state.

After enduring years of economically extractive policies, perduring efforts to deprive Bengalis of the political power their numerical strength and political coherence demanded, their continued exclusion from government and military services as well as brutal ethno-linguistic and cultural oppression, Bengalis began to demand change. Initially, they fought for greater autonomy and federalism within the framework of Pakistan. In contrast, elites in West Pakistan wanted a strong federal government.

When the Awami League contested the 1970 election, it was on Mujib's so-called 'Six Point Programme' that articulated such demands.[10] The Awami League easily won a robust majority of seats in the Parliament, which would position it to determine Pakistan's Constitution in the constituent assembly; however, to preempt this outcome, western Pakistani elites refused to let them convene the Parliament. By March 1970, Bengalis understood that West Pakistan would never treat Bengalis fairly and launched a violent insurrection. The western wing used Islamist militias, including some who were under the control of the Jamaat-e-Islami (JeI),[11] as well as the armed forces to brutally suppress Bengali agitators. Approximately three million people died in the conflict, and millions more were displaced. Many of the perpetrators of extreme violence were associated with the JeI, which aided the Pakistani army in committing atrocities against civilians in East Pakistan. Finally, in December 1971, with Indian assistance, the Bengali freedom fighters (*mukti bahini*) secured an independent Bangladesh.[12]

Neither the war nor the emergence of Bangladesh was a foregone conclusion. Had a peaceful transfer of power taken place and had the Awami League been able to forge a constitution with greater devolution of power and autonomy for all provinces and institute more inclusive governance structures, many of Pakistan's contemporary security challenges may have been forestalled, such as the sanguinary conflict with ethnic Baloch who harbour grievances similar to those of the Bengalis but, because they comprise less than five per cent of Pakistan's population, lack the demographic or political heft.[13]

Because this did not occur and because West Pakistan responded with a brutal military response, Bengalis in East Pakistan, from all social classes and religious commitments, took up arms against the West Pakistan military and their Islamist militant allies in pursuit of freedom. Bengalis who did not join the ranks of the *mukti bahini* provided material support to them. However, despite the broad basis of mobilization, there was 'no debate or consensus on the form of the state that might emerge after the war. The ideological basis of the state was imposed once the country became independent.'[14]

Despite the absence of any consensus on the ideological or philosophical basis of the state, the government hurriedly framed the Constitution in 1972 based upon Bengali nationalism, secularism, socialism and democracy, for several reasons. First, the Awami League embraced these bases of statehood, partly due to Indian prodding.[15] Pakistan came into the international system with a communal ideology, which held that Pakistan was the rightful home of South Asia's Muslims. Pakistan's national ideology was inimical to India's own beliefs, that it was a secular democracy for persons of all creeds. In considerable measure, Pakistan's state ideology not only forged a civilizational opposition to India, but it also justified Pakistan's ill-founded territorial claims to Kashmir.[16]

Second, in 'the wake of military suppression, brutalities, fire and hate, a small group of secular and radical leaders, intellectuals and students selected the symbolism of Bangladesh nationalism'.[17] In this spirit, they selected a poem by Rabindranath Tagore, purportedly composed following protests against the much-detested 1905 partition of Bengal, as the Bangladeshi national song. Third, because Mujib himself was in a Pakistani jail from 26 March 1971, when the crackdown in East Pakistan began, until 8 January 1972, most political leaders were still in Calcutta, where they began forging the contours of the new state.

Consequently, the 'polemics of the exiled leaders, the noises of independence war and radicalism of the freedom fighters were more a language of vengeance, fantasy and escape. Much of what they did were designed to tap deep into the Bengali resentment and rejection of Pakistan, lock, stock and barrel including the Muslim identity which midwife the creation of a separate Muslim state in 1947.'[18]

Finally, due to the collaborationist role that JeI and other Islamist militant groups[19] played in what historians have called the Bengali genocide in East Pakistan,[20] Mujib's government banned the organization, which became known as the Bangladesh Jamaat-e-Islami Bangladesh (BJeI).[21] The role of BJeI in the atrocities committed during the war of liberation remains a contentious issue and explains why many Bangladeshis are wary of Islamism generally and of BJeI specifically.[22]

There was no referendum to secure citizens' approval for these bases of the state due to the hurried nature of forging the Constitution and the lack of national consensus on the lineaments and foundations of the document and the state, despite contemporary concerns about this notion of secularism as a state principle.[23] In hindsight, this posited national narrative had a fundamental flaw: it rejected the simple fact that for most of the citizens of this new Bangladesh, Islam had formed the basis of their identity for hundreds of years.

Those who picked up arms against the Pakistani army did not do so to forge a 'socialist, secular society that diminished the prominence of Islam as a component of the political identity of East

Bengali Muslims, a commonly made *ex post* claim … Consequently, the 1971 independence war did not bring fundamental changes in the structural parameters of Bangladeshi Muslim society, whose contemporary identity and tradition have been evolving since the thirteenth century or much earlier.'[24] Thus, even while secularism, *dharmo niropekhkhota* (religious neutrality), was being promoted by Mujib and his Awami League, religious groups, including the reviled BJeI, opposed it, arguing that it was in fact *dharmohinata* or non-religiousness.[25] In an effort to allay some of these concerns, in 1972, Mujib explained to Parliament:

> Secularism (*dharma niropekhkhata*) does not mean absence of religion. Muslims will observe their religion and nobody in this state has the power to prevent that. Hindus will observe their religion and nobody has the power to prevent that. Buddhists and Christians will observe their respective religions and nobody can brent that. Our only objection is that nobody will be allowed to use religion as a political weapon.[26]

In other words, secularism in Bangladesh in this period is best understood as multi-theocracy.[27]

Despite being the party that birthed Bangladesh, the Awami League's popularity was short-lived because it was unable to contend with corruption, slow economic growth and general incompetence. Corrupt elections in 1973, a fragmented opposition movement, complicit legislators and the presence of an elite paramilitary force called Jatiya Rakkhi Bahini allowed the AL to remain in power despite declining support for the AL and the secular values it claimed to espouse. Over time, the resurgent importance of Bangladeshis' personal identity as Muslim made it difficult for the government to maintain its commitment to secularism.[28] While secularism allowed citizens to separate their identities as Bangladeshis (distinct from Bengalis in India) on the one hand and as Muslims on the other, it did not eliminate the importance of personal faith, and openly criticizing Islam was politically unpopular.[29]

The role of Islam deepened as Mujib sought to secure the support of other Muslim countries, the majority of which warily viewed the Bengali freedom effort as an effort to destroy Pakistan and divide the Muslim world. Mujib needed this external assistance to help develop Bangladesh's flagging economy and to prop up his legitimacy at home. In 1973, Mujib mustered considerable efforts during a meeting of the Non-Aligned Movement in Algiers to obtain formal recognition from and the eventual support of several Arab countries.[30] His efforts to emplace Bangladesh in the comity of Islamic states further fructified when Bangladesh was included in the Organization of the Islamic Conference and participated in its second summit in Lahore in 1974.

While the support of Saudi Arabia remained elusive, by the eve of the summit, Bangladesh had been recognized by Pakistan, Iran and Turkey.[31] Wary of losing newfound aid from the so-called Islamic bloc, Mujib's government abjured criticizing Islam aggressively and became more permissive of Islamist movements. The possibilities of employment for Bangladeshi expatriate labour in oil-rich Gulf states and the remittances such opportunities afforded buttressed these attitudes further. Despite the efforts of some Bangladeshi politicians to firmly embed secularism in Bangladeshi society and systems of education, Bangladeshis increasingly viewed secularism as being synonymous with dishonouring Islam and tantamount to dependence upon India.[32]

Despite Mujib's efforts to shore up the country's economy and secure external support, fragmented opposition movements—which often operated through the aforementioned aid, charity or relief organizations—consolidated as public support for secularism, the AL generally and Mujib in particular—declined.[33] Religious schools, the media and the ubiquity of Islam in family and social life subsequently contributed to a growing consensus in support of Islam and away from secularism. Huque and Akhter argue that as scepticism towards secularism grew, 'political parties and leaders competed with one another to be in tune with the society and its rulers, thus strengthening Islam as a factor in the power struggle in Bangladesh'.[34] Mujib was assassinated during an August 1975 military coup. Khandakar Moshtaque Ahmad became president for less than three months before a counter-coup brought Major General Ziaur Rahman (usually called Ziaur) to power in late 1975. He remained in power until 1981.

Bangladesh's external ties to Arab Gulf states intensified under Ziaur's tenure, in part because he believed such support was necessary for legitimacy at home and abroad. To establish more productive ties with Muslim states and to woo Saudi Arabia, Ziaur made crucial constitutional changes. He inserted a clause into Article 25 of the 1972 Constitution that formally stated Bangladesh's solidarity with other Muslim countries.[35] He also reversed the country's secular orientation by changing the Constitution in 1977 to remove the preamble's reference to secularism in favour of the words 'absolute trust and faith in the Almighty Allah'.[36] In 1978, he tried to bolster his government's legitimacy by founding the BNP as an alternative to the AL.

The BNP promoted Bangladeshi nationalism, which was 'explicitly Islamic in character', instead of the secular Bengali nationalism favoured by the AL.[37] However, the BNP lacked both ideological clarity and unity. Instead, it was born largely out of what Siddiqi calls 'the politics of grievance': its followers had little in common except a strong opposition to the AL.[38] The party became enormously influential in Bangladesh despite its ambiguous principles because it allowed the political opposition to consolidate into a party that could oppose the powerful AL. The AL and the BNP have been fierce rivals ever since.

Between 1976 and 1979, Ziaur also legalized religious political parties and allowed the Islamists who had worked with the Pakistani army during the liberation war to participate in government again. BJeI was able to publicly re-join Bangladeshi politics in 1979.[39] The changes were part of a strategy to win political popularity by appealing to Islam. What makes BJeI different from Islamists in Iran or the Islamic State, which believed in coercing their versions of Islamic law upon a resisting population, is that the BJeI rejects such top-down imposition of Sharia. BJeI (as well as the Jamaat-e-Islami in Pakistan) believes that Sharia should only be imposed after a majority of voters vote for the party and their goals of making Islamic law the basis of the state. BJeI is an inherently grassroots organization that seeks to Islamize the country from the bottom-up.[40] It is their overt Islamizing agenda that disquiets more secular Bangladeshis.

While Ziaur's efforts to appear less corrupt and more legitimate failed, he did facilitate the growth of more radical Islamist groups in the country by turning a blind eye to their criminal abuses, both because he wanted their political support and because he feared alienating Islamists and pious Bangladeshis[41] (Singh 2015). By the time Ziaur was assassinated in 1981, reliance on Islam to build nationalism and bolster the government's legitimacy was commonplace.

General Hossain Mohammad Ershad (Ershad), Bangladesh's second military dictator, who was in power from 1982 to 1990, continued consolidating Bangladesh's ties with Muslim countries and extended Ziaur's project of embedding Islam in Bangladesh's governance. Most importantly, Ershad declared Islam to be

Bangladesh's state religion and he denervated BJeI as a legitimate political actor. Ershad even appointed two war criminals from the BJeI (Abdul Mannan and Salahuddin Quader Chowdhury) to cabinet positions.[42]

From the eras of Mujib to Ershad, association with the BJeI did not just grant political legitimacy—it also made it easier to obtain aid from oil-rich Middle Eastern countries. While Arab Gulf state monies helped Bangladesh financially through aid and expatriate labour opportunities, they also financed new mosques and madrasas, the upkeep of old religious buildings, and the general propagation of Islamic values through Islamic social institutions that expanded the presence of Islam in everyday life.[43]

A popular uprising toppled Ershad's military government in 1990, and democracy replaced fifteen years of military rule. Although the leaders of the AL and the BNP had temporarily united with each other and some Islamist parties to bring Ershad down, the fissures between the AL and the BNP quickly re-emerged. By 1991, the AL and the BNP were the two main political parties in newly democratic Bangladesh. They remained intense rivals and their duelling ideologies turned vitriolic.

The BNP was victorious in the 1991 elections. Unfortunately, the chasm between the religious Bangladeshi nationalism propounded by the BNP and the secular Bengali nationalism espoused by the AL widened in subsequent years. Both parties boycotted Parliament at different times to undermine the elected government of the competition, turning to what Siddiqi calls 'violence and extra-legal means' to assert themselves.[44]

Since 1990, Bangladesh's civil societies and political actors have struggled to define the role of Islam within the polity and the state, with proponents of secularism pitted against those who want to see greater formalization of Islam in state and society.[45] With the country nearly split in its support for the two parties, neither party can win an election without coalitions. Electoral politics and Bangladesh's first-past-the post system have empowered the BJeI and other Islamist political parties as both parties have sought to align with them in an effort to secure adequate seats in the national assembly to form the government.[46]

Remarking upon the zero-sum nature of their competition, Riaz observed that 'the relentless acrimony between the AL and the BNP, since 1991, and the pursuance of the politics of expediency, by both parties, enabled the Islamists to rise as a formidable force in the political arena'.[47] Perhaps the most worrying episode occurred during the tenure of Prime Minister Khaleda Zia's bid for her second tenure as prime minister. She aligned with the BJeI to secure adequate seats to form the government.

As kingmakers, BJeI was able to exact two cabinet positions even though it won only seventeen seats in the 350-seat body and garnered a meagre 4.28 per cent of the vote.[48] It was also during Zia's tenure that Bangladesh experienced widespread Islamist terrorism. Analysts such as Raiz contend that her reliance upon Islamist parties like the BJeI, which had ties to militant groups, made her unwilling to take on Islamist terrorism in the country.[49]

Sheikh Hasina and her Awami League won the 2008 general election with an absolute majority, due in large measure to the widespread antipathy towards the BNP-BJeI government and the reign of Islamist terror it ushered. Hasina began to take steps to fulfil several electoral promises. One of her manifesto pledges was the prosecution of war criminals from the 1971 war. In 2009, her government revivified a procedure in the 1973 Constitution for prosecuting war criminals, which became known as the International Crimes Tribunal. In 2010, the first indictment was issued against Mr Delawar Hossain Sayedee, a BJeI leader and parliamentarian.

In February 2013, he was found guilty of genocide, murder and rape during the 1971 war and was sentenced to death. His death sentence sparked protests throughout the country, leaving more than 100 persons dead. In 2014, his sentenced was commuted to life in prison.[50]

Between 2010 and 2018, the tribunal delivered judgments in thirty-four cases against eighty-three alleged war criminals, resulting in fifty-two death sentences.[51] Cases are still being heard and new complaints investigated. The majority of the convicted are from the Awami League's key political opponents: the BJeI and the BNP. Hasina now stands accused of using the tribunal as an effective way to eliminate her political foes as she consolidates one-woman rule over the country.[52]

In 2011, her government moved to restore secularism. This move was facilitated by two Supreme Court rulings in 2011 which declared General Zia's controversial fifth and General Ershad's eighth amendments as unconstitutional and void, restoring the 1972 Constitution's four basic principles of democracy, nationalism, socialism and secularism. The court argued that these 'changes were fundamental in nature and changed the very basis of our war for liberation and also defaced the Constitution altogether', while transforming Bangladesh into a 'theocratic state' and 'betray(ing) one of the dominant causes for the war of liberation of Bangladesh'.[53]

However, Hasina approved a bill that sought to retain 'Islam as the state religion' and the phrase 'Bismillahir Rahmanir Rahim', over the objection of two ministers who opposed this move on the simple argument that retaining them was in violent opposition to the principle of secularism. Hasina defended her decision to retain these two provisions on the basis of 'ground reality'.[54]

Since then, Hasina has continued her relentless war on the BJeI and the BNP with considerable public support; however, she has had to continue retrenching from her commitment to secularism following robust protests by HI, which was a previously unknown Deobandi Islamist movement moored in the country's unregulated *qawmi* madrasas. Hasina quickly moved to not only appease but also co-opt the group, both as a means to quell allegations that she and her party are anti-Islam and pro-India, and to ensure that the organization does not undertake destabilizing activities.[55] This has resulted in what Lorch has described as Islamization by otherwise purportedly secular elites.[56]

Bangladesh's Coexistence Problem

As discussed above, Bangladesh's Constitution embraces secularism as one of the fundamental principles of state policy; however, Article 2(a) declares that 'The state religion of the Republic is Islam, but the State shall ensure equal status and equal rights in the practice of the Hindu, Buddhist, Christian and other religions.' Moreover, while Article 41 protects 'freedom of religion', including the 'right to profess, practice or propagate any religion' and the right of 'every religious community or denomination … to establish, maintain and manage its religious institutions'; these rights are 'subject to law, public order and morality'. In 2015, the Supreme Court rejected a petition challenging Islam's status as the state religion. The US Commission on International Religious Freedom routinely identifies the various challenges faced by Bangladesh's religious minorities.[57]

Communal and sectarian strife has a long history in what is today Bangladesh. According to the 1941 census (the last census prior to Partition), the areas that were to become Pakistan had a combined population of 70.3 million, of which 15.5 million were Hindus (22 per cent) and another 4 per cent which were Christian and 'others'. Of those 15.5 million Hindus, 11.7 million lived in East Pakistan and were overwhelmingly Bengali. While the partition of the Punjab garners the most attention in studies of Partition-related violence, the partition of Bengal into the Indian state of West Bengal and East Pakistan was also accompanied by communal brutality (Roy 2018).[58]

During the chaotic and sanguinary Partition process, Sikhs and Hindus who were living in areas that would become Pakistan were brutally killed or driven into what would be India while Muslims in areas that were to become India were killed or driven into what would become Pakistan. After Partition, many Hindus and Sikhs who somehow managed to survive Partition and stayed in Pakistan concluded that living in Pakistan would be difficult, and they too moved, resulting in fewer minorities in the country by the time Pakistan conducted its first census in 1951 (Zaidi 1988).[59]

According to Pakistan's 1951 census, the overall population was about 75 million, with 33.7 million in West Pakistan and 42 million in East Pakistan. In 1951, non-Muslims comprised 1.6 per cent of the overall population of West Pakistan and 23.2 per cent of East Pakistan. Hindus, who were 12.9 per cent of Pakistan's overall population, were predominantly concentrated in East Pakistan, where they were 22 per cent of the population (Rizvi 1981).[60]

A decade later, per the 1961 census, religious minorities were 10.7 per cent of the overall population of Pakistan, which numbered 94 million. Hindus constituted about 10 million of that minority population, 9.4 million of whom lived in East Pakistan, where they were 18.4 per cent of the population there. In West Pakistan, religious minorities remained steady at 1.6 per cent of the population, the vast majority of whom were Christian (Rizvi 1981; Sanaullah 1962).[61]

After Bangladesh's independence, the Hindu population continued to dwindle for several reasons. In addition to communal violence and ethnic cleansing, Bangladeshi law (such as the Vested Property Act) has permitted Hindu property to be stolen by Muslims.

Additionally, in retaliation for Hindu violence against Muslims in India, Bangladeshi Muslims have retaliated against their Hindu citizens. Consequently, Barket et al. assess that 'over the last 40 years, the relative share of Hindu population declined from 18.4% of the total population in 1961 to 12.1% in 1981, to 10.5% in 1991 and further down to 9.2% in 2001. There was a corresponding rise in the relative share of Muslim population from 80.4% in 1961 to 86.7% in 1981, 88.3% in 1981 and 89.7% in 1991' (Barkat et al, cited by Guhathakurta 2012, p. 292).[62]

According to the most recent Bangladeshi census of 2011, Hindus, Buddhists and Christians comprised 8.5 per cent, 0.6 per cent and 0.3 per cent, respectively, of the population (Haider, Rahman and Kamal 2019).[63] The ongoing oppression and even ethnic cleansing of Hindus in Bangladesh has largely gone unremarked by western scholars (Feldman 2016).[64] Buddhists as well as Christians have also been affected by the ongoing erosion of religious freedom (Akins 2020).[65]

While communal violence has been a long-standing concern in Bangladesh, so is sectarianism. In Bangladesh, sectarianism has had two guises. The first is ongoing violence against Ahmadis (also called Ahmadiyya, Ahmedis), whom many Muslims throughout the world revile as blasphemers (among other equally unsavoury monikers), because they do not recognize the ordinal finality of the Prophet and recognize a nineteenth-century prophet, Mirza Ghulam Ahmad (1835–1908). For this reason, some countries, such as Pakistan, have legally declared them to be non-Muslim and prohibit them from calling themselves Muslim; calling their holy book the Quran; calling their prayer namaz; or their houses of worships mosques, among other similar restrictions. Ahmadis throughout the Muslim world have been subject to harassment, violence and even murder.

Bangladesh has not legally declared them to be non-Muslims despite calls from Muslim thought leaders to do so, but it did ban their publications in 2004 (for this reason, we consider this kind of violence to be sectarian rather than communal). Attacks on Ahmadi mosques and persons are all too common in Bangladesh. Even their graves are subject to desecration if they are buried in a Muslim cemetery, as most are (Human Rights Watch 2005; Kabir 2016).[66]

Sufis are also the subject of sectarian attacks by extremists because they too engage in practices that Salafists abjure, such as attributing to the Prophet Mohammad aspects which are reserved for Allah. Sufis, for example, tend to assert that the Prophet had no shadow as he was made of light. And Salafists accuse them of engaging in practices that resemble worship of the Prophet in the way that Christians worship Jesus. For such Muslims, these practices constitute shirk. For these reasons, extremists have targeted Bangladesh's various Sufi shrines and those who worship in them (Akins 2020).[67]

In addition to the Vested Property Act, religious minorities' religious freedoms have also been affected by the October 2018 Digital Security Act (DSA), which specifically criminalizes activities in the digital space, ostensibly to increase digital security. However, many of the law's provisions limit civil rights, including freedom of expression and freedom of religion or belief. As the US Commission on International Religious Freedom notes,

> While Bangladesh's Penal Code punishes blasphemy with up to two years in prison and a fine, the DSA further criminalizes blasphemy as a nonbailable offense and increases the penalties. Article 28 of the new law prohibits 'Publication, Broadcast, etc. of such information in any website or in any electronic format that hampers the religious sentiment or values.' It further reads that any person or group will be considered to have committed a criminal offense under this overly vague provision if they 'intentionally or knowingly with the aim of hurting religious

> sentiments or values or with the intention to provoke publish or broadcast anything by means of any website or any electronic format which hurts religious sentiment or values.' The DSA sets as the punishment not more than seven years for the first offense and not more than 10 years for repeat offenses.[68]

One notable victim of this law is the Sufi folk singer Shariat Sarker, who was arrested in January 2020 under the DSA after an Islamic scholar filed charges that comments made by Sarker, and uploaded to YouTube after a December 2019 performance, hurt the 'religious sentiments' of Muslims.

The offending remarks included arguments that the Qur'an does not prohibit music and statements he has made against religion being used as a political tool. Sarker was jailed for six months and remains in hiding following death threats. Other Sufi singers, such as Rita Dewan, have also been targeted under this law; she too lives in incessant fear of death threats from vigilantes who have called for her beheading, among other forms of murder.[69]

Data and Analytical Methods

To exposit sectarian and communal intolerance in Bangladesh, we employ survey data derived from a face-to-face, nationally representative survey of 4,067 Bangladeshis (547 of whom were non-Muslim), fielded in Bangla (Bengali), which is the country's national language, by gender-appropriate teams. The survey was conducted under IRB supervision on behalf of the United States Agency for International Development (USAID) and executed by the RESOLVE NETWORK, under the auspices of the United States Institute of Peace (USIP).

The survey effort was led by two co-principal investigators (C. Christine Fair and Ali Riaz), who developed the instrument, oversaw the quality control of the translation, identified and worked with a highly regarded Bangladeshi survey firm (which wishes to remain un-named due to Bangladesh's political environment) to conduct focus groups about the instrument and pre-test it to ensure that it performed as expected. The instrument collected demographic information for the respondents as well as their beliefs about an array of issues including religion, governance and violent extremism. The firm conducted the survey between 12 and 30 April 2017. For this analysis, we use only the Muslim respondents.

The local contractor, who wishes to remain anonymous given the hostile climate for such research in Bangladesh, employed a stratified random sampling design that was nationally representative at division levels (Bangladesh has eight divisions). Sample ratios were 50 per cent male and 50 per cent female and 75 per cent rural and 25 per cent urban, which are in accord with the 2011 Bangladesh Population Census. Samples at the division level were assigned in line with the proportionate distribution of the population, including religion, as provided by the 2011 Census (Bangladesh Bureau of Statistics). The survey response rate was 70 per cent, which is similar to comparable surveys in Bangladesh which have a recorded response rate of 75 per cent.

The study team originally sought to sample 8,000 respondents; however, nearly halfway through the survey effort, local authorities objected to survey questions about the Bangladesh Jamaat-e-Islami and insisted that those be removed as a condition of permitting the study to continue. The team discontinued further enrolments, both for scientific reasons and because the distribution of the sample that had been collected was representative of Bangladesh's eight administrative divisions with reference to gender, religion and urban/rural residence.

The original margin of error for the survey, with a sample size of 8,000, was about 1.10 per cent at a 5 per cent level of significance. The margin of error for the reduced sample was 1.54 per cent at a 5 per cent level of significance. While the resultant sample is smaller than planned, it is still four times larger than other publicly available surveys, including Pew's Global Attitudes Survey.[70]

Variables Analysis

First, we assess several questions about Bangladeshi preferences for governance and religious influence in the same. To exposit respondents' preferred models of governance, we use Q910, which asks respondents about their governance preferences, specifically whether they preferred a 'democratic leader'; 'non-democratic, strong, secular leader'; 'democratically elected religious leader'; or a 'non-democratic religious leader'. These response categories reflect Bangladesh's past and contemporary political reality. For many, Sheikh Hasina represents the category of 'non-democratic, strong, secular leader' (Fair and Patel 2019).[71] The response category of 'democratically elected religious leader' reflects the political philosophy of BJeI, which is to Islamize Bangladesh with the consent of the public through fair elections.[72] 'Non-democratic religious leader', in contrast, reflects the aspirations of the country's Islamist revolutionaries such as the Islamic State and al-Qaeda Indian Subcontinent. Results are in Table 1.

We next use Q178, which asks respondents whether non-Muslims should be subjected to Islamic law. This survey item directly addresses whether respondents accept non-Muslims' fundamental rights, guaranteed in the Constitution, to live their lives per their own religious beliefs and commitments even when they are irreconcilable with some persons' interpretations of Islam. Results are in Table 2.

We use several questions to understand respondents' preferences for religious leadership and Islam in the daily lives of citizens as they interact with the state. For example, Q915 asks respondents 'how much influence should (Islamic) religious leaders (ulema, maulvis) have in matters of political governance?' This is yet another measure of respondents' desire to impose their religio-political preferences upon other Muslims as well as non-Muslims. Similarly, Q970 queries respondent support for giving Muslim leaders, such as imams, 'the power to decide family and property disputes'. This not only speaks to Muslim respondents' desire to assert interpretations of Muslim family law over other Muslims, who may prefer that such matters be referred to secular courts, as well as non-Muslims. Q985 asks if respondents favour or oppose using physical punishments (hudood punishments) such as whippings and cutting off hands for various crimes such as theft. Q990 similarly asks respondents whether they favour or oppose stoning persons who commit adultery, which is another hudood punishment. Results are in tables 3, 4, 5 and 6, respectively.

We use two questions to assess respondent beliefs about the extent to which laws in Bangladesh follow the prescriptions of Sharia (Q175) and another (Q176) which asks them whether they believe that this current state of affairs is good or bad. This allows us to identify persons who want the laws of the country to align more with Sharia and those who want less alignment. Presumably those who want more Sharia are unwilling to concede autonomy to other Muslims who have different political and juridical preferences as well as non-Muslims who are forced to live under a legal regime that explicitly privileges the tenets of Islam (this question cannot address the very robust and often violent difference of opinion about which school of Islamic jurisprudence should be the standard of sharia in Bangladesh. While most Muslims in Bangladesh are adherents to the Hanafi school, there are very serious disagreements among them which cannot be reconciled and have often precipitated violent clashes). These combined results are in Tables 7a–7c.

Second, we employ several survey items that first assess communal intolerance, that is to say, Muslim intolerance towards non-Muslims. Our first measure of communal intolerance is from D300, which asks whether the respondent believes 'Non-Muslims and Muslims should be allowed to inter-marry freely' (Table 8). To understand respondents' willingness to let non-Muslims pursue their faith aspirations, we use question Q930, which queries respondents whether they believe 'Muslims have a duty to try and convert others to Islam' (Table 9).

Presumably one of the most foundational ways of othering of fellow citizens is a belief that non-Muslims will not go to heaven in the afterlife. Survey item Q935 (Table 10) addresses this foundational othering. It asks respondents whether 'Islam is the one, truth faith leading to eternal life in heaven' or whether 'many religions can lead to eternal life in heaven' or 'neither/both equally'. This question speaks directly to the notion discussed above of 'minimalist tolerance'.

Third, we assess survey items for sectarian intolerance, that is to say, intolerance towards Muslims who follow different interpretative traditions. The first question that we use to assess sectarian intolerance is D310, which asks respondents whether 'Sunnis and Shias should be allowed to inter-marry freely' (Table 11). For many Muslims, it is apostasy and punishable by death to leave Islam. To assess Bangladeshi Muslims' support for other Muslims to pursue their own religious interests, we use Q975, which asks respondents whether they 'favour or oppose the death penalty for Bangladesh Muslims who leave Islam' (Table 12).

A second, related question pertains to Muslims' willingness to embrace—not just tolerate—internal differences within Islam. Q940 asks respondents whether they believe 'There is only one true way to interpret the teachings of Islam' or 'There is more than one true way to interpret the teachings of Islam' or 'neither/both equally' (Table 13).

We analyse these survey items principally through analysis of frequency distributions, unless otherwise noted. All empirical results are in the following tables:

Table 1. Tabulation of Q910

Q910: Some feel that we should rely on a democratic form of government to solve …	Freq.	Percentage	Cum.
Democratic leader	1784	51.15	51.15
Non-democratic, strong, secular leader	151	4.33	55.48
Democratically elected religious leader	1521	43.61	99.08
Non-democratic religious leader	32	0.92	100.00
Total	3488	100.00	

Table 2. Tabulation of Q178

Q178: In your opinion, should Muslims and non-Muslims in Bangladesh be subject to the Sharia (or Islamic law), or should only be applied to Muslims?	Freq.	Per cent	Cum.
Both Muslims and non-Muslim	1809	51.86	51.86
Muslims only	1679	48.14	100.00
Total	3488	100.00	

Table 3. Tabulation of Q915

Q915: In your opinion, how much influence should religious leaders have?	Freq.	Per cent	Cum.
Large influence	1460	41.86	41.86
Some influence	1546	44.32	86.18
Not too much influence	326	9.35	95.53
No influence at all	156	4.47	100.00
Total	3488	100.00	

Table 4. Tabulation of Q970

Q970: Do you favour or oppose giving Muslim leaders such as imams, the power to …	Freq.	Per cent	Cum.
Completely favour	1421	40.74	40.74
Somewhat favour	1134	32.51	73.25
Somewhat oppose	406	11.64	84.89
Completely oppose	527	15.11	100.00
Total	3488	100.00	

Table 5. Tabulation of Q985

Q985: Do you favour or oppose punishments like whippings and cutting off of hands …	Freq.	Per cent	Cum.
Completely favour	1944	55.73	55.73
Somewhat favour	687	19.70	75.43
Somewhat oppose	402	11.53	86.96
Completely oppose	455	13.04	100.00
Total	3488	100.00	

Table 6. Tabulation of Q990

Q990: Do you favour or oppose stoning people who commit adultery?	Freq.	Per cent	Cum.
Completely favour	2308	66.17	66.17
Somewhat favour	586	16.80	82.97
Somewhat oppose	250	7.17	90.14
Completely oppose	344	9.86	100.00
Total	3488	100.00	

Table 7a. Tabulation of Q175

Q175: In your opinion, how closely, if at all, do the laws in Bangladesh follow …	Freq.	Per cent	Cum.
Very closely	887	25.43	25.43
Somewhat closely	1547	44.35	69.78
Not too closely	740	21.22	91.00
Not at all closely	314	9.00	100.00
Total	3488	100.00	

Table 7b. Tabulation of Q176

Q176: And, in your opinion, is this good thing or a bad thing?	Freq.	Per cent	Cum.
Good thing	2448	70.18	70.18
Bad thing	979	28.07	98.25
Neither	61	1.75	100.00
Total	3488	100.00	

Table 7c. Tabulation of Q176, Q175b

Q176: And, in your opinion, is this good thing or a bad thing?	Are Bangladesh' Laws Sharia Compliant		
	Yes	No	Total
Good thing	2224	224	2448
Bad thing	178	801	979
Neither	32	29	61
Total	2434	1054	3488

Table 8. Tabulation of D300

D-300: In your opinion, should non-Muslims and Muslims be allowed to inter-marry	Freq.	Per cent	Cum.
Yes	246	7.05	7.05
No	3242	92.95	100.00
Total	3488	100.00	

Table 9. Tabulation of Q930

Q930: Here is a statement. Muslims have a duty to try and convert others to Islam. Do you …	Freq.	Per cent	Cum.
Completely agree	2452	70.30	70.30
Mostly agree	571	16.37	86.67
Mostly disagree	158	4.53	91.20
Completely disagree	307	8.80	100.00
Total	3488	100.00	

Table 10. Tabulation of Q935

Q935: Now I'm going to read you two statements. Please tell me whether the …	Freq.	Per cent	Cum.
Islam is the one, true faith leading to eternal life in heaven	2641	75.72	75.72
Many religions can lead to eternal life in heaven	780	22.36	98.08
Neither/both equally	67	1.92	100.00
Total	3488	100.00	

Table 11. Tabulation of D310

D-310: In your opinion, should Sunnis and Shia be allowed to intermarry freely?	Freq.	Per cent	Cum.
Yes	1404	40.25	40.25
No	2084	59.75	100.00
Total	3488	100.00	

Table 12. Tabulation of Q975

Q975: Do you favour or oppose the death penalty for Bangladesh Muslims who …	Freq.	Per cent	Cum.
Completely favour	1911	54.79	54.79
Somewhat favour	526	15.08	69.87
Somewhat oppose	437	12.53	82.40
Completely oppose	614	17.60	100.00
Total	3488	100.00	

Table 13. Tabulation of Q940

Q940: Now I'm going to read you two additional statements. Please tell me ...	Freq.	Per cent	Cum.
There is only *one* true way to interpret the teachings of Islam	1393	39.94	39.94
There is *more* than one true way to interpret the teachings of Islam	2084	59.75	99.68
Neither/both equally	11	0.32	100.00
Total	3488	100.00	

Results

What do these survey items tell us about respondents' preferences for governance and religious influence in the same? From Q910 (Table 1), we see that while a slim majority (51.15 per cent) preferred a democratic leader, a large minority (43.61) preferred a democratically elected religious (Muslim) leader.

When asked whether non-Muslims should be subject to Islamic law (Q178, Table 2), respondents were neatly divided, with a majority (51.86 per cent) saying that both should be subject to Islamic law and 48.14 per cent indicating that it should only apply to Muslims. Analysis of Q915 (Table 3) demonstrates that a large majority of respondents also believe that religious leaders should have 'a large influence' (41.86 per cent) or 'some influence' in matters of political governance while a meagre 4.47 per cent said 'no influence at all'.

The distribution of responses to Q970 shows that a large majority either 'completely favour' (40.74) or 'somewhat favour' (32.51 per cent) giving Muslim imams the power to decide family and property disputes, with 15.11 per cent completely oppose doing so (Table

4). Large majorities (55.73 per cent) also favour or 'somewhat favour' (19.70 per cent) using physical punishments (whipping, amputations), whereas 13.04 per cent oppose doing so (Q985, Table 5). Large majorities also 'completely favour' (66.17 per cent) or 'somewhat favour' (16.80 per cent) stoning persons for adultery while fewer than one in ten (9.8 per cent) oppose doing so (Q990, Table 6).

Our conjoint analysis of Q175 and Q176 (Tables 7a-7c) assesses respondent beliefs about the degree to which Bangladeshi laws accord with Islamic law or Sharia. On the issue of compliance, respondents were split: about one in four (25.43 per cent) believe Bangladeshi laws 'very closely' follow Islamic law, while 21.22 per cent and 9.00 per cent indicated that laws are 'not too closely' or 'not at all closely' aligned with Islamic law, respectively. The plurality (44.35 per cent) indicated that they 'somewhat' align (Table 7a). Of the 2,434 respondents who indicated that Bangladeshi laws are sharia-compliant, the vast majority (2,224) believed this is a good thing. Of the 1,054 respondents who thought the country's laws were not Sharia-compliant, most (801) thought this was a bad thing.

What do these survey data tell us about sectarian intolerance? Per our analysis of D300, the vast majority (92.95) of Bangladeshis oppose Muslims and non-Muslims freely intermarrying (Table 8). We learn from responses to Q930 (Table 9) that the vast majority of Muslim Bangladeshis are not content letting non-Muslims pursue their faith aspirations, as a vast majority either 'completely agree' (70.30 per cent) or 'mostly agree' (16.37 per cent) that Muslims have a duty to convert non-Muslims, whereas 4.53 per cent 'mostly disagree' and 8.80 per cent 'totally disagree' that Muslims have such a duty.

Consistent with the belief that Muslims should convert non-Muslims, analysis of Q935 (Table 10), a solid majority (75.72 per cent) said that they believe that Islam is the 'one, truth faith leading to eternal life in heaven' whereas 22.36 per cent thought that 'many religions can lead to eternal life in heaven' (the balance of 1.92 per cent did not commit to either position). This finding strongly undermines even a basic level of tolerance for those with different religious beliefs, with most respondents believing that non-Muslims will not go to heaven in their afterlife. This is arguably one of the most foundational otherings that can exist in a polity.

Our analyses show that while respondents are extremely intolerant of non-Muslims, they are also intolerant towards Muslims of differing sectarian commitments, although sectarian intolerance is less severe than communal intolerance. As responses to D30 illustrates (Table 11), Bangladeshi Muslims were more divided on the issue of intermarriage between Sunnis and Shias than they were about Muslims marrying non-Muslims: 40.25 per cent believe that they should be able to freely intermarry while the majority (59.75 per cent) opposed such intermarriage.

A solid majority of respondents (54.79 per cent) said they 'completely favour' and another 15.08 per cent said they 'somewhat favour' the death penalty for those Muslims who leave the faith, whereas 12.53 per cent 'somewhat oppose' and another 17.60 per cent 'completely oppose' doing so.

Whereas we saw the vast majority of Bangladeshi Muslims cannot countenance the idea that non-Muslims will experience an eternal life in heaven, they are somewhat more tolerant when it comes to the beliefs of other Muslims. Responses to Q940 show that a majority (59.75 per cent) believed there is plurality in the teachings of Islam while 39.94 per cent believed that there is only one true way to interpret Islam's teachings (eleven respondents [0.32 per cent] refused to commit to either position).

Implications and Conclusions

Despite Bangladesh's reputation for being a so-called 'moderate Muslim country' with a robust tradition of secularism and democracy,[72] there is very little evidence of this often-lauded moderate Islam. The various survey items that we analyse here show a consistent set of patterns.

First, Bangladeshis overwhelmingly prefer more Sharia in governance of their country and larger roles for religious leaders. They also support harsh punishments which are often called hudood punishments, such as whipping, amputation and stoning. Our survey data show overwhelming support for applying these laws to non-Muslims as well. While the respondents in our survey evince severe intolerance towards non-Muslims using an array of measures, they are somewhat less intolerant of differences across sects of Islam.

There is little in these data that motivate optimism. As our background review of Bangladesh shows, the country's experiments with democracy and secularism were seriously eroded by the end of the 1970s. Despite Supreme Court rulings that vacated the Islamizing amendments under the military regimes of Zia and Ershad, Sheikh Hasina did not exploit these rulings to return Bangladesh to the secular democracy that the 1972 Constitution envisioned. Instead, she has chosen to retain Islam as the state religion and, in her zeal to extirpate the BJeI, she has chosen to patronize an equally dangerous suite of Islamist actors for her own purposeful gains.

About the Contributors

Husain Haqqani served as Pakistan's ambassador to the United States and is director for South and and Central Asia at the Hudson Institute. He is co-chair of its project on the 'Future of the Muslim World' as well as co-editor of the journal *Current Trends in Islamist Ideology* published from Washington DC. Haqqani's books include *Pakistan: Between Mosque and Military; Magnificent Delusions: US, Pakistan and an Epic History of Misunderstanding; India vs Pakistan: Why Can't We Just Be Friends*? and *Reimagining Pakistan: Transforming a Dysfunctional Nuclear State.*

Haqqani served as Pakistan's ambassador to the United States from 2008–2011 and has been a journalist, academic and diplomat in addition to serving as advisor to four Pakistani prime ministers.

A. Faizur Rahman is an India-based independent researcher, and founder and secretary-general of the Islamic Forum for the Promotion of Moderate Thought, which counters, through the re-interpretation of Islamic scriptures, all forms of extremism and Islamophobia in society. He holds a bachelor's degree in civil engineering and a master's degree in Islamic studies. His essays and research papers have appeared in various national and international publications including *The Hindu, The Times of India, Hindustan Times, The Indian Express,* and *Current Dialogue* published by the World Council of Churches, Geneva.

Niranjan Sahoo is a senior fellow at Observer Research Foundation, New Delhi. Sahoo's specialization is in areas of democracy, governance, conflicts and human rights. A recipient of Ford Asia Fellowship (2009) and Sir Ratan Tata Fellow (2010), Sahoo is South Asia expert for the Carnegie Rising Democracies Network, Washington DC, and regional coordinator of Asia Democracy Research Network (ADRN), Seoul.

Maya Mirchandani is an award-winning Indian journalist. She now teaches media studies at Ashoka University and is a senior fellow at the Delhi-based Observer Research Foundation, where her research is focused on 'Preventing and Countering Violent Extremism' (P/CVE), de-radicalization, misinformation and hate speech. Before joining the world of academia, Maya was foreign affairs' editor at NDTV, India's pioneering broadcast news network. She has won the prestigious Ramnath Goenka Award for Excellence in Journalism twice, the RedInk Award for reporting on human rights, and the Exchange for Media Broadcast Journalism Award for best international affairs' reporting.

Neil DeVotta is a professor in politics and international affairs at Wake Forest University. His research interests include Asian security and politics, ethno-religious nationalism, ethnic conflict resolution, and democratic transition and consolidation. He is the author of *Blowback: Linguistic Nationalism, Institutional Decay, and Ethnic Conflict in Sri Lanka* and has authored numerous articles. He has also consulted for the United States Agency for International Development, Freedom House, Bertelsmann Stiftung and Global Center for Pluralism.

Gehan Gunatilleke is a lawyer specializing in international human rights and constitutional law, and a junior research fellow at Pembroke College, University of Oxford. He is a founding partner at LexAG, a law firm based in Colombo, Sri Lanka, and a visiting lecturer at the Centre for the Study of Human Rights, University of Colombo. He is also a former advisor to the Ministry of Foreign Affairs in Sri Lanka, where he specialized in international treaty compliance. Gehan's current research focuses on the relationship between identity politics, constitutional discourse, and ethno-religious violence in Sri Lanka.

Michael Nazir-Ali is a Pakistani-born British Roman Catholic priest and former Anglican bishop who served as the 106th Bishop of Rochester from 1994 to 2009 and, before that, as Bishop of Raiwind in Pakistan. He is currently the director of the Oxford Centre for Training, Research, Advocacy and Dialogue. In 2021, he was received into the Catholic Church and was ordained as a priest for the Ordinariate of Our Lady of Walsingham on October 2021.

Mohammad Taqi is a Pakistani–American columnist and analyst. He hails from Peshawar, Pakistan, and has a long-standing association with the progressive Pashtun nationalist politics in

Pakistan. His columns have appeared in Pakistan, India and the US. Taqi's focus include Pakistan, Afghanistan and US affairs, culture and religion. He is currently based in Florida.

Ali Riaz is a distinguished professor of political science at Illinois State University, USA, and a nonresident senior fellow of the Atlantic Council. His primary area of interests are South Asian politics, democratization, violent extremism, political Islam, and Bangladeshi politics. His recent publications include *More than Meets the Eye: Essays on Bangladeshi Politics* (2022), *Voting in A Hybrid Regime: Explaining the 2018 Bangladeshi Election* (2019), and an edited volume, *Religion and Politics in South Asia* (2021).

Parina Patel is an associate teaching professor in the Edmund A. Walsh School of Foreign Service at Georgetown University. She holds a PhD in political science and a MS in statistics. Her recent collaborations can be found in academic journals including *Politics and Religion*, *Democraziation*, *Political Science Quarterly* and *Small Wars and Insurgency*.

Christine Fair C. Christine Fair is a professor in the security studies programme, Edmund A. Walsh School of Foreign Service, Georgetown University. She previously served as a senior political scientist with the RAND Corporation, a political officer with the United Nations Assistance Mission to Afghanistan in Kabul, and a senior research associate at the United States Institute of Peace. She has authored, co-authored and co-edited several books, including *In Their Own Words: Understanding Lashkar-e-Tayyaba* (2019), *Pakistan's Enduring Challenges* (2015), *Fighting* *to the End: The Pakistan Army's Way of War* (2014), *Policing Insurgencies: Cops as Counterinsurgents* (2014); *Political Islam and Governance in Bangladesh* (2010); *Treading on Hallowed Ground: Counterinsurgency Operations in Sacred Spaces* (2008); *The Madrassah Challenge: Militancy and Religious Education in Pakistan* (2008), and *The Cuisines of the Axis of Evil and Other Irritating States* (2008), among others.

Notes

Introduction

1. Conrad Hackett, 'By 2050, India to have world's largest populations of Hindus and Muslims', Pew Research Center, 21 April 2015, https://www.pewresearch.org/fact-tank/2015/04/21/by-2050-india-to-have-worlds-largest-populations-of-hindus-and-muslims/
2. 'Citizenship Amendment Bill: India's new "anti-Muslim" law explained', BBC News, 11 December 2019, https://www.bbc.com/news/world-asia-india-50670393
3. Yogita Limaye, 'Amnesty International to halt India operations', BBC News, 29 September 2020, https://www.bbc.com/news/world-asia-india-54277329
4. Jayshree Bajoria, 'CoronaJihad is only the latest manifestation: Islamophobia in India has been years in the making', Human Rights Watch, 1 May 2020, https://www.hrw.org/news/2020/05/01/coronajihad-only-latest-manifestation-islamophobia-india-has-been-years-making

5. Billy Perrigo, 'It was already dangerous to be Muslim in India. Then came the coronavirus', *Time*, 3 April 2020, https://time.com/5815264/coronavirus-india-islamophobia-coronajihad/
6. Arushi Thapar and Zaid Wahidi, '"Unjust and unfair": What three High Courts said about the arrests of Tablighi Jamaat members', Scroll.in, 24 August 2020, https://scroll.in/article/971195/unjust-and- unfair-what-three-high-courts-said-about-the-arrests-of-tablighi- jamaat-members
7. 'Stan Swamy: India outrage over death of jailed activist', BBC News, 7 July 2021, https://www.bbc.com/news/world-asia-india-57718361
8. Haroon Janjua, 'Eight-year-old becomes youngest person charged with blasphemy in Pakistan', *The Guardian* (UK), 10 August 2021, https://www.theguardian.com/global-development/2021/aug/09/eight-year-old-becomes-youngest-person-charged-with-blasphemy-in-pakistan
9. 'Pakistan: Hindu temple damaged in attack returned after repairs', Al Jazeera, 10 August 2021, https://www.aljazeera.com/news/2021/8/10/temple-attacked-in-pakistan-returned-to-hindus-after-repairs
10. Shafique Khokhar, 'Muslim mob attacks a Christian village. Houses looted, men and women beaten and injured', Asia News, 18 May 2021, https://www.asianews.it/news-en/Muslim-mob-attacks-a-Christian-village.-Houses-looted,-men-and-women-beaten-and-injured-(VIDEO)-53169.html '"When the blood starts": Spike in Ahmadi persecution in Pakistan', Al Jazeera, 26 July 2021, https://www.aljazeera.com/ news/2021/7/26/ahmadi-persecution-pakistan-blasphemy-islam
11. 'Hardline Islamist group's followers attack Hindu homes in Bangladesh', Press Trust of India, 20 March 2021, https://timeso findia.indiatimes.com/world/ rest-of-world/hardline-islamist-groups-followers-attack- hindu-homes-in-bangladesh/articleshow/81597987.cms;

12. Ruma Paul, 'Bangladesh violence spreads after Modi's visit, attacks on Hindu temples, train', Reuters, 28 March 2021, https://www.reuters.com/world/asia-pacific/bangladesh-violence-spreads-after-modi-visit-attacks-hindu-temples-train-2021-03-28/
13. Joanna Slater and Amantha Perera, 'At least 290 killed in Easter Sunday attacks on churches and hotels', *The Washington Post,* 22 April 2019, https://www.washingtonpost.com/world/coordinated-explosions-rock-three-churches-and-two-hotels-in-sri-lanka-on-easter-sunday/2019/04/21/a09002a0-63f6-11e9-9ff2-abc984dc9eec_story.html
14. Joanna Slater and Hafeel Farisz, 'After Sri Lankan attacks, Muslims face boycotts and violence', *The Washington Post*, 7 July 2019, https://www.washingtonpost.com/world/asia_pacific/after-easter-Sunday-attacks-muslims-face-boycotts-and-violence-in-sri-lanka/2019/07/06/3e4a405a-91f6-11e9-956a-88c291ab5c38_story.html
15. 'Sri Lanka to allow COVID burials for Muslims after outcry', Al Jazeera, 10 February 2021, https://www.aljazeera.com/news/2021/2/10/sri-lanka-allows-first-covid-burial
16. Farzana Haniffa, 'What is behind the anti-Muslim measures in Sri Lanka?', Al Jazeera, 12 April 2021, https://www.aljazeera.com/opinions/2021/4/12/what-is-behind-the-anti-muslim-measures-in-sri-lanka

1: Religious Majoritarianism in a Diverse Region

1. Angana P. Chatterji, Thomas Blom Hansen and Christophe Jaffrelot, eds., *Majoritarian State: How Hindu Nationalism is Changing India* (New Delhi: HarperCollins India, 2019).
2. India Population Census, Census of India, https://censusindia.gov.in/census.website/.
3. '2020 Report on international religious freedom: India', Office of International Religious Freedom, Department of State, May 2021.

4. Nafisa Hoodbhoy, 'Pakistan's religious minorities say they were undercounted in census', Voice of America, 1 July 2021, https://www.voanews.com/a/extremism-watch_pakistans-religious- minorities-say-they-were-undercounted-census/6207724.html.
5. '2020 Report on international religious freedom: Pakistan', Office of International Religious Freedom, Department of State, May 2021.
6. Ibid.
7. 'Eight-year-old becomes youngest person charged with blasphemy in Pakistan,' *The Guardian*, 9 August 2021, https://www.theguardian.com/global-development/2021/aug/09/eight-year-old-becomes-youngest-person-charged-with-blasphemy-in-pakistan
8. Ibid.
9. '2020 Report on international religious freedom: Bangladesh', Office of International Religious Freedom, Department of State, May 2021.
10. Ibid.
11. Ibid.
12. Ibid.
13. Ibid.
14. Ibid.
15. '2020 Report on international religious freedom: Sri Lanka', Office of International Religious Freedom, Department of State, May 2021.
16. Ibid.
17. Sunil Khilnani, *The Idea of India* (New York: Farrar, Straus, Giroux, 1997): pp. 5–9.
18. Kanchan Chandra, 'The triumph of Hindu majoritarianism: A requiem for an old idea of India', Foreign Affairs, 23 November 2018, https://www.foreignaffairs.com/articles/india/2018-11-23/triumph-hindu-majoritarianism

19. V.D. Savarkar, 'Hindutva: Who is a Hindu?' (Bombay: S.S. Savarkar, 1925).
20. Ibid, p. 83.
21. M.S. Golwalkar, *We or Our Nationhood Defined* (Nagpur: Bharat Publications, 1939), p. 100.
22. Ibid, p. 5.
23. Ibid, p. 51.
24. Tora Agarwala, 'CAA, NRC not a Hindu-Muslim issue, says RSS chief Mohan Bhagwat', *The Indian Express*, 21 July 2021, https://economictimes.indiatimes.com/news/politics-and-nation/caa-nrc-nothing-to-do-with-hindu-muslim-divide-rss-chief-mohan-bhagwat/articleshow/84611043.cms
25. Chatterji, *Majoritarian State*, 2019.
26. Kanchan Chandra, 'The triumph of Hindu majoritarianism', *ForeignAffairs*, 23 November 2018, https://www.foreignaffairs.com/articles/india/2018-11-23/triumph-hindu-majoritarianism.
27. Jawaharlal Nehru on discussion on citizenship, Constituent Assembly of India Debates (Proceedings), Volume 9, 12 August 1949, http://cadindia.clpr.org.in/ constitution_assembly_debates/volume/9/1949-08-12
28. '2020 Report on international religious freedom: India', Office of International Religious Freedom, Department of State, May 2021.
29. Faisal Devji, *Muslim Zion: Pakistan as a Political Idea* (Cambridge: Harvard University Press, 2013), p. 3.
30. Venkat Dhulipala, *Creating a New Medina: State Power, Islam and the Quest for Pakistan in Late Colonial North India* (Delhi: Cambridge University Press, 2015), p. 4.
31. Muhammad Ali Jinnah's first presidential address to the Constituent Assembly of Pakistan, Constituent Assembly of Pakistan Debates, 11 August 1947.
32. Ibid.

33. 'Quaid-i-Azam lays stress on need for technical training', *Dawn*, 19 April 1948.
34. Herbert Feldman, *From Crisis to Crisis: Pakistan 1962-1969* (London: Oxford University Press, 1972), p. 42.
35. Hasan Akhtar, 'Daily prayer for officials in Pakistan', *The Times* (London edition), 28 January 1978.
36. 'The President on Pakistan's ideological basis', address by President General Zia-ul-Haq at the inauguration of Shariat Faculty at the Quaid-i-Azam University, Islamabad, 8 October 1979 (Islamabad: Ministry of Information and Broadcasting, n.d.), p. 2; Cited in CGP Rakisits, 'Center province relations in Pakistan under President Zia: The government's and opposition's approaches', *Pacific Affairs*, Volume 61, Number 1 (1988), p. 79.
37. Saad Sayeed, 'Pakistan's long-persecuted Ahmadi minority fear becoming election scapegoat', Reuters, 15 November 2017, https://www.reuters.com/article/uk-pakistan-election-ahmadis-idUKKBN1DG04N.
38. Shah Meer Baloch, 'Pakistani Shias live in terror as sectarian violence increases', *The Guardian*, 21 October 2020, https://www.theguardian.com/world/2020/oct/21/pakistani-shias-live-in-terror-as-sectarian-violence-increases
39. Neil DeVotta, *Sinhalese Buddhist Nationalist Ideology: Implications for Politics and Conflict Resolution in Sri Lanka* (Washington: East-West Center, 2007), p. 11.
40. Harshana Rambukwella, *Politics and Poetics of Authenticity: A Cultural Genealogy of Sinhala Nationalism* (UK: UCL Press, 2018), p. 55.
41. Neil DeVotta and Jason Stone, 'Jathika Heia Urumaya and ethno-religious politics in Sri Lanka', *Pacific Affairs*, Volume 81, Number 1 (spring, 2008), p. 35.
42. 'Sri Lanka: Sinhala Nationalism and the Elusive Southern Consensus', International Crisis Group, Report 141 Asia,

November 2007, p. 18, https://www. crisisgroup.org/asia/south-asia/sri-lanka/sri-lanka-sinhala-nationalism-and-elusive-southern-consensus

43. Emily Schmall, 'Buddhist nationalists claim victory in Sri Lankan election', AP News, 26 November 2019, https://apnews.com/article/mountains-ap-top-news-reinventing-faith-weekend-reads-race-and-ethnicity-bf051a4b2673484f8460131a7500b0ec
44. Sanjay Kumar, 'The Rise of Buddhist Nationalism in Sri Lanka', *The Diplomat*, 9 July 2014, https://thediplomat.com/2014/07/the-rise-of-buddhist-nationalism-in-sri-lanka/
45. Barana Waidyatilake and Myra Sivaloganathan, 'Can Buddhist values overcome nationalism in Sri Lanka', Carnegie Endowment for International Peace, 25 July 2018, https://carnegieindia.org/2018/07/25/can-buddhist-values-overcome-nationalism-in-sri-lanka-pub-76922
46. Krishnadas Rajagopal, 'Majoritarian tendencies must be questioned against background of constitutive promise, says Justice Chandrachud', *The Hindu*, 17 July 2021, https://www. Thehindu.com/news/national/majoritarian-tendencies-must-be- questioned-against-background-of-constitutive-promise-says-justice-chandrachud/article35384129.ece

2: Muslimophobia in India—Reasons and Remedy

1. Azeem Ibrahim, 'Modi's Slide Toward Autocracy', *Foreign Policy*, 13 July 2020, https://foreignpolicy.com/2020/07/13/modi-india-anglade-hindu-nationalism-autocracy/.
2. Shashi Tharoor, *The Battle of Belonging: On Nationalism, Patriotism, And What it Means to Be Indian* (Delhi: Aleph Book Company, 2020).
3. '2020 Report on international religious freedom: India', Office of International Religious Freedom, Department of State, May

2021, https://www.state.gov/reports/2020-report-on-international religious-freedom/india/.

4. U.S. Commission on International Religious Freedom, 2020 Annual Report (Washington DC: USCIRF, 2020), p. 20.
5. Ibid.
6. Ibid.
7. Abhishek Angad, 'Jharkhand man dies days after he was assaulted for "theft", made to chant Jai Shri Ram', *The Indian Express*, 24 June 2019, https://indianexpress.com/article/india/anglades-man-dies-days-after-he-was-assaulted-for-theft-made-to-chant-jai-shri-ram-5796230/.
8. 'Every third Indian cop thinks mob violence over cow slaughter is "natural": new survey', IndiaSpend, 28 August 2019, https://www.Indiaspend.com/every-third-indian-cop-thinks-mob-violence-over-cow-slaughter-is-natural-new-survey/.
9. 'India slams USCIRF report claiming it targets minorities', The *Hindustan Times*, 29 April 2020, https://www.hindustantimes.com/india-news/india-slams-uscirf-report-on-religious-freedom-violations/story-FqbIafgWH4MkkQR68QMp1O.html.
10. Suhasini Haidar, 'News analysis: U.S. Commission of International Religious Freedom's report may prompt concerns', *The Hindu*, 2 May 2020, https://www.thehindu.com/news/national/news-analysis-us commission-of-international-religious-freedoms-report-may-prompt-concerns/article31491165.ece
11. Faizan Mustafa, 'The US report on religious freedom in India calls for reflection', *The Indian Express*, 1 June 2020, https://indianexpress.com/article/ opinion/columns/uscirf-report-on-religious-freedom-in-india-anti-caa-protests-gujarat-northeast-delhi-riots-6436322/
12. 2021 Annual Report, United States Commission on International Religious Freedom, Department of State, April 2021, https://www.uscirf.gov/publication/2021-annual-report

13. Syed Sajjad Ali, 'Three youths lynched in Tripura', *The Hindu*, 20 June 2021, https://www.thehindu.com/news/national/other-states/three- youths-lynched-in-tripura/article34869466.ece
14. 'Coronavirus: Islamophobia concerns after India mosque outbreak', BBC News, 3 April 2020, https://www.bbc.com/news/world-asia-india-52147260
15. Gayathri Mani, 'Muslim man brutally thrashed on suspicion of spreading coronavirus', *The New Indian Express*, 9 April 2020, https://www.Newindianexpress.com/nation/2020/apr/09/muslim-man-brutally-thrashed-on-suspicion-of-spreding-coronavirus 2127927.html
16. 'Muslim traders not allowed', reads poster in Indore village; police file case', Scroll.in, 3 May 2020, https://scroll.in/latest/960924/muslims-not-allowed-reads-poster-in-indore-village-police-file-case
17. 'UP medical college principal calls Tablighis terrorists, says they got VIP treatment', *India Today*, 3 June 2020, https://www.indiatoday.in/india/story/up-medical-college-principal-calls-tablighis-terrorists-says-they-got-vip-treatment-1684852-2020-06-03
18. Hannah Ellis-Peterson and Shaikh Azizur Rahman, 'Coronavirus conspiracy theories targeting Muslims spread in India', *The Guardian*, 13 April 2020, https://www.theguardian. com/world/2020/apr/13/coronavirus-conspiracy-theories- targeting-muslims-spread-in-india
19. Jeffrey Gettleman, Kai Schultz and Suhasini Raj, 'In India, Coronavirus fans religious hatred', *The New York Times*, 12 April 2020, https://www.nytimes.com/2020/04/12/world/asia/ india-coronavirus-muslims-bigotry.html
20. Joanna Slater and Niha Masih, 'As the world looks for coronavirus scapegoats, Muslims are blamed in India', *The Washington Post*, 23 April 2020, https://www.washingtonpost.com/world/asia_pacific/as- world-looks-for-coronavirus-scapegoats-

india-pins-blame-on muslims/2020/04/22/3cb43430-7f3f-11ea-84c2-0792d8591911_ story.html.

21. Perrigo, 'It was already dangerous', 2020.
22. 'Islamophobia is rising in India, says Organization of Islamic Cooperation', *The Hindu*, 19 April 2020, https://www.thehindu.com/news/national/islamophobia-is-rising-in-india-says-angladeshi-of-islamic-cooperation/article31383624.ece
23. 'Criminal Write Petition No. 548 of 2020', Bombay High Court, Aurangabad Bench: Cri.W.P. 548/20 & Ors para 35, 21 August 2020, https://images. Assettype.com/barandbench/2020-08/f61e07e4-273b-42fe- 9ead-2de545c33787/Konan_Kodio_Ganstone_and_Ors__v__ State_of_Maharashtra Allied_Petitions Judgment_dated_ August_21_.pdf
24. For full judgment see: https://indiankanoon.org/doc/71965246/>
25. UPSC stands for Union Public Service Commission, and under Article 320 of the Indian Constitution, the commission is, inter alia, required to be consulted on all matters relating to recruitment to civil services and posts.
26. S. Meghnad, 'Powered by Amul and UP government, Suresh Chavhanke asks if 40 crore Muslims got scared of a 30-sec promo', Newslaundry, 29 August 2020, https://www.newslaundry.com/2020/08/29/powered-by-amul-and-up-government-suresh-chavhanke-asks-if-40-crore-muslims-got-scared-of-a-30-sec- promo
27. 'SC stops show on "UPSC jihad": Bid to vilify Muslims with untruths', *The Indian Express*, 16 September 2020, https://indianexpress.com/article/india/sc-stops-show-on-upsc-jihad-bid- to-vilify-muslims-with-untruths-6597662/
28. HYPERLINK "https://thewire.in/communalism/there-is-growing-religious-fanaticism-under-the-cover-of-constitution-rss"
29. Apurva Vishwanath, '3 states, 3 anti-conversion laws: what's similar, what's different', *The Indian Express*, 3 January 2021,

https://indianexpress.com/article/explained/religion-conversion- bill-bjp-7129285/

30. Madan B. Lokur, 'An ill-conceived, overbroad and vague ordinance', *The Hindu*, 2 January 2021, https://www.thehindu com/opinion/lead/an-ill-conceived-overbroad-and-vague- ordinance/article33475179.ece
31. Bhavya Dore, 'Hindu nationalists see Muslim jihad everywhere in India', Religion News Service, 5 October 2020, https://religionnews.com/2020/10/05/hindu-nationalists-see-muslim- jihad-everywhere-in-india/
32. Neha Sahgal, et al., 'Religion in India: Tolerance and Segregation', PewResearchCenter.org, 29 June 2021, https://www.pewforum.org/2021/06/29/religion-in-india-tolerance-and-segregation/
33. Prithviraj Singh, 'If needed, we can kill them'— Hindu seers issue call to arms against Muslims at Haridwar meet', The Print, 23 December 2021, https://theprint.in/india/if-needed-we-can-kill-them-hindu-seers-issue-call-to-arms-against-muslims-at-haridwar-meet/786583/>
34. Letters of Swami Vivekananda, Advaita Ashrama, Kolkata, pp. 379–380, https://en.wikisource.org/wiki/The_Complete_Works_of_Swami_Vivekananda/Volume_6/Epistles_-_Second_Series/CXLII_Friend>
35. Jawaharlal Nehru, *The Discovery of India* (Delhi: Oxford University Press, 1989), pp. 335–336.
36. Roger Ballard, *Desh Pardesh: The South Asian Presence in Britain* (London: Hurst & Company, 1994), p. 64.
37. N. Gerald Barrier, 'The Punjab Government and Communal Politics, 1870-1908', *The Journal of Asian Studies*, Volume 27, Number 3 (1968), p. 528.
38. Neeti Nair, *Changing Homelands: Hindu Politics and the Partition of India* (Harvard University Press, 2011), p. 134.

39. Ibid, p.78.
40. Ibid, p.17.
41. Ibid, p.77.
42. Chetan Bhatt, *Hindu Nationalism: Origins, Ideologies and Modern Myths* (Oxford: Berg, 2001), pp. 25–26.
43. Julius J. Lipner, *Anandamath, or The Sacred Brotherhood* (India: Oxford University Press, 2005), pp. 189–261. Emphasis added.
44. Snigdhendu Bhattacharya, *Mission Bengal: A Saffron Experiment* (Delhi: HarperCollins India, 2020).
45. V.D. Savarkar, 'Hindutva: Who is a Hindu?' (Bombay: Veer Savarkar Prakashan, 1969), pp. 84, 113, 119, 129–131, 134.
46. Ibid, pp. 84–116.
47. Har Bilas Sarda, *Hindu Superiority: An Attempt to Determine the Position of The Hindu Race in the Scale of Nations* (Ajmer: Rajputana Printing Press, 1906), pp. 29–30.
48. Ibid, pp. 433–454.
49. Tony Ballantyne, *Orientalism and Race: Aryanism in the British Empire* (India: Palgrave Macmillan, 2002), p. 42, 172, 177 and 179.
50. Ibid, p. 186.
51. Kabir Agarwal, 'L.K. Advani, the provocateur in chief', The Wire, 30 September 2020, https://thewire.in/politics/the-provocateur- in-chief-l-k-advani.
52. Aroon Purie's interview with Narasimha Rao, 'I don't think any PM would have acted differently under the circumstances: Narasimha Rao', *India Today*, 15 January 1993, https://www.indiatoday.in/magazine/cover-story/story/19930115- i-I-think-any-prime-minister-would-have-acted-differently-under-the-circumstances-says-narasimha-rao-810564-1993-01-15
53. A. Faizur Rahman, 'Seeking harmony and moderation in Ayodhya talks', *The Hindu*, 30 September 2019, https://www.thehindu.

com/opinion/lead/seeking-harmony-and-moderation-in-ayodhya-talks/article29550460.ece

54. 'Babri Masjid demolition verdict: All 32 accused acquitted', The *Hindustan Times*, 30 September 2020, https://www.hindustantimes.com/india-news/babri-masjid-demolition-verdict-all-32-accused-acquitted/story-pEH3vJXWUCxhkfZ44kCnaI.html
55. Manogya Loiwal, 'Ayodhya verdict: Retired SC judge says minorities have been wronged', *India Today*, 10 November 2019, https://www.indiatoday.in/india/story/ayodhya-verdict-retired-sc-judge-slams-final-verdict-1617561-2019-11-10; 'Babri demolition: "Travesty of justice," says Opposition as special court acquits LK Advani, others', Scroll.in, 30 September 2020, https://scroll.in/ latest/974515/babri-demolition-verdict-vindicates-beliefs-says-anglavani-muslim-leaders-left-criticise-order.
56. Alok Deshpande, 'Hindutva is essence of country's selfhood: Mohan Bhagwat', *The Hindu*, 25 October 2020, https://www.thehindu.com/news/citanglamangladeutva-is-essence-of-countrys-selfhood-mohan- bhagwat/article32939866.ece
57. Abhinav Rajput, 'Inside a VHP bike rally for temple funds: Businessman, insurance execs, children', *The Indian Express*, 28 January 2021, https:// indianexpress.com/article/cities/delhi/inside-a-vhp-bike-rally-for- temple-funds-businessman-insurance-execs-children-7164435/
58. Nair, *Changing Homelands*, 2011, p. 55.
59. Ibid, pp. 46–53.
60. Dhulipala, *Creating a New Medina*, 2015, pp. 135–136.
61. Ibid, p. 137.
62. Ibid, p. 144.
63. Ibid, pp. 146–147.
64. 'VHP sees "purpose" in Muslim population growth', *The Times of India*, 7 September 2004, https://timesofindia.indiatimes.

com/india/VHP-sees-purpose-in-Muslim-population-growth/articleshow/842314.cms.

65. 'VHP leader Ashok Singhal's remark "Hindus must bear five children" stirs controversy', DNA, 14 February 2014, https://www.dnaindia.com/india/report-vhp-leader-ashok-singhal-s-remark- hindus-must-bear-five-children-stirs-controversy-1964465.

66. '"Hindutva" won't be safe unless population control laws are made: BJP lawmaker', *Financial Express*, 29 October 2019, https://www. financialexpress.com/india-nangladeutva-wont-be-safe-unless-population-control-laws-are-made-bjp-lawmaker/1749104/.

67. Gireesh Chandra Prasad, 'Explosive population growth a concern: Modi', *Mint*, 15 August 2019, https://www.livemint.com/news/india/explosive-population-growth-a-concern-modi-1565844038431.html

68. 'The Population Regulation Bill, 2019', Bill No XVIII of 2019, Rajya Sabha, Introduced 12 July 2019, http://164.100.47.4/BillsTexts/RSBillTexts/asintroduced/population-E-12719.pdf; Private Member's Bill to Regulate Population Withdrawn in Rajya Sabha', Press Trust of India, 1 April 2022, https://www.ndtv.com/india-news/private-members-bill-to-regulate-population-withdrawn-in-rajya-sabha-2857719

69. Adila Matra, 'BJP rally calls for check on Muslim population, Twitter reacts', The Quint, 15 July 2019, https://www.thequint.com/elections/ social-dangal/bjp-rally-calls-for-a-check-on-muslim-population- twitter-reacts#read-more

70. Utpal Parashar, 'Assam CM tells Muslims to adopt "decent family planning" measures', *Hindustan Times*, 11 June 2021, https://www.hindustantimes.com/india-news/assam-cm-tells-muslims-to-adopt-decent-family-planning-measures 101623348919528.html

71. 'Population control, religion-based population balance can no longer be ignored: RSS chief Mohan Bhagwat', *The Hindu*,

5 October 2022, https://www.thehindu.com/news/national/population-control-religion-based-population-balance-can-no-longer-be-ignored-rss-chief-mohan-bhagwat/article65971011.ece?homepage=true>

72. Nayantara Sheoran, 'Why the 2019 "Population Regulation Bill" has dangerous consequences for India', The Wire, 18 July 2020, https://science.thewire.in/health/india-2019-population-regulation-biangladeshiontion-womens-rights/

73. Gurdeep Singh Sappal, 'Gurdeep Singh Sappal punctures holes in BJP's propaganda on CAA-NPR-NRIC', *National Herald*, 17 January 2020, https:// www.nationalheraldindia.com/opinion/gurdeep-singh-sappal- punctures-holes-in-bjps-propaganda-on-caa-npr-nric.

74. Yusra Husain, 'All Muslim Personal Law Board calls passing of Triple Talaq bill as Indian democracy's black day', *The Times of India*, 30 July 2019, https://timesofindia.indiatimes.com/india/all-muslim-personal-law-board-calls-passing-of-triple-talaq-bill-as-indian-democracys- black-day/articleshow/70456250.cms

75. 'Bihar poll results: AIMIM wins 5 seats in Seemanchal, makes inroad into Grand Alliance's stronghold', Scroll.in, 11 November 2020, https://scroll.in/latest/978199/bihar-poll-results-aimim-wins-5-seats-in-seemanchal-makes-inroad-into-grand-alliances-stronghold.

76. 'Asad visits Furfura Sharif, says MIM to contest in Bengal', *The Hindu*, 3 January 2021, https://www.thehindu.com/news/cities/Hyderabad/asad-visits-furfura-sharif-says-mim-to-contest-anglangal/article33488300.ece.

77. Akshaya Nath, 'Will AIMIM be a threat to Muslim allies of DMK?', *India Today*, 8 January 2021, https://www.indiatoday.in/news-analysis/story/aimim-threat-muslim-allies-dmk-tamil-nadu 1756927-2021-01-08

78. 'Form political party, move to Kerala, leave country: Zakir Naik's survival guide for Indian Muslims amid "suppression"', Moneycontrol, 23 August 2020, https://www.moneycontrol.com/news/india/form-political-party-move-to-kerala-leave-country-zakir-naiks-survival-guide-for-indian-muslims-amid-suppression-5743691.html
79. Asim Ali, 'We are the true inheritors of the nationalist legacy!', The India Forum, 17 April 2020, https://www.theindiaforum.in/article/meaning-anti-caa-protests
80. Yogendra Yadav, 'Asaduddin Owaisi's rise is just the opportunity Hindutva politics is waiting for', The Print, 18 November 2020, https://theprint.in/opinangladesddin-owaisis-rise-is-just-the-opportunity-hindutva- politics-is-waiting-for/546837/
81. Kancha Ilaiah Shepherd, 'Asaduddin Owaisi's success in carving out a Muslim constituency will benefit BJP and bleed the Congress', *The Indian Express*, 14 December 2020, https://indianexpress.com/article/opinion/ coluangladesddin-owaisi-aimim-hyderabad-muslims- rss-7103600/
82. 'Hindutva a cultural idea, not religious: RSS chief Mohan Bhagwat', *The New Indian Express*, 13 October 2019, https:// www.newindianexpress.com/states/odisha/2019/oct/13/hindutva- a-cultural-idea-not-religious-rss-chief-mohan-bhagwat-2046752. html
83. Arun Anand, 'Muslims are most happy in India, Constitution ensured space to all—RSS chief Mohan Bhagwat', The Print, 9 October 2020, https://theprint.in/india/muslims-are-most-happy- in-india-constitution-ensured-space-to-all-rss-chief-mohan-bhagwat/520032/
84. 'Most content Muslims are in India … we created a space for them: RSS chief Mohan Bhagwat', *The Indian Express*, 10 October 2020, https://indianexpress.com/article/india/rss-chief-mohan-bhagwat-remark-muslims-hindus-india-6719384/

85. Faizan Mustafa, 'Metrics of world happiness and the Muslims of India', *The Hindu*, 24 October 2020, https://www.thehindu.com/opinion/op-ed/metrics-of-world-happiness-and-the-muslims-of-india/article32932909.ece
86. Rajmohan Gandhi, 'India's victory against divisive politics will come when everyday Hindus say enough', *The Indian Express*, 19 January 2021, https:// indianexpress.com/article/opinion/columns/indias-victory-against-divisive-politics-will-come-when-everyday-hindus-say-enough-7151952/
87. 'Does India belong to only Hindus? Nearly 75% of Hindus say "No", finds CSDS survey', *National Herald*, 14 June 2019, https://www.nationalheraldindia.com/india/does-india-belong-to-only-hindus-nearly-75-of-hindus-say-no-csds-survey
88. Sahgal, 'Religion in India', 2021.
89. Census of India 1941, Volume I (Government of India Press: Shimla, 1943), pp. 98–99.
90. 'Muslim population growth at 20-year low', IndiaSpend, 27 August 2015, https://www.indiaspend.com/muslim-population-growth-at-20-year-low-90625
91. 'Social, Economic and Educational Status of the Muslim Community of India, A Report', Prime Minister's High Level Committee, Cabinet Secretariat, Government of India, November 2006, p. 47, http://14.139.60.153/ handle/123456789/113
92. S.E. Vollset, et al., 'Fertility, mortality, migration, and population scenarios for 195 countries and territories from 2017 to 2100: a forecasting analysis for the Global Burden of Disease Study', *The Lancet*, 14 July 2020, https://www.thelancet.com/article/S0140-6736(20)30677-2/ fulltext#tbl1
93. 'China's two-child policy', Bloomberg, 22 January 2020, https://www.bloomberg.com/quicktake/china-s-two-child-policy.

94. Islamuddin Sajid, 'China planning incentives for more births', Anadolu Agency, 23 November 2020, https://www.aa.com.tr/en/asia-pacific/china- planning-incentives-for-more-births/2053144#:~:text=China%20 is%20planning%20 to%20further,state%2Drun%20media%20 reported%20 Monday.&text=The%20country%20released%20 its%20 five,population%20development%20earlier%20this%20 month
95. 'China population: three-child policy will not "drastically raise birth rate", top Chinese economist says', *South China Morning Post,* 13 June 2021, https://www.scmp.com/economy/china-economy/article/3136890/china-population-three-child-policy-will-not-drastically
96. Roshan Kishore, 'Why India can shed its population obsession', *Hindustan Times*, 23 June 2021, https://www.hindustantimes.com/india-news/why-india-can-shed-its-population-obsession-101624388140227.html
97. Richard M. Eaton, *India's Islamic Traditions, 711–1750* (Delhi: Oxford University Press, 2003), pp. 9–16
98. Ibid, p. 15.
99. Ibid, pp. 19–21.
100. Tony Joseph, *Early Indians: The Story of Our Ancestors and Where We Came From* (Delhi: Juggernaut Books, 2018).
101. Citing a peer-reviewed 2019 paper co-authored by 117 scientists titled *The Formation of Human Populations in South and Central Asia*, and another study titled *An Ancient Harappan Genome Lacks Ancestry from Steppe Pastoralists or Iranian Farmers* co-authored by twenty-eight scientists)
102. Tony Joseph, 'New reports clearly confirm "Arya" migration into India', *The Hindu*, 13 September 2019, https://www.thehindu.com/society/ history-and-culture/theres-no-confusion-the-new-reports-clearly-confirm-arya-migration-into-india/article29409611.ece

103. Joseph, *Early Indians,* 2018, p. 203.

104. Tony Joseph, '"The Indian population is a result of four migrations": Tony Joseph', *The Hindu,* 1 February 2020, https://www.thehindu.com/books/the-indian-population-is-a-result-of-four-migrations-tony- joseph/article30701183.ece.

105. Richard Barrett, 'Beyond the caliphate: foreign fighters and the threat of returnees', The Soufan Centre, October 2017, https://thesoufancenter.org/wp-content/uploads/2017/11/Beyond-the-Caliphate-Foreign-Fighters-and-the-Threat-of-Returnees-TSC-Report-October- 2017-v3.pdf.

106. 'Indian Muslims will live and die for the nation: Modi', *The Hindu,* 19 September 2014, https://www.thehindu.com/news/national/indian-muslims-will-not-dance-to-tunes-of-alqaeda-prime-minister-narendra-modi-says/article6426331.ece

107. 'ISIS failed in India despite country's large Muslim population: Rajnath Singh', *India Today,* 4 June 2017, https://www.indiatoday.in/india/story/isis-failed-in-india-despite-countrys-large-muslim-population-rajnath-singh-980791-2017-06-03.

108. 'Al-Qaeda in the Indian Subcontinent (Aqis): The Nucleus of Jihad in South Asia', The Soufan Center, January 2019, p. 32, https://thesoufancenter.org/wp-content/uploads/2019/01/Al-Qaeda-in-the-Indian-Subcontinent-AQIS.pdf.

109. I.H. Qureshi, *Ulema in Politics* (Delhi: Renaissance Publishing House, 1985), pp. 74–98.

110. Ibid, pp. 113–114.

111. Ibid, pp. 138–139.

112. Ahmet T. Kuru, *Islam, Authoritarianism, and Underdevelopment: A Global and Historical Comparison* (Cambridge University Press, 2019), p. 170.

113. Ibid, p. 177.

114. Qureshi, *Ulema in Politics,* 1985.

115. 'No Happy Diwali No Holi ... you can say Eid Mubarak', Youtube video, 3.30, 24 October 2017, https:// www.youtube.com/watch?v=rjfaZgN3yGQ
116. Internet Hindu, 'Zakir Naik insults Lord Ganesha and Lord Shiva', Youtube video, 4.30, 7 July 2016, https://www.youtube.com/watch?v=cQmmaiF-OPo.
117. 'Darul Ifta', Darul Uloom Deoband, https://darulifta-deoband.com/home/en/H–al--Haram/9850
118. 'No heaven for non-Muslims, only Muslims go to heaven', says Islamic preacher Zakir Naik', DailyHunt, 9 July 2020, https://m.dailyhunt.in/news/india/eng%20angladlish/east+coast+daily+eng-epaper-eastco/no+heaven+for+non+muslims+only+muslims+go+to+he%20aven+says+isl%20angladamic+preacher+zakir+naik-newsid-n197117626
119. 'Are Non Muslims allowed to build their places of worship in Islamic State?', Youtube video, 3.32, 18 August 2010, https://www.youtube.com/watch?v=Qoz4hAPCb8Q
120. 'Dr. Zakir Naik stance on building Hindu Temple in Islamabad, Pakistan', Youtube video, 6.16, https://www.youtube.com/watch?v=ma9DQ0ByIjw
121. 'Dr Zakir's Views on Erdogan converting Hagia Sophia from a Museum to a Mosque?', DailyMoition video, 23.09, https://www.dailymotion.com/video/x7v108h
122. Quran 22:40; 'Dr Zakir's Views on Erdogan converting Hagia Sophia from a Museum to a Mosque?', Youtube video, 3.32, https://www.youtube.com/watch?v=IITaIhDT-2c
123. A. Faizur Rahman, 'Is blasphemy a capital crime in Islam?', *Daily Times*, 14 January 2011, https://dailytimes.com.pk/112436/is-blasphemy-a-capital- crime-in-islam/.
124. Qazi Faraz Ahmad, 'AIMPLB removes controversial tweet comparing Hagia Sophia to Babri Masjid after backlash', News

18, 7 August 2020, https://www.news18.com/news/india/aimplb-removes-controversial-tweet-comparing-hagia-sophia-to-babri-masjid-after-backlash-2765799.html

125. Narrated by an-Nasaa'i (hadith number 3175) and Imam Ahmad in al-Musnad (37/81). Classified as Hasan (good) by the commentators on al-Musnad, and classed as Sahih (authentic) by al-Albaani in as-Silsilah as-Saheehah (number 1934).
126. Quran 11:31.
127. Ibid, 10:20.
128. Ibid, 46:9.
129. 'What is Gazwa-e-Hind & why is it invoked?', *Organiser*, 28 February 2020, https://www.organiser.org/Encyc/2020/2/28/What-is-Gazwa-e-Hind-Why-is-it-invoked-.html
130. A. Faizur Rahman, 'Hindu Rashtra versus Darul Harb', *The Hindustan Times*, 28 March 2009, https://www.hindustantimes.com/india/hindu-rashtra-versus-darul-harb/story-o3lbx8HhvEoMVP3ajXH3lK.html
131. Quran 2:163-164.
132. Yahya Cholil Staquf, 'How to make the Islamic world less radical', *The Wall Street Journal*, 14 January 2021, https://www.wsj.com/articles/how-to-make-the- islamic-world-less-radical-11610665933
133. Sarah Dadouch, 'Saudi Arabia has been scrubbing its textbooks of anti-Semitic and misogynistic passages', *The Washington Post*, 30 January 2021, https://www.washingtonpost.com/world/middle_east/saudi- arabia-textbooks-education-curriculum/2021/01/30/28ebe632-5a54-11eb-a849-6f9423a75ffd_story.html
134. The bharud is an old poetic form used by sixteenth century poets in Maharashtra to compose devotional songs. On most occasions, these narrative songs, or drama-poems, carried double meanings, with the deeper spiritual meaning disguised in meanings at the surface level.

135. Eka Janardan was the pen name of Sant Eknath.
136. Richard Eaton, ed., 'A medieval encounter between Hindu and Muslim: Eknath's drama-poem Hindu-Turk Samvad', *India's Islamic Traditions, 711–1750*, pp. 64–82.

3: Hindu Majoritarianism and Unmaking the Idea of India

1. Christophe Jaffrelot, *The Hindu Nationalist Movement and Indian Politics: 1925 to the 1990s* (London: C. Hurst & Co., 1996).
2. B.D. Graham, 'The Congress and Hindu Nationalism'; D.A. Low, ed., *The Indian National Congress: Centenary Hindsights* (Delhi: Oxford University Press, 1988), pp. 170–87; Gyanendra Pandey, *The Construction of Communalism in Colonial North India* (Delhi: Oxford University Press, 1990)
3. The ideological roots of Hindu nationalism can be found in religious revivalist and reform movements that emerged among educated Hindus in the nineteenth century. Two prominent figures behind these movements were Ram Mohan Roy and Dayananda Saraswati. Although the former was keen to reform an ossified, caste-ridden Hindu religion, the latter focused on reviving religious dimensions of the Vedic Golden Age and promoting Sanskrit as the fount of Indo-European languages. These reformers sought to 'purify' Hinduism, make it look more civilized in Western eyes, and revive its lost glories. This movement later got a fillip from nationalists such as Tilak and Lajpat Rai, who began promoting the idea of a Hindu rashtra. See Arun R. Swamy, 'Ideology, organization and electoral strategy of Hindu nationalism: what's religion got to do with it?' in Satu P. Limaye, Mohan Malik and Robert G. Wirsing, eds., *Religious Radicalism and Security in South Asia* (Honolulu: Asia-Pacific Center for Security Studies, 2004),

pp. 73–100; Christophe Jaffrelot, 'Hindu nationalism: strategic syncretism in ideology building', *Economic and Political Weekly*, Volume 28, Number 12–13 (1993); Ramchandra Guha, *Gandhi: The Years That Changed the World, 1914–1948* (Delhi: Penguin Random House India, 2018).

4. Christophe Jaffrelot, ed., *Hindu Nationalism: A Reader* (Princeton, N.J.: Princeton University Press, 2007).
5. Christophe Jaffrelot, *The Hindu Nationalist Movement and Indian Politics* (New Delhi: Penguin Books, 1999); Swamy, 'Ideology, organisation, and electoral strategy'.
6. Savarkar's writings on Hindutva were in large part a reaction to the pan-Islamic mobilization of the Khilafat Movement (1919–24). Most of his thoughts derived from his deep distrust of Islam and its followers. For him, Muslims, who constituted one-fifth of the population, were loyal to Mecca and Istanbul rather than to India. Through Hindutva, he strove to unify Hindus, who historically had been subject first to Muslim and then to British rulers. See Richard Gordon, 'The Hindu Mahasabha and the Indian National Congress, 1915 to 1926', *Modern Asian Studies*, Volume 9, Number 2 (1975), pp. 145–203; Ashutosh Varshney, 'Contested meaning: India's national identity, Hindu nationalism, and the politics of anxiety', *Daedalus*, Volume 122, Number 3 (1993), pp. 227–261.
7. Pandey, *The Construction of Communalism*, 1990
8. Walter K. Anderson and Sridhar K. Damle, *The Brotherhood in Saffron: The Rashtriya Swayamsevak Sangh and Hindu Revivalism* (New Delhi: Vistaar Publications, 1987).
9. For an excellent illustration of the Sangh Parivar, see Gautam Mehta, 'Changing Character of Sangh Parivar', *The Hindu BusinessLine*, 5 December 2017, https://www.thehindubusinessline.com/opinion/columns/changing-character-of-sangh-parivar/article9983293.ece

10. The Hindu right suspected that Gandhi was inclined to favour Muslim Pakistan. See Guha, *Gandhi*, 2018.
11. Thomas Blom Hansen, *The Saffron Wave: Democracy and Hindu Nationalism in Modern India* (Princeton, N.J.: Princeton University Press, 1999); Walter K. Anderson and Sridhar K. Damle, *The RSS: A View to the Inside* (Delhi: Penguin, 2018).
12. For a detailed reading of Hindu personal laws, see Partha S. Ghosh, 'Politics of Personal Law in India: The Hindu-Muslim Dichotomy', *South Asia Research*, Volume 29, Number 1 (February 2009), https://journals.sagepub.com/doi/10.1177/026272800802900101
13. For a detailed reading of Hindu personal laws, see Ibid, p. 1–17.
14. Kuldip Nayar, *The Judgement: Inside Story of the Emergency in India* (Delhi: Vikas Publishing House, 1977); Pandey, *The Construction of Communalism*, 1990.
15. In dealing with Muslim personal law, in 1985, the Indian Supreme Court, in the Shah Bano case, upheld the lower court's ruling directing Shah Bano's husband to pay maintenance under the alimony provision of Indian law applicable to all communities. This path-breaking ruling created a huge uproar within the Muslim community, especially among Muslim males, which prompted the Rajiv Gandhi government to quickly enact the Muslim Women (Protection of Rights on Divorce) Act in 1986 to roll back the progressive judgment and appease members of the minority community. For more, see 'What Is Shah Bano Case', *The Indian Express*, 23 August 2017, https://indianexpress.com/article/what- is/what-is-shah-bano-case-4809632/.
16. Hansen, *The Saffron Wave*, 1999.
17. Anderson and Damle, *The RSS,* 2018.
18. Together with more than a dozen regional parties, the BJP formed a coalition called the National Democratic Alliance to form governments in 1998 and 1999.

19. Among other things, it invented terms such as 'Hindu terror' and 'saffron terror' to stir up fears about the BJP. For a detailed account, see Padmashree Pande, ed., 'How "saffron terror" was coined: a rundown of 2008 Malegaon blasts', The Quint, 5 June 2018, www.thequint.com/ videos/news-videos/how-saffron-terror-was-coined-a-rundown-of- 2008-malegaon-blasts.
20. Milan Vaishnav, 'Religious nationalism and India's future', Carnegie Endowment for International Peace, 4 April 2019, https://carnegieendowment.org/2019/04/04/religious-nationalism-and-india-s-future-pub-78703.
21. Ashutosh Varshney, '2014, like 1952', *The Indian Express*, 19 May 2014, https://indianexpress.com/article/opinion/columns/2014- like-1952/.
22. For instance, in the Hindi-speaking states such as UP, Bihar, Rajasthan, Madhya Pradesh, Chhattisgarh, Haryana, Delhi, Jharkhand, Himachal Pradesh and Uttarakhand, the BJP won as many as 190 out of 225 seats. In UP, the BJP broke all past records by capturing seventy-three out of eighty seats.
23. The Gujarat riots happened in 2002 when Modi was the chief minister of the state. The state-wide communal riots led to more than a thousand deaths, mostly within the Muslim community. Although the Supreme Court appointed a special investigation team that exonerated Modi in 2012, many accuse him of not taking sufficient action to quell the violence against Muslims. For an update, see Manas Dasgupta, 'SIT finds no proof against Modi, says court', *The Hindu*, 10 April 2012, https://www.thehindu.com/news/national//article60478487.ece
24. However, the saffron party received a major jolt in 2018 when it lost three key Hindi heartland states to the Congress. The BJP's tally now comes down to sixteen states. See also Suhas Palshikar, 'Towards hegemony: BJP beyond electoral dominance', *Economic and Political Weekly,* Volume 53, Number 33 (August 2018),

https://www.epw.in/journal/2018/33/indias-democracy-today/towards-hegemony.html

25. Sagarika Ghosh, 'With Pragya Thakur in the fray, Hindutva no longer needs to wear mask', *The Times of India*, 28 April 2019, https://timesofindia.indiatimes.com/blogs/bloody-mary/with- pragya-thakur-in-the-fray-hindutva-no-longer-needs-to-wear-a- mask/
26. Data have been collected since 2010. See Alison Saldanha, '2017 deadliest year for cow-related hate crime since 2010, 86% of those killed Muslim', The Wire, 8 December 2017, https://thewire.in/communalism/cow-vigilantism-violence-2017-muslims-hate-crime
27. Murali Krishnan, '"Not in my name"– Indians protest vigilante attacks on Muslims', Deutsche Welle, 29 June 2017, https://www.dw.com/en/not-in-my-name-indians-protest-vigilante-attacks-on-muslims/a-39456019
28. Debashis Roy Chowdhury, 'Laws against "Love Jihad" are yet another serious attack on India's once secular democracy', *Time*, 30 November 2020, https://time.com/5915872/love-jihad-india-democracy/
29. Kiran Bhatty and Nandini Sundar, 'Sliding from majoritarianism to fascism: Educating India under the Modi regime', *International Sociology*, September 2020, https://journals.sagepub.com/doi/10.1177/0268580920937226
30. Christophe Jaffrelot and Gilles Varniers, 'The dwindling minority', *The Indian Express*, 30 July 2018, https://indianexpress.com/article/opinion/columns/muslims-politicians-in-india-angladeendra-modi-government-5282128/
31. Rasheed Kidwai, 'Need for CVE program to engage with Muslim community', ORF Analysis, 20 June 2018, www.orfonline.org/expert-speak/need-for-major-cve-programme-to-engage-with- muslim-community/

32. '2019 Lok Sabha election results: Only 27 Muslim MPs elected to Parliament, none from the BJP', Scroll.in, 24 May 2019, https://scroll.in/ latest/924627/2019-lok-sabha-election-results-only-24-muslim- mps-elected-to-parliament-none-from-the-bjp.
33. Safoora, 'Saumitra Khan lone Muslim face of BJP, community number goes up to 27', *The Siasat Daily*, 26 May 2019, https://www.siasat.com/saumitra-khan-lone-muslim-face-bjp-community-number- goes-27-1500532/
34. Nissim Mannathukkaren, 'The fast disappearing Muslim in the Indian republic', *The Indian Express*, 22 January 2018, https://indianexpress.com/article/opinion/the-fast-disappearing-muslim- in-the-indian-republic-bjp-mla-hindu-saffron-religion-5034205/
35. Prabhash K. Dutt, 'Triple Talaq Bill in Rajya Sabha: Do you know why it is controversial', *India Today*, 30 July 2019, https://www.indiatoday.in/news-analysis/story/triple-talaq-bill-in-rajya-sabha- do-you-know-why-it-is-controversial-1575100-2019-07-30.
36. Milan Vaishnav, op cit.
37. 'Article 370 no more: BJP on way to fulfill its long-standing promise', *The Economic Times*, 5 August 2019, https://economictimes.indiaangladeshtimes.com/news/politics-andnation/article-370-no-more-bjp-on-the-way-to-fulfill-its-long-standing-promise/ articleshow/70531929.cms
38. Pooja Changoiwala, 'India's Muslims are terrified of being deported', *Foreign Policy*, 21 February 2020, https://foreignpolicy.com/2020/02/21/india-muslims-deported-terrified-citizenship-amendment-act-caa/
39. 'Citizenship Amendment Bill: India's new anti-Muslim law explained', BBC, 11 December 2019, https://www.bbc.com/news/world-asia-india-50670393.
40. See Pallavi Ghosh, 'From flag is my religion to Shiv Bhakt', News 18, 20 September 2018, https://www.news18.com/news/politics/

from-flag-is-my-religion-to-shiv-bhakt-how-rahul-gandhi-is-using-hindutav-lite-to-make-a-comeback-1883195.html.

41. Rohan Venkataramakrishnan, 'Despite BJP's defeat is Arvind Kejriwal's huge win in Delhi also a victory for Hindutva', Scroll.in, 14 February 2020, https://scroll.in/article/953046/despite-bjps-defeat-is-arvind-kejriwals-huge-win-in-delhi-also-a-victory-for-hindutva
42. 'The return of identity politics and its hefty cost', Livemint, 10 April 2018, www.livemint.com/Opinion/x42E8WuLHwYaGk1N1DoiiN/The-return-of-identity-politics-and-its-hefty-cost.html.

4: The Indian Media's Role in Fuelling Communal Violence: Media Divides and Hates for Profit

1. Criminal writ petition number 548 OF 2020 on 21 August 2020.
2. Arabinda Padhee, Basanta Kar and Pranab Choudhury, 'The lockdown revealed the extent of poverty and misery faced by migrant workers', The Wire, 16 July 2020, https://thewire.in/labour/covid-19-poverty-migrant-workers.
3. Arjun Appadurai, *Fear of Small Numbers: An Essay on the Geography of Anger* (Durham: Duke University Press, 2006).
4. Noam Chomsky and Edward S. Herman, *Manufacturing Consent: The Political Economy of the Mass Media* New York: Pantheon Books, 1988).
5. Samarth Bansal, 'Narendra Modi App Has A Fake News Problem', HuffPost, 27 January 2019, https://www.huffpost.com/archive/in/entry/narendra-modi-app-has-a-fake-news-problem_in_5c4d5c86e4b0287e5b8b6d52; Piyasree Dasgupta, '"It's Like Frankenstein's Monster": The Founder Of BJP's IT Cell Says PM Modi's Team Started The Rot Prodyut Bora set up the BJP's IT Cell in 2007 under Rajnath Singh's tutelage',

HuffPost, 25 June 2018, https://www.huffpost.com/archive/in/entry/its-like-frankensteins-monster-the-father-of-the-bjps-it-cell-says-team-modi-started-the-rot_in_5c10c957e4b09dcd67fc57bb; Swati Chaturvedi, *I Am A Troll: Inside the Secret World of the BJP's Digital Army* (Delhi: Juggernaut, 2016).

6. 'Misinformation' is inadvertent sharing of false content while 'disinformation' is deliberate sharing with an intent to deceive.
7. Cherian George, *Hate Spin: The Manufacture of Religious Offense and Its Threat to Democracy* (MIT Press, 2016).
8. Shweta Desai and Amarnath Amarasingam, '#CoronaJihad COVID-19, misinformation, and anti-Muslim violence in India,' Strong Cities, May 2020, https://strongcitiesnetwork.org/en/wp-content/uploads/sites/5/2020/05/CoronaJihad.pdf.
9. Aditya Menon, 'Attacks on Muslims in the name of COVID-19 surge across India', Quint, 8 April 2020, https://www.thequint.com/news/india/coronavirus-muslims-attacked-covid19-karnataka-haryana#read-more; Alok Pandey, 'Abused, stopped from selling vegetables, allege Muslim vendors in UP', NDTV, 13 April 2020, https://www.ndtv.com/india-news/coronavirus-uttar-pradesh-abused-stopped-from-selling-vegetables-allege-muslim-vendors-in-up-2210963
10. Maya Mirchandani, 'Elections 2019: Democracy in the face of majoritarianism', Observer Research Foundation, 13 May 2019, https://www.orfonline.org/expert-speak/elections-2019-democracy-face-majoritarianism/.
11. Amulya Gopalakrishnan, 'Dog-whistling, the BJP's art form of choice', *Times of India*, 16 October 2016. https://timesofindia.indiatimes.com/blogs/to-name-and-address/dog-whistling-the-bjps-art-form-of-choice/
12. Neelam Pandey, 'BJP MP says Shaheen Bagh protesters will "rape, kill" as party makes it Delhi poll plank', Print, 28 January 2020,

https://theprint.in/politics/bjp-mp-says-shaheen-bagh-protesters-will-rape-kill-as-party-makes-it-delhi-poll-plank/355438/;

13. Nazia Erum, *Mothering a Muslim* (Delhi: Juggernaut Publication, 2017).
14. Marshall McLuhan, *Understanding Media: The Extensions of Man* (McGraw-Hill, 1964).
15. Mohd. Ahmed Khan vs. Shah Bano Begum, also called the Shah Bano case, is viewed as one of the landmark judgments in Muslim women's battle for rights in India and the fight against the set Muslim personal law. It laid the groundwork for a Muslim woman to make claims for maintenance, which they were not permitted to do previously.
16. Bhadra Sinha, 'In 2017, govt said criminalising marital rape would harm marriage. Now it's reviewing stance', The Print India, 3 February 2022. https://theprint.in/judiciary/in-2017-govt-said-criminalising-marital-rape-would-harm-marriage-now-its-reviewing-stance/819853/
17. Lata Jha, 'Bhajan renditions, temple replicas mark news TV coverage of Ayodhya event', Livemint, 5 August 2020, https://www.livemint.com/industry/media/bhajan-renditions-temple-replicas-mark-news-tv-coverage-of-ayodhya-event-11596628692303.html
18. Manisha Pande, 'Bloodlust TV: Calling out India's hate media', Newslaundry, 12 October 2019, https://www.newslaundry.com/2019/10/21/bloodlust-tv-calling-out-indias-hate-media
19. Shuddhabrata Sengupta, 'Kumbh 2021: Astrology, mortality and the indifference to life of leaders and stars', The Wire, 20 April 2021, https://thewire.in/government/kumbh-2021-astrology-mortality-and-the-indifference-to-life-of-leaders-and-stars
20. The Kumbh Mela is a Hindu religious festival that takes place over several weeks and is celebrated four times over the course of twelve

years at four different pilgrimage spots on four different 'sacred' rivers in India. The spots are identified on the basis of where drops of amrit, or the holy nectar of immortality, fell on the earth after a struggle between gods and demons. Attendees come from different religious sects within Hinduism to take a dip in the river in their quest for purity and immortality. Each site hosts a Kumbh Mela once in twelve years, making the event especially significant for the hosts. In addition, a Great (Maha) Kumbh Mela is held every 144 years at the confluence of the rivers Ganga, Yamuna and (the mythical) Saraswati in Prayagraj (formerly Allahabad). However, Uttar Pradesh Chief Minister Yogi Adityanath had declared that a Kumbh Mela held at the same spot after twelve years will also be called a 'maha kumbh'.

21. Sandeep Rawat, '9.1 million thronged Mahakumbh despite Covid-19 surge: Govt data', *Hindustan Times*, 30 April 2021, https://www.hindustantimes.com/cities/dehradun-news/91-million-thronged-mahakumbh-despite-covid-19-surge-govt-data-101619729096750.html.; Lalmani Verma, 'Promised testing, sanitization and distancing was not maintained', *The Indian Express*, 13 April 2021, https://indianexpress.com/article/india/at-kumbh-mela-covid-guard-slips-no-thermal-screening-few-masks-102-test-positive-7270853/.
22. 'After Kumbh, Uttarakhand sees 1800% jump in COVID-19 cases', The Quint, 8 May 2021, https://www.thequint.com/coronavirus/spike-covid-cases-uttarakhand-haridwar-maha-kumbh-mela.
23. Stuart Hall, *Representation: Cultural Representations and Signifying Practices* (Sage Publications, 1997).
24. Firoz Iqbal Khan vs. Union of India and others on 18 September 2020, WP(C) No.956/2020.
25. '"Communal, irresponsible": IPS association condemns Sudarshan TV's "UPSC Jihad" trailer', The Wire, 27 August 2020, https://

thewire.in/communalism/sudarshan-news-tv-ips-association-upsc-muslims-jihad; 'IPS association denounces Sudarshan News video targeting Muslims in the civil services.' Scroll, 27 August 2020, https://scroll.in/latest/971570/ips-association-denounces-sudarshan-news-video-targeting-muslims-in-the-civil-services

26. Prachi Bhardwaj, 'SC stays the telecast of Sudarshan News' "UPSC Jihad" show; says it prima facie appears like an attempt to vilify the Muslim community', SCCOnline, 15 September 2020, https://www.scconline.com/blog/post/2020/09/15/sc-stays-the-telecast-of-sudarshan-news-upsc-jihad-show-says-it-prima-facie-appears-like-an-attempt-to-vilify-the-muslim-community/
27. The Programme and Advertising Codes prescribed under the Cable TV Network Rules, 1994, lists what cannot be carried by a cable service. Restrictions include content that offends 'good taste or decency, contains attack on religions or communities or visuals or words contemptuous of religious groups or which promote communal attitudes'.
28. '16 key statements by Supreme Court in the Sudarshan TV case', The Leaflet, 20 September 2020, https://theleaflet.in/16-key-statements-by-supreme-court-in-the-sudarshan-tv-case/
29. Vikas Pandey, 'Nupur Sharma: Prophet Muhammad remarks deepen India's diplomatic crisis.' BBC, 7 June 2022, https://www.bbc.com/news/world-asia-india-61701908.
30. 'Supreme Court condemns hate speech aired on TV', *The Hindu*, 22 September 2022. https://www.thehindu.com/news/national/duty-of-tv-anchors-is-to-prevent-hate-speech-supreme-court/article65918224.ece
31. Eric Schmidt and Jared Cohen, 'The digital disruption: connectivity and the diffusion of power', Council on Foreign Relations, December 2010, https://www.jstor.org/stable/20788718?seq=1 .
32. Punya Prasun Bajpai, 'Exclusive: Punya Prasun Bajpai reveals the story behind his exit from ABP News', The Wire, 6 August

2018, https://thewire.in/media/punya-prasun-bajpai-abp-news-narendra-modi.

33. 'Hindustan Times pulls down its Hate Tracker', Newslaundry, 25 October 2017, https://www.newslaundry.com/shorts/hindustan-times-pulls-down-its-ht-hate-tracker
34. 'Cobrapost sting: big media houses say yes to Hindutva, black money, paid news', The Wire, 26 May 2018, https://thewire.in/media/cobrapost-sting-big-media-houses-say-yes-to-hindutva-black-money-paid-news
35. Geeta Pandey, 'Why does Indian PM Narendra Modi follow trolls on Twitter?' BBC News, 10 October 2017, https://www.bbc.com/news/world-asia-india-41549756; 'The Followed', *Indian Express*, 12 September 2017, https://indianexpress.com/article/opinion/editorials/the-followed-gauri-lankesh-narendra-modi-social-media-trolls-4834866/
36. 'Don't want my child to inherit an India built on hate: Rajiv Bajaj on blacklisting TV channels', *The Economic Times*, 13 October 2020, https://economictimes.indiatimes.com/industry/services/advertising/rajiv-bajaj-pulls-out-advertisements-says-will-not-endorse-channels-with-toxic-content/articleshow/78635013.cms?from=mdr.
37. Raj Kamal Jha and Ravish Tiwari, 'Prime Minister Narendra Modi Interview to Indian Express: "Khan Market gang hasn't created my image, 45 years of tapasya has … you cannot dismantle it"', *The Indian Express*, 13 May 2019, https://indianexpress.com/elections/pm-narendra-modi-interview-to-indian-express-live-lok-sabha-elections-2019-bjp-5723186/
38. Media censorship during the Emergency (1975–1976) was rampant: the Indira Gandhi-led government issued guidelines to crack down on any form of dissent. Various journalists were threatened and arrested for criticizing the government's policies.

5: Islamophobia and Sinhalese Buddhist Nationalism in Sri Lanka

1. A Muslim school principal quoting a Muslim woman who had just given birth. Zahran Hashim was the mastermind behind the 2019 Easter Sunday bombings that killed 269 people in Sri Lanka. Author interview, Dharga Town, August 2019.
2. Neil DeVotta, 'Liberation Tigers of Tamil Eelam and the lost quest for separatism in Sri Lanka', *Asian Survey*, Volume 49, Number 6 (November/December 2009), pp. 1021–1051. There were some Muslims in Eastern Province who joined the Tamil rebels in the 1980s, but such support ceased when the LTTE began persecuting Muslims.
3. The worst attacks took place in August 1990 when 147 Muslims were killed while praying in two mosques in Kattankudy in Batticaloa District.
4. K.M. DeSilva, 'The Muslim minority in a democratic polity: the case of Sri Lanka: Reflections on a theme', M.A.M. Shukri, ed., *Muslims of Sri Lanka: Avenues to Antiquity* (Beruwala, Sri Lanka: Jamiah Naleemia Institute, 1986), pp. 443–52.
5. A.R.M. Imtiyaz and Amjad Mohamed-Saleem, 'Muslims in post-war Sri Lanka: Understanding Sinhala-Buddhist mobilization against them', *Asian Ethnicity*, Volume 16, Number 2 (2015), pp. 186–202.
6. Quoted in Samanth Subramanian, *This Divided Island: Stories from the Sri Lankan War* (Delhi: Penguin Books, 2015), p. 226.
7. Neil DeVotta, 'Sri Lanka: From turmoil to dynasty', *Journal of Democracy*, Volume 22, Number 2 (April 2011), pp. 130–144.
8. Scott Thomas, *The Global Resurgence of Religion and the Transformation of International Relations: The Struggle for the Soul of the Twenty-First Century* (New York: Palgrave Macmillan, 2005), pp. 39–40.

9. Groups like the BBS do not have to look too far for anti-Muslim strategies, given the pervasive Islamophobia in neighbouring India. The chief executive of the BBS has claimed that his organization has relations with India's RSS and BJP and is inspired by their activities and Indian PM Narendra Modi. He notes that 'There are lots of similarities between India and Sri Lanka. Both of us face threats from Muslims and minorities who are actively engaged in conversions. When Sinhalese families have a child or two, minorities have half a dozen or more. When foreign money plays behind such activities, we need to resist. So, Modi and his party is a great inspiration for us.' Quoted in Arun Janardhanan, 'Hardline Lanka Buddhists to launch party, say inspired by BJP, RSS', *The Indian Express*, 20 January 2015, http://indianexpress.com/article/india/politics/hardline-lanka- buddhists-to-launch-party-say-inspired-by-bjp-rss/.
10. Tanya Basu, 'What does 'Islamophobia' actually mean?', *The Atlantic,* 15 October 2014, https://www.theatlantic.com/international/archive/2014/10/is-islamophobia-real-maher-harris-aslan/381411/.
11. 'Islamophobia: A Challenge for Us All: Report of the Runnymede Trust Commission on British Muslims and Islamophobia', Runnymede Trust, 1997, p. 1, https://www.runnymedetrust.org/publications/islamophobia-a-challenge-for-us-all.
12. Ibid.
13. Simon Kuper, 'The myth of Eurabia', *Financial Times*, Life and Arts Section, US edition (3–4 October 2009), pp. 1–2.
14. Carl W. Ernst, *Islamophobia in America: The Anatomy of Intolerance* (New York, NY: Palgrave Macmillan, 2013); Peter Gottschalk and Gabriel Greenberg, *Islamophobia: Making Muslims the Enemy* (Lanham: Roman and Littlefield Publishers, 2008); Todd H. Green, *The Fear of Islam: An Introduction to Islamophobia in the West* (Minneapolis: Fortress Press, 2015).

15. Victoria Schofield, *Kashmir in Conflict: India, Pakistan and the Unending War* (London: I.B. Tauris, 2010).
16. Neil DeVotta and David Timberman, *Violent Extremism and Insurgency in Bangladesh: A Risk Assessment* (Washington, D. C.: United States Agency for International Development, 2012).
17. Hansen, *The Saffron Wave*, 1999.
18. Kunal Pradhan and Kaushik Deka, 'Angst and aspiration', *India Today*, 17 March 2014, https://www.indiatoday.in/magazine/cover-story/story/20140317-muslims-community-india-growth-not-the-politics-of-division-800432-2014-03-07.
19. Stanley J. Tambiah, *Buddhism Betrayed?: Religion, Politics, and Violence in Sri Lanka* (Chicago: University of Chicago Press, 1992); Neil DeVotta and Jason Stone, 'Jathika Hela Urumaya and ethno-religious politics in Sri Lanka', *Pacific Affairs*, Volume 81, Number 1 (spring 2008), pp. 31–51.
20. Jeyadeva Uyangoda, 'Ethnicity, Nation and State Formation in Sri Lanka: Antinomies of Nation-Building', *Pravada*, Volume 3 (1994), p. 14.
21. E.B. Denham, Ceylon at the Census of 1911 (Colombo: Government Printer, 1912), pp. 196 and 245; 'Sri Lanka Census of Population and Housing 2011', Department of Census and Statistics, Sri Lanka, 2011, http://www.statistics.gov.lk/PopHouSat/CPH2011/index. php?fileName=pop43&gp=Activities&tpl=3
22. For population figures, see 'Census of Population and Housing 2012', Department of Census and Statistics, Sri Lanka, pp. 20-21, http://statistics.gov.lk/PopHouSat/CPH2011/index.php?fileName=Key_E&gp=Activities&tpl=3
23. Dennis B. McGilvray, 'Rethinking Muslim Identity in Sri Lanka', in John Clifford Holt, ed., *Buddhist Extremists and Muslim Minorities: Religious Conflict in Contemporary Sri Lanka* (New York: Oxford University Press, 2016), p. 69.

24. Farah Mihlar, 'The state of Sri Lanka's Muslims', *Economic and Political Weekly*, Volume 44, Number 38 (September 2009), p. 24.
25. Author interviews with Muslim and Tamil community members in Eastern Province, June 2014.
26. Ameer Ali, 'Political Buddhism, Islam orthodoxy and open economy: The toxic triad in Sinhalese-Muslim relations in Sri Lanka', *Journal of Asian and African Studies*, Volume 49, Number 3 (June 2014), p. 299. Also see Dennis B. McGilvray, 'Sri Lankan Muslims: Between ethnonationalism and the global ummah', *India Review*, Volume 17, Number 1 (January 2011), pp. 45–64.
27. Farzana Haniffa, 'Piety as politics among Muslim women in contemporary Sri Lanka', *Modern Asian Studies*, Volume 42, Number 2/3 (March-May 2008), pp. 347–75.
28. Victor Mallet, 'Madrassas: behind closed doors', *Financial Times*, Life and Arts Section, US edition, 30 October 2015, https://www.ft.com/content/d807f15a-7db0-11e5-98fb-5a6d4728f74e; Farhan Bokhari, '"Saudi-isation" debate grips Pakistan amid terror fears', *Financial Times*, US edition, 30 December 2015; Pervez Hoodbhoy, 'Saudizing Pakistan: How Pakistan is changing and what this means for South Asia and the world', in Aparna Pande, ed., *Routledge Handbook of Contemporary Pakistan* (London: Routledge, 2017), pp. 466–78; Farahnaz Ispahani, 'Pakistan's descent into religious intolerance', in ibid, pp. 336–50.
29. Meghan O'Sullivan, 'Conflict as a catalyst: The changing politics of the Sri Lankan Muslims', in Siri Gamage and I.B. Watson, eds., *Conflict and Community in Contemporary Sri Lanka* (New Delhi: Sage Publications, 1999), pp. 268–69.
30. In most instances, one can figure out an establishment's ethnic links based on the name of the proprietor or business. Advertising an establishment's Sinhalese Buddhist ownership merely reinforces the call to boycott non-Buddhist establishments.

31. Quoted from the letter Muslim parliamentarians sent President Maithripala Sirisena. See 'Muslim Parliamentarians Forum wants action against Gnanasara for blaspheming Allah', Colombo Telegraph, 13 December 2016, https://www.colombotelegraph.com/index.php/muslim-parliamentarians-forum-wants-action-against-gnanasara-for-blaspheming-allah/.
32. Shreen Saroor, 'Denying justice while dehumanizing a community at large', *Groundviews*, 21 April 2021, https://groundviews.org/2021/04/21/denying-justice-while-dehumanizing-a-community-at-large/.
33. Ibid. For instance, one person was arrested for merely listening to a sermon by the group that perpetrated the Easter Sunday bombings while another man was arrested for transporting food in an autorickshaw for an individual who turned out to be a suicide bomber.
34. Author interviews with numerous Muslim civil society activists and community leaders in 2018 and 2019 made it clear that they believed the Easter Sunday attacks were unlikely to have taken place, especially in such a coordinated fashion involving so many suicide bombers, if not for the post-civil war anti-Muslim agitprop.
35. Hashim appears to have maintained links with certain Sri Lankan intelligence officials, which is why some suggest the Easter Sunday bombings were part of a conspiracy that included certain politicians and security personnel. That noted, the extremism Hashim espoused and used to recruit followers was IS-inspired.
36. These include putting military personnel, as opposed to competent and qualified health officials, in charge of tackling the spread of the virus and prematurely opening up sectors like the garment and tourist industries to generate scarce foreign currency.
37. Neil DeVotta, 'Promoting covenantal pluralism amidst embedded majoritarianism in Sri Lanka', *Journal of Faith and International Affairs*, Volume 18, Number 4 (Winter 2020), pp. 49–62.

6: Fear, Radicalism and Violence: Sri Lanka's Cyclical Crisis

1. Amresh Gunasingham, 'Sri Lanka attacks: An analysis of the aftermath', *Counter Terrorist Trends and Analyses*, Volume 11, Number 2 (2019), pp. 8, 11.
2. Department of Census and Statistics, *Census of Population and Housing of Sri Lanka* (Colombo: Government of Sri Lanka, 2012), p. 141.
3. Ibid.
4. Verité Research and NCEASL, *Silent Suppression: Restrictions on Religious Freedoms of Christians (1994-2014)* (Colombo: National Christian Evangelical Alliance of Sri Lanka, 2015), pp. 21–24.
5. Farzana Haniffa, Harini Amarasuriya and Vishakha Wijenayake, *Where Have All the Neighbours Gone? Aluthgama Riots and its Aftermath: A Fact-Finding Mission to Aluthgama, Dharga Town, Valipanna and Beruwela* (Colombo: Law & Society Trust, 2014), p. 1.
6. Roshini Wickremesinhe, *Confronting Intolerance: Continued Violations against Religious Minorities in Sri Lanka* (London: Minority Rights Group International, 2016), p. 15.
7. Hilmy Ahmed, 'Escalating violence: Renewed assaults on the Muslim community', *Groundviews*, 22 May 2017, http://groundviews.org/2017/05/22/escalating-violence-renewed- assaults-on-the-muslim-community/
8. Dharisha Bastians, 'Gintota and the shadows of extremism', *Daily FT*, 23 November 2017, www.ft.lk/opinion/Gintota-and-the-shadows-of-extremism/14-643843.
9. Maneshka Borham, 'Kandy communal violence: Main suspect arrested', *The Daily News*, 9 March 2018, https://www.dailynews.lk/2018/03/09/local/145064/kandy-communal-violence-main-suspect-arrested.

10. Pamela Constable and Joanna Slater, 'Brothers of Sri Lanka bombing mastermind said to be killed in safe house battle; 'Catholics watch Mass on TV', *The Washington Post*, 28 April 2019, https://www.washingtonpost.com/world/asia_pacific/brothers-of- sri-lanka-bombing-mastermind-said-to-be-dead-in-safe-house- battle-catholics-watch-mass-on-tv/2019/04/28/426d1e9c-6932- 11e9-a698-2a8f808c9cfb_story.html.
11. Farzana Haniffa, 'How the Easter bombings left Sri Lanka's Muslims with no path forward', The Wire, 18 October 2019, https://thewire.in/communalism/how-the-easter-bombings-left-sri-lankas-muslims-with-no-path-forward
12. Meera Srinivasan, 'Mobs attack mosques, Muslim-owned shops and homes in Sri Lanka's Kurunegala District', *The Hindu*, 14 May 2019, https://www.thehindu.com/news/international/mobs-attack-mosques-muslim-owned-shops-and-homes-in-sri-lankas-kurunegala-district/article27119473.ece.
13. Gehan Gunatilleke, 'The constitutional practice of ethno-religious violence in Sri Lanka', *Asian Journal of Comparative Law*, Volume 13, Number 2 (2018), pp. 359, 370.
14. DeVotta, *Sinhalese*, 2007p. 5; Gananath Obeyesekere, *The Work of Culture: Symbolic Transformation in Psychoanalysis and Anthropology* (Chicago: University of Chicago Press, 1990), p. 147.
15. Anne M. Blackburn, *Locations of Buddhism: Colonialism and Modernity in Sri Lanka* (Chicago: The University of Chicago Press, 2010) for an in-depth discussion on the work of early revivalists such as Hikkaduwe Sri Sumangala Thera.
16. Richard Gombrich and Gananath Obeyesekere, *Buddhism Transformed: Religious Change in Sri Lanka* (New Jersey: Princeton University Press, 1988), pp. 202–38.
17. Ayesha Zuhair, *Dynamics of Sinhala Buddhist Ethno-Nationalism in Post-War Sri Lanka* (Colombo: Centre for Policy Alternatives,

2016), p. 13. Also see Kalana Senaratne, 'Jathika Chinthanaya and the executive presidency', in Asanga Welikala, ed., *Reforming Sri Lankan Presidentialism: Provenance, Problems and Prospects* (Colombo: Centre for Policy Alternatives, 2015), p. 208.

18. Meera Srinivasan, 'Rajapaksas win super majority in Sri Lanka parliamentary poll', *The Hindu*, 7 August 2020, https://www.thehindu.com/news/international/sri-lanka-polls-rajapaksas-slpp-secures-big-win/article32290424.ece.
19. Sasanka Perera, *The Ethnic Conflict in Sri Lanka: A Historical and Sociopolitical Outline* (Colombo: World Bank, 2001), p. 4.
20. DeVotta, *Sinhalese*, 2007, p. 6.
21. Stanley J. Tambiah, *Sri Lanka: Ethnic Fratricide and the Dismantling of Democracy* (Chicago: Chicago University Press, 1986), pp. 92–93.
22. Department of Census and Statistics, Census of Population and Housing of Sri Lanka (Colombo: Government of Sri Lanka, 2012).
23. Mohamed Faslan and Nadine Vanniasinkam, *Fracturing Community: Intra-group Relations among the Muslims of Sri Lanka* (Colombo: International Centre for Ethnic Studies, 2015).
24. Ibid.
25. Anagarika Dharmapala, 'The richest legacy in the universe' in Ananda Guruge, ed., *Return to Righteousness: A Collection of Speeches, Essays, and Letters of the Anagarika Dharmapala* (Colombo: Ceylon Government Press, 1965).
26. Ahilan Kadirgamar, 'The political economy of anti-Muslim attacks', *The Island*, 2 March 2013, http://www.island.lk/ index.php?page_cat=article-details&page=article-details&code_ title=73829.
27. Newton Gunasinghe, 'The open economy and its impact on ethnic relations in Sri Lanka', in Deborah Winslow and Michael D. Woost, eds., *Economy, Culture, and Civil War in Sri Lanka* (Bloomington: Indiana University Press, 2004), p. 99.

28. See letter by the Wennappuwa Pradeshiya Sabha, 24 June 2019. 'Wennappuwa – A Land of Its Own? Pradeshiya Sabha Bans Muslim Vendors', *The Colombo Telegraph*, 25 June 2019, https://www.colombotelegraph.com/index.php/wennapuwa-a-land-of-its-own-pradeshiya-sabha- bans-muslim-vendors/.
29. The certification system was characterized by militant groups such as BBS as a means for Muslims to maintain market monopolies, as the requirement of prior certification could have the effect of discouraging Muslim customers from purchasing products from non-Muslim producers. See Gehan Gunatilleke, *The Chronic and the Acute: Post-War Religious Violence in Sri Lanka* (Colombo: Equitas and ICES, 2015), p. 35.
30. According to Richard Gombrich, the practice of cattle slaughter is virtually exclusive to the Muslim community, as butcheries have been historically run by Muslims. See Richard Gombrich, *Buddhist Precept and Practice: Traditional Buddhism in the Rural Highlands of Ceylon* (Delhi: Motilal Banarsidass, 1991).
31. Shamara Wettimuny, 'On Kandy: How myths about minorities underlie violence', *Groundviews*, 9 March 2018, https:// groundviews.org/2018/03/09/on-kandy-how-myths-about-minorities-underlie-violence; Gehan Gunatilleke, *The Chronic and the Entrenched: Ethno-religious Violence in Sri Lanka* (Colombo: Equitas and ICES, 2018), p. 43.
32. Benjamin Schonthal, '"Environments of law": Islam, Buddhism, and the state in contemporary Sri Lanka', *The Journal of Asian Studies*, Volume 75, Number 1 (2016), pp. 137–56, 144. Also see Qadri Ismail, 'Unmooring identity: The antinomics of elite Muslim self-representation in modern Sri Lanka', in Pradeep Jeganathan and Qadri Ismail, eds., *Unmaking the Nation: The Politics of Identity and History in Modern Sri Lanka* (Colombo: ICES 1995), pp. 55–105.

33. P.K Balachandran, 'Rise of Wahabism in Eastern Sri Lanka', *The Hindustan Times*, 26 April 2007, https://www.hindustantimes.com/world/rise-of-wahabism-in-eastern-sri-lanka/story-AJuCl7hu8Dt2bEvky3FarO.html.
34. Lecture delivered by Ash-Sheik Muneer Mulafer, Committee Member of the Coexistence National Shoora Council, on 18 September 2017 at a conference titled 'Religious Freedom in Sri Lanka: Confrontation or Cooperation' organized by the National Christian Council of Sri Lanka held in Negombo from 18 to 20 September 2017.
35. Farzana Haniffa, 'Piety as politics amongst Muslim women in contemporary Sri Lanka', *Modern Asian Studies*, Volume 42, Number 2/3 (2008), pp. 347, 357.
36. Ibid.
37. M.A. Nuhman, *Sri Lankan Muslims: Ethnic Identity within Cultural Diversity* (Colombo: ICES, 2007), p. 205.
38. Gunasingham, 'Sri Lanka Attacks', p. 8.
39. Faslan, et al, *Fracturing Community*, p. 3.
40. Amresh Gunasingham, 'Arrest of influential religious hardliner and religious extremism in Sri Lanka', *Counter Terrorist Trends and Analyses*, Volume 10, Number 8 (2018), pp. 7–9.
41. Dennis McGilvray, 'Sri Lankan Muslims: Between ethno-nationalism and the global ummah', *Nations and Nationalism*, Volume 17, Number 1 (2011), pp. 45–64.
42. Faslan et al, *Fracturing Community*; Dennis McGilvray and Mirak Raheem, 'Muslim perspectives on the Sri Lankan conflict', *Policy Studies*, Volume 41 (2007).
43. Faslan, et al, *Fracturing Community*, pp. 15–16.
44. See Shamara Wettimuny, 'A brief history of anti-Muslim violence in Sri Lanka', *History Workshop*, 22 July 2019, https://www.

historyworkshop.org.uk/a-brief-history-of-anti-muslim-violence-in-sri-lanka/.

45. Borham, 'Kandy communal violence', 2018; 'Kandy incidents created new international challenges: PM', *The Daily Mirror*, 11 March 2018, www.dailymirror.lk/147104/Kandy-incidents-created-new- international-challenges-PM.
46. Smruti S. Pattanaik, 'Sri Lanka: Securitising minority alienation', The Manohar Parrikar Institute for Defence Studies and Analyses, 29 April 2019, https://idsa.in/idsacomments/sri-lanka-securitising-minority_sspattanaik-290419.
47. Emma Green, 'How Sri Lanka's Christians became a target', *The Atlantic*, 24 April 2019, https://www.theatlantic.com/international/archive/2019/04/sri-lankas-christians-faced-new-persecution/587842. For an interesting discussion on this issue in the Indonesian context, see Melissa Crouch, 'Regulating places of worship in Indonesia: Upholding freedom of religion for religious minorities', *Singapore Journal of Legal Studies*, Volume 96 (2007), pp. 96–116. For a discussion on the Nigerian context, see Lang Michael Kpughe, 'Christian churches and the Boko Haram insurgency in Cameroon: Dilemmas and responses', *Religions*, Volume 8, Number 8 (2017), p. 143.
48. 'Textbooks pave the way to sustainable development', UNESCO Global Education Monitoring Report, Policy Paper No. 28, 11 December 2016, https://en.unesco.org/ gem-report/textbooks-pave-way-sustainable-development.
49. Michael Ignatieff, *The Ordinary Virtues: Moral Order in a Divided World* (Cambridge, MA: Harvard University Press, 2017).
50. Abdullahi An-Na'im, 'Universality of human rights: Mediating paradox to enhance practice', in Miodrag A. Jovanovic and Ivana Kristic, eds., *Human Rights Today - 60 Years of The Universal Declaration* (The Hague: Eleven International Publishing, 2010).

7: Christians in Pakistan: Retrospect and Prospect

1. John Rooney, *Shadows in the Dark* (Rawalpindi: Christian Study Centre, 1984); William Young, *Handbook of Source Materials* (Serampore: ISPCK, 2009); M. Nazir-Ali, *From Everywhere to Everywhere: A World View of Christian Mission*, (London: Collins, 1990).
2. Alexander Mar Thoma, *The Marthoma Church: Heritage and Mission* (Kottayam: Ashram Press, 1986), p. 1; William Taylor, The Syrians of Syria and South India, in Henry Hill, *Light from the East* (Toronto: Anglican Book Centre, 1988), p. 88; Rooney, op cit., p. 42.
3. William G. Young, *Patriarch, Shah and Caliph: A Study of the Relationships of the Church of the East with the Sassanid Empire and the Early Caliphates up to 800 AD* (Rawalpindi, Christian Study Centre, 1974).
4. See further John Rooney, 'The Hesitant Dawn: Christianity in Pakistan, 1579-1760', *Christian Study Centre Pakistan Christian History Monograph*, Number 2 (1984); M.L. Roy Choudhry and Roy Chaudhry Sastri, 'Position of Christians in the Mughal Empire', *Indian History Congress*, Volume 5 (1941), pp. 347–353.
5. Majid Sheikh, 'Harking Back: Jesuit missions to Lahore and the first wooden church', Dawn, 8 May 2016, https://www.dawn.com/news/1256997
6. Ibid, p. 31, 57.
7. Ibid, p. 68, 87, 91.
8. Ibid, p. 71; Khalid Anis Ahmed, ed., *Intercultural Encounter in Mughal Miniatures* (Lahore: National College of the Arts, 1995), pp. 37, 79.
9. On all of this see Stephen Neill, *A History of Christian Missions* (London: Penguin, 1986), p. 223; Jocelyn Murray, *Proclaim the*

Good News: a short history of the Church Missionary Society (London: Hodder, 1985), p. 24.

10. D. Barrett, G. Kurian & T.M. Johnson, *World Christian Encyclopedia* (New York: Oxford University Press, 2001), p. 570; J. Rooney, *On Heels of Battles: A History of the Catholic Church in Pakistan 1780- 1886* (Rawalpindi: Christian Study Centre 1986).
11. J. Massey, 'Christians in North India', *Religion and Society Journal*, Volume 34, Number 3 (1987), p. 88; Stephen Neill, op cit., p. 309; F. and M. Stock, *People Movements in the Punjab* (South Pasadena: William Carey Library, 1975).
12. World Christian Encyclopedia, op cit., p. 570.
13. Wayne McLintock, 'A Sociological Profile of the Christian Minority in Pakistan', *Missiology Journal*, Volume 20, Number 3 (1992), pp. 343–353.
14. See further George Felix, *Christians in Pakistan: The Battle for Justice* (Salford: Agape Press, 2001); Ralph Braibanti, *Chief Justice Cornelius of Pakistan* (Karachi: Oxford University Press, 1999).
15. Ibid p. 18.
16. See M. Nazir-Ali, 'Islamic Law, Fundamental Freedoms and Social Cohesion: Retrospect and Prospect', in Rex Ahdar and N. Aroney, *Shari'a in The West* (Oxford: Oxford University Press, 2010), p. 71.
17. On church buildings, see Safdar Ali Shah and Syed Javaid Kazi, *Churches of Pakistan* (Lahore: Constellation, 2010).
18. World Christian Encyclopedia, op cit., p. 570.
19. Home Office, Country Policy and Information Note on Pakistan's Christians and Christian Converts, London, 2018, p. 14.

8: Genesis of the Shia Predicament in Pakistan

1. Rudrangshu Mukherjee, *Awadh in Revolt, 1857-1858: A Study of Popular Resistance* (United Kingdom: Anthem, 2002).

2. Rakesh Bhasin, *Dastan-e-Awadh: A Momentous Journey from Faizabad to Lucknow* (Chennai: Notion Press, 2018).
3. Sajjad Rizvi, 'Faith deployed for a new Shi'i polity in India: The theology of Sayyid Dildar "Ali Nasirabadi"', *Journal of the Royal Asiatic Society*, Volume 24, Number 3 (2014), pp. 363–80.
4. Aslam Mahmud, *Awadh Symphony: Notes on a Cultural Interlude* (Delhi: Rupa Publications India, 2017), Kindle edition.
5. Muhammad Amir Ahmad Khan, 'Local nodes of a transnational network: A case study of a Shi'i family in Awadh, 1900-1950', *Journal of the Royal Asiatic Society*, Volume 24, Number 3 (2014), pp. 397–413.
6. Meir Litvak, 'Money, religion, and politics: The Oudh bequest in Najaf and Karbala, 1850-1903', *International Journal of Middle East Studies*, Volume 33, Number 1 (2001), pp. 1–21.
7. Veena Talwar Oldenburg, *The Making of Colonial Lucknow, 1856-1877* (United States: Princeton University Press, 2014).
8. Andreas Rieck, *The Shias of Pakistan* (Karachi: Oxford University Press, 2016), Kindle edition, p. 33.
9. Ibid.
10. Justin Jones, *Shi'a Islam in Colonial India* (Cambridge, UK: Cambridge University Press, 2011), Kindle Edition, p. 117.
11. Laurence Louër, *Sunnis and Shi'a: A Political History* (Princeton, NJ: Princeton University Press, 2020), Kindle edition, p. 143.
12. Jones, *Shi'a Islam in Colonial India*, 2011, p. 117.
13. Wilfred Cantwell Smith, *Modern Islam in India* (United Kingdom: Read Books, 2006).
14. Louër, *Sunnis and Shi'a*, 2020, p. 139.
15. Syed Akbar Hyder, *Reliving Karbala: Martyrdom in South Asian Memory*, (India: Oxford University Press, 2008), Kindle edition.
16. Louër, *Sunnis and Shi'a*, 2020, p. 136.

17. 17 Andreas Rieck, *The Shias of Pakistan: An Assertive and Beleaguered Minority* (United States: Oxford University Press, 2016).
18. Mushirul Hasan, *Legacy of A Divided Nation: India's Muslims from Independence to Ayodhya* (United States: Taylor & Francis, 2019).
19. Rieck, *The Shias of Pakistan*, 2016, p. 51.
20. Jones, *Shi'a Islam in Colonial India*, 2011, p. 159.
21. Ibid.
22. Ibid, p. 153.
23. Rieck, *The Shias of Pakistan,* p.43.
24. Ahmad Khan, 'Local nodes of a transnational network', 2014, pp. 397–413.
25. Mahomed Ali Jinnah, *The Quaid-e-Azam [M. A. Jinnah] Papers, 1940* (Pakistan: East & West Publishing Company, 1976).
26. Rieck, op cit., pp. 52–53.
27. Ahmad Khan, op cit., pp. 397–413.
28. Gulam Allana, *Pakistan Movement: Historic Documents* (Pakistan: Paradise Subscription Agency, 1967).
29. 'Constituent Assembly of Pakistan Debates', National Assembly Archive, http://www.na.gov.pk/ uploads/ documents/1434604126_750.pdf
30. Ibid.
31. 'The Objectives Resolution', *Islamic Studies*, Volume 48, Number 1 (2009), pp. 89–118.
32. Ibid.
33. Ibid.
34. Martin Lau, *The Role of Islam in the Legal System of Pakistan* (Netherlands: M. Nijhoff, 2006).
35. Selig S. Harrison, *In Afghanistan's Shadow: Baluch Nationalism and Soviet Temptations* (United States: Carnegie Endowment for International Peace, 1981).

36. Huseyn Shaheed Suhrawardy, 'Political stability and democracy in Pakistan', *Foreign Affairs*, Volume 35, Number 3 (1957), pp. 422–31.
37. Mohammed Ayub Khan, 'Pakistan perspective', *Foreign Affairs*, Volume 38, Number 4 (1960), pp. 547–56.
38. Husain Haqqani, *Pakistan: Between Mosque and Military* (US: Brookings Institution Press, 2005), Kindle edition, p. 40.
39. Shuja Nawaz, *Crossed Swords: Pakistan, Its Army, and the Wars Within* (Pakistan: Oxford University Press, 2018).
40. Christophe Jaffrelot, *The Pakistan Paradox: Instability and Resilience* (Karachi: Oxford University Press, 2015), Kindle edition.
41. Rieck, op cit., p. 110.
42. Seyyed Vali Reza Nasr, *The Vanguard of the Islamic Revolution: The Jama'at-i Islami of Pakistan* (United States: University of California Press, 1994).
43. Abdul Rehman Siddiqi, *East Pakistan the end game: an onlooker's journal 1969-1971* (Pakistan: Oxford University Press, 2004).
44. Abdur Rahman Siddiqi, *The Military in Pakistan, Image and Reality* (Pakistan: Vanguard, 1996).
45. Jalal Alamgir and Bina D'Costa, 'The 1971 genocide: War crimes and political crimes', *Economic and Political Weekly*, Volume 46, Number 13 (2011), pp. 38–41, http://www.jstor. org/stable/41152283.
46. Haqqani, op cit., p. 55.
47. Louër, op cit., pp. 142–143.

9: Pakistan's Legal Framework and Treatment of Religious Minorities

1. 'PM Imran says 'foreign-funded conspiracy' out to topple his govt, claims to have evidence in writing,' *Dawn*, 27 March 2022, https://www.dawn.com/news/1682104

2. Imran Khan, *Pakistan: A Personal History* (London: Random House, 2012), Preface.
3. Kathy Gannon, 'Minorities under attack as PM pushes 'tolerant' Pakistan,' Associated Press, 16 July 2020, https://apnews.com/article/ap-top-news-pakistan-international-news-islam-weekend-reads-796138f9b99b6104ea59705aa96749ce
4. Ibid.
5. Ibid.
6. 'Sindh High Court Validates Christian Girl's Forced Marriage to Alleged Abductor,' Naya Daur TV, 6 February 2020, https://nayadaur.tv/2020/02/sindh-high-court-validates-christian-girls-forced-marriage-to-alleged-abductor/
7. 'Pakistan high court forces 13-y-o Christian girl to return to captor's home as his 'wife',' Christian Post, July 10, 2021, https://www.christianpost.com/news/pakistan-court-forces-christian-girl-to-return-to-captors-home.html
8. 'Abductions, Forced Conversions, and Forced Marriages of Religious Minority Women and Girls in Pakistan,' November 2021 Report by All-Party Parliamentary Group for Pakistani Minorities, House of Commons, UK, https://appgfreedomofreligionorbelief.org/appg-for-the-pakistani-minorities-abductions-forced-conversions-and-forced-marriages-of-religious-minority-women-and-girls-in-pakistan/
9. O. H. K. Spate, 'Partition of India and Prospects for Pakistan,' *Geographical Review*, Volume 38, Number 1 (January 1948), pp. 5–29; Kingsley Davis, 'India and Pakistan: Demography of Partition', *Pacific Affairs* Volume 2, Number 3 (September 1949), pp. 254–264.
10. M.A. Jinnah's speech, 11 August 1947, in Constituent Assembly of Pakistan Debates, Volume 1.
11. 'The Objectives Resolution,' *Islamic Studies*, Volume 48, Number 1 (Spring 2009), pp. 91–119.

12. G.W. Choudhury, *Documents and Speeches on the Constitution of Pakistan* (Dacca: Green Book House, 1967)
13. Ibid
14. Ibid
15. Khalid Bin Sayeed, 'Pakistan's Constitutional Autocracy', Pacific Affairs 36, number 4 (Winter 1963–1964), pp. 368–369
16. 'The Constitution of Pakistan,1973,' National Assembly of Pakistan, Documents, Adopted 10 April 1973. https://na.gov.pk/uploads/documents/1549886415_632.pdf
17. 'Qadianis declared minority: preaching against finality of Prophethood by a Muslim made punishable', *Dawn*, 7 September 1974.
18. 1973 Constitution of Pakistan, http://www.pakistani.org/pakistan/constitution/.
19. W. Eric Gustafson, 'Pakistan 1978: At the brink again?', *Asian Survey*, Volume 19, number 2 (February 1979), pp. 159–162.
20. Ordinance XX of 26 April 1984.
21. Ibid.
22. Ibid.
23. 'Pakistan: Human Rights after Martial Law, Chapter VIII: Rights of Religious and Other Minorities', International Commission of Jurists' 1987 report, Geneva, pp. 98–105.
24. Pakistan Penal Code: Act XLV of 1860, as amended from time to time.
25. 'Pakistan: Blasphemy charges against Ahmadis' (London: Amnesty International, April 1994).
26. Ibid; 'Pakistan: 5 Ahmadi journalists charged with Blasphemy,' Amnesty International Report ASA 33/03/1994, London, https://www.amnesty.org/en/wp-content/uploads/2021/06/asa330031994en.pdf

27. 'Pakistan: Violation of Human Rights of Ahmadis' (London: Amnesty International, September 1991). 'Pakistan: Violations of Human Rights of Ahmadis,' Amnesty International Report ASA 33/15/1991. London, https://www.amnesty.org/en/wp-content/uploads/2021/06/asa330151991en.pdf
28. 'Text of Musharraf speech', *Dawn*, 17 October 1999.
29. 'Church expects Musharraf to honor promises to religious minorities', Union of Catholic Asian News, 24 February 2000, http://www.ucanews.com/story-archive/?post_name=/2000/02/24/church-expects-musharraf-to-honor-promises-to-religious-minorities&post_id=15486.

10: Understanding the Radicalization of Bangladeshi Society and Politics

1. 'Bangladesh siege: Twenty killed at Holey Artisan Bakery in Dhaka', BBC News, 2 July 2016, http:// www.bbc.com/news/world-asia-36692613
2. Maher Sattar, 'Bombing at Bangladesh's largest Eid gathering kills at least 3', *The New York Times*, 7 July 2016, https:// www.nytimes.com/2016/07/08/world/asia/bangladesh-bomb-eid-sholakia-eidgah.html
3. Maaz Hussain, 'Anti-terror fatwa endorsed by 100,000 Bangladeshi Islamic scholars', Voice of America (VoA), 21 June 2016, https://www.voanews.com/east-asia-pacific/anti-terror-fatwa-endorsed-100000-bangladeshi- islamic-scholars.
4. Donatella della Porta, 'Radicalization: A relational perspective', *Annual Review of Political Science*, Volume 21, Number 1 (2008), pp. 461–74.
5. Alex P. Schmid, 'Radicalisation, de-radicalisation, counter-radicalisation: A conceptual discussion and literature review', *ICCT Research Paper*, Volume 97, Number 1 (2013), p. 7.

6. Porta, 'Radicalization', p. 74.
7. Schmid, 'Radicalisation', p. 8.
8. Porta, 'Radicalization', p. 462.
9. Tore Bjørgo and John Horgan, eds., *Leaving Terrorism Behind: Individual and Collective Disengagement* (New York: Routledge, 2009).
10. Randy Borum, 'Radicalization into violent extremism I: a review of social science theories', *Journal of Strategic Security*, Volume 4, Number 4 (2012), pp. 7–36.
11. Peter R. Neumann, 'The Trouble with Radicalization', *International Affairs*, Volume 89, Number 4 (2013), pp. 873–93.
12. Ibid.
13. Schmid, 'Radicalisation', p. 8.
14. Joshua Sinai, 'Radicalisation into extremism and terrorism', *Intelligencer: Journal of U.S. Intelligence Studies*, Volume 19, Number 2 (2012).
15. Simona Trip et al., 'Psychological mechanisms involved in radicalization and extremism. A rational emotive behavioral conceptualization', *Frontiers in Psychology*, Volume 10, Number 437 (2019), doi:10.3389/fpsyg.2019.00437, https://www.frontiersin.org/articles/10.3389/fpsyg.2019.00437/full.
16. Porta, op cit., p. 463.
17. Talukdar Maniruzzaman, *Radical Politics and the Emergence of Bangladesh* (Dhaka: Bangladesh Books, 1975).
18. Ali Riaz, *Bangladesh: A Political History since Independence* (London/New York: I.B. Tauris, 2016).
19. Ibid; Syed M. Ali, *Understanding Bangladesh* (London: Hurst, 2010).
20. For details, see, Ali Riaz, 'Political Parties, Elections and Party Systems', in Ali Riaz and Md Sajjadur Rahman, eds., *Routledge Handbook of Contemporary Bangladesh* (London: Routledge, 2016).

21. 'August 21 attack: "State-backed crime" punished', *The Daily Star*, 11 October 2018, https://www.thedailystar.net/august-21-carnage/21-august-grenade-attack-verdict-tarique-rahman-awarded-life-1645090.
22. Dina Mahnaz Siddiqi, 'Political culture in contemporary Bangladesh: Histories, ruptures and contradictions' in Ali Riaz and C. Christine Fair, eds., *Political Islam and Governance in Bangladesh* (London: Routledge, 2010), p. 13.
23. For 2018 election, see Ali Riaz, *Voting in a Hybrid Regime: Explaining the 2018 Bangladeshi Election* (Singapore: Palgrave Pivot, 2019).
24. Ali Riaz, *Islamist Militancy in Bangladesh: A Complex Web* (London: Routledge, 2008).
25. Schmid, 'Radicalisation', p. 5.
26. Porta, 'Radicalization', p. 464.
27. C. Christine Fair and Wahid Abdallah, 'Islamist militancy in Bangladesh public awareness and attitudes', *RESOLVE Network Research Brief*, Number 4 (September 2017), https://resolvenet.org/system/files/2017-09/RSVE_04BangladeshBrief_MilitantSupport2017.pdf
28. 'Total Extra-judicial killings from 2001–2019', Odhikar, 2010 http://odhikar.org/wp-content/uploads/2020/02/ Statistics_EJK_2001-2019.pdf
29. 'Enforced disappearances (2009–2019)', Odhikar, 2020, http://odhikar.org/wp-content/uploads/2020/02/Statistics_Disappearance_2009-2019.pdf.
30. Pinak Ranjan Chakravarty, 'Shadow of India, Hasina government's corruption, repression of BNP looms over Bangladesh polls', Observer Research Foundation, 5 September 2018, https://www.orfonline.org/research/43844-shadow-of-india-hasina-governments-corruption-repression-of-bnp-looms-over-bangladesh-polls/

31. 'Transformation Index 2018: Polarization and repression increase', Bertelsmann Stiftung International 2018 Report, Executive Summary, 2018, http://www.uni- heidelberg.de/md/politik/personal/croissant/forschung/bti_2018_ executive_summary_english.pdf
32. 'Bangladesh: New Digital Security Act is attack on freedom of expression', Amnesty International, 12 November 2018, https://www.amnesty.org/en/latest/news/2018/11/bangladesh-muzzling-dissent-online/
33. Alexandra Pfefferle, 'Political bipartisanship and violence in Bangladesh', ACLED, 16 June 2015, https://acleddata.com/2015/06/16/political-bipartisanism-and-violence-in-bangladesh-2/
34. Fazlur Rahman Raju, 'Five years of political violence: 1,028 deaths and 52,000 injuries', *Dhaka Tribune*, 20 November 2017, https://www.dhakatribune.com/ bangladesh/2017/11/20/1028-deaths-53000-injuries/
35. Lorenzo Bosi and Donagh Davis, 'What is to be done?' Agency and the causation of transformative events in Ireland's 1916 Rising and 1969 Long March', *Mobilization*, Volume 22, Number 2 (2017), pp. 223–43.
36. Anupam Debashish Roy, 'Shahbag stolen? Third force dynamics and electoral politics in Bangladesh', *South Asia Research,* Volume 38, Number 3 (2018), pp. 1–24.
37. 'Bangladesh: Investigate deaths in protest clashes to prevent more bloodshed', Amnesty International, 7 May 2013, https://www.amnesty.org/en/latest/news/2013/05/bangladesh-investigate-deaths-protest-clashes-prevent-more- bloodshed/
38. Zakir Kibria, 'An Adivasi speaks: What brings me to Shahbag, what pulls me back from it', *Alal-O-Dulal*, 25 February 2013, https://alalodulal.org/2013/02/25/shahbag-what-pulls-back/.

39. Vikrom Sood, 'Bangladesh: A battle for its secular soul', Blogspot, 17 April 2013, http://soodvikram.blogspot. com/2013/04/ bangladesh-battle-for-its-secular-soul.html
40. Photo posted in an unnamed blog post, Somewhereinblog. net, http://www.somewhereinblog.net/blog/ mamunhussain2/29813002.
41. Yannis Gabriel, 'The other and othering: A short introduction', Yiannis Gabriel, 10 September 2012, http://www. yiannisgabriel.com/2012/09/the-other-and-otheringshort. html#:~:text=Othering%20is%20the%20process%20 of,frequently%2C%20vilification%20of%20this%20Other.
42. Naeem Mohaimeen, 'Shahbag: The forest of symbols', *Alal-O-Dulal*, 22 February 2013, http://alalodulal. org/2013/02/22/ Shahbag-symbols/
43. Kibria, 'An Adivasi speaks', 2013.
44. Seuty Sabur, 'Postcard from Shahabag', *International Sociological Association*, Volume 3, Number 1 (2013), https://www.isa-sociology.org/uploads/files/EBul-Sabur- March2012.pdf

11: Religious Intolerance in Bangladesh

1. This article is the culmination of several previous publications by C. Christine Fair and Parina Patel, which include:

   'Support for Domestic Islamist Terrorism in Bangladesh: Insights from a Novel Survey', *Politics and Religion*, pp. 1–27.

   'Barriers to Covenantal Pluralism in Bangladeshi Public Opinion', *The Review of Faith & International Affairs*, Volume 19, Number 2 (2021) 40–55;

   'Rational Islamists: Islamism and regime preferences in Bangladesh', *Journal of Democratization*, Volume 27, Number 4 (2020), pp. 547–569; and

C. Christine Fair, 'Bangladesh in 2019: Hasina Consolidates One-Woman Rule', *Asian Survey*, Volume 60, Number 1 (March 2020), pp. 189–195.

2. 'Interactive Data Table', CIA World Fact Book: Bangladesh, Pew.
3. Ala Uddin, 'Politics of Secularism and the State of Religious Pluralism in Bangladesh', *Journal of South Asian and Middle Eastern Studies*, Volume 38, Number 3 (Spring 2015), p. 47–48.
4. Uddin, 'Politics of Secularism', 2015; Ali Riaz, *God Willing: The Politics of Islamism in Bangladesh* (Lanham: Rowman & Littlefield Publishers, 2004).
5. Freedom in the World, Freedom House, 2020, https://freedomhouse.org/reports/freedom-world/faq-freedom-world.
6. Md Nazrul Islam and Md Saidul Islam, 'Islam, politics and secularism in Bangladesh: Contesting the dominant narratives.' *Social Sciences*, Volume 7, Number 3 (2018), p. 37.
7. C. Fair, A. Hamza & R. Heller, 'Who Supports Suicide Terrorism in Bangladesh? What the Data Say', *Politics and Religion,* Volume 10, Number 3 (2017), pp. 622–661.
8. Some orthodox Muslims are adamant that Ahmadis are not Muslim because they do not respect the ordinal finality of the prophethood. Some even argue that any Ahmadi self-identifying as Muslim is committing blasphemy (see Kabir, 2016).
9. Bruce Vaughn, 'Bangladesh', Congressional Research Service Report, 22 June 2020, p. 1, https://fas.org/sgp/crs/row/IF10214.pdf
10. Craig Baxter, 'Pakistan Votes--1970', *Asian Survey,* Volume 11, Number 3 (1971), pp. 197–218.
11. Yelena Biberman, *Gambling with Violence: State Outsourcing of War in Pakistan and India* (New York: Oxford University Press, 2019).
12. Gary Bass, *The Blood Telegram* (New York: Alfred A. Knopf, 2013).

13. Katharine Adeney, 'A step towards inclusive federalism in Pakistan? The politics of the 18th amendment', *Publius: The Journal of Federalism,* Volume 42, Number 4 (2012), pp. 539–565; Manzoor Ahmed, 'The Dynamics of (Ethno) Nationalism and Federalism in Postcolonial Balochistan, Pakistan', *Journal of Asian and African Studies,* (2020), 0021909619900216.
14. Akhand Akhtar Hossain, 'Contested national identity and political crisis in Bangladesh: Historical analysis of the dynamics of Bangladeshi society and politics', *Asian Journal of Political Science,* Volume 23, Number 3 (2015), pp. 366–396.
15. M. Rashiduzzaman, 'Islam, Muslim Identity and Nationalism in Bangladesh', *Journal of Asian and Middle Eastern Studies,* Volume XVIII, Number 1 (Fall 1994), pp. 36–60.
16. H. Tinker, 'Pressure, persuasion, decision', *The Journal of Asian Studies,* Volume 36, Number 4 (1977), pp. 695–704; Indian Independence Act of 1947, The National Archives, 1947, available at https://www. legislation.gov.uk/ukpga/1947/30/pdfs/ukpga_19470030_en.pdf;
17. Rashiduzzaman, 'Islam, Muslim Identity', 1994, p. 40.
18. Ibid, p. 39.
19. Biberman, 'Gambling with Violence', 2019.
20. Bass, *The Blood Telegram,* 2013.
21. Ahmed Shafiqul Huque and Muhammad Yeahia Akhter, 'The ubiquity of Islam: religion and society in Bangladesh', *Pacific Affairs,* Volume 60, Number 2 (1987), pp. 200–225.
22. Riaz, *God Willing,* 2004.
23. Hossain, 'Contested national identity', 2015.
24. Ibid; Richard Maxwell Eaton, *The Rise of Islam and The Bengal Frontier, 1204–1760* (Berkeley: University of California Press, 1993).

25. For many South Asian Muslims, secularism is often translated as a 'lack of religion' (*ladiniyaat*). Consequently, many Muslims in South Asia are discomfited by this concept.
26. Government of Bangladesh, Parliament Debates, 12 October 1972 (Dhaka: Government of Bangladesh, 1972), p. 20. Cited by Uddin, 'Politics of Secularism', p. 44.
27. Uddin, op cit.
28. Huque and Akhter, op cit.
29. Dina Mahaz Siddiqui, *Political culture in contemporary Bangladesh: Histories, ruptures and contradictions* (London: Routledge, 2010).
30. Iftikhar A. Chowdhury, 'Strategy of a small power in a subsystem: Bangladesh's external relations', *Australian Outlook*, Volume 34, Number 1 (1980), https://www.tandfonline.com/doi/citedby/10.1080/10357718008444696?scroll=top&needAccess=true; Huque & Akhter, op cit; Jagir Kaur, 'Foreign policy of Bangladesh: continuity and change (1975-1996)', PhD diss. (Jawaharlal Nehru University, 2000), http:// hdl.handle.net/10603/19030
31. Chowdhury, 'Strategy of a small power in a subsystem', 1980; Kaur, 'Foreign policy of Bangladesh', 2000; Syed Anwar Hussain, 'Bangabandhu's Contribution to Normalising Relations with Muslim Countries', *Bangladesh Quarterly*, Volume 18, Number 3 (1998), pp. 12–16.
32. Huque and Akhter, op cit.
33. Huque and Akhter, op cit, p. 205.
34. 33. Ibid, p. 224.
35. Zillur R. Khan, 'Leadership, Parties and Politics in Bangladesh', *Western Political Quarterly*, Volume 29, Number 1 (1976), pp. 102–125, https://journals.sagepub.com/doi/10.1177/106591297602900108?icid=int.sj-abstract. similar-articles.2
36. Riaz, 'Bangladesh', p. 79.

37. Siddiqi, 'Political Culture in Contemporary Bangladesh', p. 19.
38. Ibid.
39. Riaz, 'Bangladesh'.
40. Sanjay Kumar, 'Islamic Fundamentalists Terrorize Minorities in Bangladesh', *The Diplomat*, 15 January 2014, https://thediplomat.com/2014/01/islamic-fundamentalists- terrorize-minorities-in-bangladesh/
41. Binodkumar Singh, 'Islamic Fundamentalism in Bangladesh', *Himalayan and Central Asian Studies,* Volume 19, Number 1/2 (January–June 2015), pp. 55–64, https:// www.proquest.com/openview/c8d5b972af4ce5cd385d47535556 3ffa/1?pq-origsite=gscholar&cbl=1036373
42. Praveen Swami, 'What India can learn from Bangladesh's Jamaat-e-Islami ban', Firstpost, 3 August 2013, https://www.firstpost.com/world/what-india-can-learn-from- bangladeshs-jamaat-e-islami-ban-1007303.html
43. Mubashar Hasan, 'Historical Developments of Political Islam with Reference to Bangladesh', *Journal of Asian and African Studies,* Volume 47, Number 2 (2015), p. 161.
44. Siddiqi, 'Political Culture in Contemporary Bangladesh', p. 15.
45. Rashiduzzaman, 'Islam, Muslim Identity', 1994; Humayun Kabir, 'The "Othering" of the Ahmadiyya Community in Bangladesh', November 2016, http://dx.doi.org/10.1057/978-1-349-94966-3_15; Jawad Syed, Edwina Pio, Tahir Kamran and Abbas Zaidi, eds., *Faith-Based Violence and Deobandi Militancy in Pakistan* (London: Palgrave Macmillan, 2016), pp. 423–452; Md Maidul Islam, 'Secularism in Bangladesh: An Unfinished Revolution', *South Asia Research,* Volume 38, Number 1 (2018), pp. 20–39.
46. Siddiqi, 'Political Culture in Contemporary Bangladesh', p. 19–20.
47. Ali Riaz, 'Traditional Institutions as Tools of Political Islam in Bangladesh', *Journal of Asian and African Studies*, Volume 40, Number 3 (2005), pp. 171–196.

48. Kumar, 'Islamic Fundamentalists Terrorize Minorities in Bangladesh', 2015.
49. Riaz, *God Willing,* 2004.
50. Suzannah Linton, 'Completing the circle: accountability for the crimes of the 1971 Bangladesh war of liberation', *Criminal Law Forum,* Volume 21, Number 2 (2010); Morten Bergsmo and Elisa Novic, 'Justice after decades in Bangladesh: National trials for international crimes', *Journal of Genocide Research,* Volume 13, Number 4 (2011), pp. 503–510; Md Awal Hossain Mollah, 'War Crimes Trials in Bangladesh: Justice or Politics?', *Journal of Asian and African Studies,* Volume 55, Number 5 (2020), pp. 652–665.
51. Ashif Islam Shaon, 'Eight years of war crimes trials', The *Dhaka Tribune,* 18 August 2018, https:// archive.dhakatribune.com/bangladesh/war-crimes/2018/08/18/eight-years-of-war-crimes-trials
52. C. Christine Fair, 'Bangladesh in 2019: Hasina Consolidates One-Woman Rule', *Asian Survey,* Volume 60, Number 1 (2020), pp. 189–195.
53. Haroon Habib, 'Bangladesh: Restoring Secular Constitution', *The Hindu,* 25 June 2011, https://www.thehindu. com/opinion/lead/bangladesh-restoring-secular-constitution/ article2132333.ece.
54. Habib, 'Bangladesh: Restoring Secular Constitution', 2011.
55. Fair, 'Bangladesh in 2019', 2020.
56. Jasmin Lorch, 'Islamization by secular ruling parties: The case of Bangladesh', *Politics and Religion,* Volume 12, Number 2 (2019), pp. 257–282.
57. Harrison Akins, 'Bangladesh Country Update: Challenges to Religious Freedom in Bangladesh', US Commission on International Religious Freedom, May 2020, https://www.uscirf.gov/sites/default/files/2020%20Bangladesh%20Country%20Update.pdf

58. Anwesha Roy, *Making Peace, Making Riots: Communalism and Communal Violence, Bengal 1940-1947* (Cambridge University Press, 2018).
59. S. Akbar Zaidi, 'Religious minorities in Pakistan today', *Journal of Contemporary Asia,* Volume 18, Number 4 (1988), pp. 444–457, doi. org/10.1080/00472338880000331
60. Hasan Askari Rizvi, *Internal Strife and External Intervention: India's Role in the Civil War in East Pakistan (Bangladesh)* (Lahore: Progressive Publishers, 1981).
61. Ibid; M. Sanaullah, 'Review: Second and Third Release from the Second Population Census of Pakistan, 1961', *The Pakistan Development Review,* Volume 2, Number 1 (Spring 1962), pp. 106–113, www.jstor.org/stable/41258062.
62. Barkat, et al, cited by Meghna Guhathakurta, 'Amidst the winds of change: the Hindu minority in Bangladesh', *South Asian History and Culture,* Volume 3, Number 2 (2012), p. 292, doi: 10.1080/19472498.2012.664434.
63. M. Moinuddin Haider, Mizanur Rahman, and Nahid Kamal, 'Hindu population growth in Bangladesh: A demographic puzzle', *Journal of Religion and Demography,* Volume 6, Number 1 (2019), pp. 123–148, doi:10.1163/2589742X-00601003.
64. Shelley Feldman, 'The Hindu as Other: State, Law, and Land Relations in Contemporary Bangladesh', *South Asia Multidisciplinary Academic Journal,* Volume 13 (2016), pp. 1–19, https://journals.openedition.org/samaj/4111, doi.org/10.4000/samaj.4111.
65. Harrison Akins, 'Challenges to Religious Freedom in Bangladesh By Harrison Akins, Policy Analyst', U.S. Commission on International Religious Freedom, May 2020, https://www.uscirf.gov/sites/default/files/2020%20Bangladesh%20Country%20Update.pdf

66. 'Breach of Faith: Persecution of the Ahmadiyya Community in Bangladesh', Human Rights Watch, 15 June 2005, https://www.hrw.org/report/2005/06/15/breach-faith/persecution-ahmadiyya-community-bangladesh; Kabir, 'The "Othering" of the Ahmadiyya Community', 2016; Syed, *Faith-Based Violence,* 2016, pp. 423–452.
67. Akins, 'Challenges to Religious Freedom in Bangladesh', 2020.
68. US Commission on International Religious Freedom, 'Bangladesh Country Update', p. 3.
69. 'Bangladeshi star's comeback after Islamist death threats', Bangkok Post, 13 November 2020, https://www.bangkokpost.com/world/2019155/bangladeshi-stars-comeback-after-islamist-death-threats
70. 'International Methodology', Pew Foundation, 8 January 2019, https://www.pewresearch.org/methods/interactives/international-methodology/global-attitudes-survey/ bangladesh/2014/
71. C. Christine Fair and Parina Patel, 'Explaining Why Some Muslims Support Islamist Political Violence', *Political Science Quarterly,* Volume 134, Number 2 (2019), pp. 245–276, doi.org/10.1002/polq.12897.
72. Ibid.
73. Annie Gowen, 'Bangladesh's political unrest threatens economic gains, democracy', *The Washington Post,* March 22, https://www.washingtonpost.com/world/bangladeshs-political-unrest-threatens-economic-gains democracy/2014/03/22/baf1807c-a369-11e3-84d4-e59b1709222c_story.html; Vaughn, 'Bangladesh', 2020.

About the Editor

Farahnaz Ispahani is a global fellow at the Woodrow Wilson Center and a Steering Group Member of the International Parliamentarians Panel for Freedom of Religion or Belief (IPPFORB). She also serves on the Anti-Defamation League Task Force on Middle East Minorities.

She has been a leading voice for women and religious minorities in Pakistan for the past twenty-five years, first as a journalist, then as a member of Pakistan's National Assembly and, most recently, as a scholar based in the United States.

Ispahani served as a spokesperson and international media coordinator for the Pakistan People's Party, working alongside the late Benazir Bhutto. During her tenure in Parliament (2008–2012), she was a member of the Foreign Affairs and Human Rights Committees and of the Women's Parliamentary Caucus. She concurrently served as media advisor to the President of Pakistan.

She has authored *Purifying the Land of the Pure: A History of Pakistan's Religious Minorities* (2017).

30 Years *of*

HarperCollins *Publishers* India

At HarperCollins, we believe in telling the best stories and finding the widest possible readership for our books in every format possible. We started publishing 30 years ago; a great deal has changed since then, but what has remained constant is the passion with which our authors write their books, the love with which readers receive them, and the sheer joy and excitement that we as publishers feel in being a part of the publishing process.

Over the years, we've had the pleasure of publishing some of the finest writing from the subcontinent and around the world, and some of the biggest bestsellers in India's publishing history. Our books and authors have won a phenomenal range of awards, and we ourselves have been named Publisher of the Year the greatest number of times. But nothing has meant more to us than the fact that millions of people have read the books we published, and somewhere, a book of ours might have made a difference.

As we step into our fourth decade, we go back to that one word – a word which has been a driving force for us all these years.

Read.